J2EE™ Technology in Practice

The Java™ Series

Lisa Friendly, Series Editor
Tim Lindholm, Technical Editor
Ken Arnold, Technical Editor of The Jini™ Technology Series
Jim Inscore, Technical Editor of The Java™ Series, Enterprise Edition

Ken Arnold, James Gosling, David Holmes
The Java™ Programming Language, Third Edition

Joshua Bloch
Effective Java™ Programming Language Guide

Greg Bollella, James Gosling, Ben Brosgol, Peter Dibble,
Steve Furr, David Hardin, Mark Turnbull
The Real-Time Specification for Java™

Mary Campione, Kathy Walrath, Alison Huml
The Java™ Tutorial, Third Edition:
A Short Course on the Basics

Mary Campione, Kathy Walrath, Alison Huml,
Tutorial Team
The Java™ Tutorial Continued:
The Rest of the JDK™

Patrick Chan
The Java™ Developers Almanac 2000

Patrick Chan, Rosanna Lee
The Java™ Class Libraries, Second Edition, Volume 2:
java.applet, java.awt, java.beans

Patrick Chan, Rosanna Lee
The Java™ Class Libraries Poster, Sixth Edition, Part 1

Patrick Chan, Rosanna Lee
The Java™ Class Libraries Poster, Sixth Edition, Part 2

Patrick Chan, Rosanna Lee, Doug Kramer
The Java™ Class Libraries, Second Edition, Volume 1:
java.io, java.lang, java.math, java.net, java.text, java.util

Patrick Chan, Rosanna Lee, Doug Kramer
The Java™ Class Libraries, Second Edition, Volume 1:
Supplement for the Java™ 2 Platform,
Standard Edition, v1.2

Kirk Chen, Li Gong
Programming Open Service Gateways with Java™
Embedded Server

Zhiqun Chen
Java Card™ Technology for Smart Cards:
Architecture and Programmer's Guide

Li Gong
Inside Java™ 2 Platform Security:
Architecture, API Design, and Implementation

James Gosling, Bill Joy, Guy Steele, Gilad Bracha
The Java™ Language Specification, Second Edition

Jonni Kanerva
The Java™ FAQ

Doug Lea
Concurrent Programming in Java™, Second Edition:
Design Principles and Patterns

Rosanna Lee, Scott Seligman
JNDI API Tutorial and Reference:
Building Directory-Enabled Java™ Applications

Sheng Liang
The Java™ Native Interface:
Programmer's Guide and Specification

Tim Lindholm and Frank Yellin
The Java™ Virtual Machine Specification, Second Edition

Vlada Matena and Beth Stearns
Applying Enterprise JavaBeans™:
Component-Based Development for the J2EE™ Platform

Roger Riggs, Antero Taivalsaari, Mark VandenBrink
Programming Wireless Devices with the Java™ 2
Platform, Micro Edition

Henry Sowizral, Kevin Rushforth, and Michael Deering
The Java 3D™ API Specification, Second Edition

Kathy Walrath, Mary Campione
The JFC Swing Tutorial:
A Guide to Constructing GUIs

Seth White, Maydene Fisher, Rick Cattell,
Graham Hamilton, and Mark Hapner
JDBC™ API Tutorial and Reference, Second Edition:
Universal Data Access for the Java™ 2 Platform

Steve Wilson, Jeff Kesselman
Java™ Platform Performance:
Strategies and Tactics

The Jini™ Technology Series

Eric Freeman, Susanne Hupfer, Ken Arnold
JavaSpaces™ Principles, Patterns, and Practice

Jim Waldo/Jini™ Technology Team
The Jini™ Specifications, Second Edition,
edited by Ken Arnold

The Java™ Series, Enterprise Edition

Rick Cattell, Jim Inscore, Enterprise Partners
J2EE™ Technology in Practice:
Building Business Applications with the Java™ 2 Platform,
Enterprise Edition

Patrick Chan, Rosanna Lee
The Java™ Class Libraries Poster, Enterprise Edition,
version 1.2

Nicholas Kassem, Enterprise Team
Designing Enterprise Applications with the Java™ 2
Platform, Enterprise Edition

Bill Shannon, Mark Hapner, Vlada Matena, James
Davidson, Eduardo Pelegri-Llopart, Larry Cable,
Enterprise Team
Java™ 2 Platform, Enterprise Edition:
Platform and Component Specifications

http://www.javaseries.com

J2EE™ Technology in Practice

Building Business Applications with the
Java™ 2 Platform, Enterprise Edition

Rick Cattell
Jim Inscore
Enterprise Partners

ADDISON-WESLEY

Boston • San Francisco • New York • Toronto • Montreal
London • Munich • Paris • Madrid
Capetown • Sydney • Tokyo • Singapore • Mexico City

The publisher offers discounts on this book when ordered in quantity for special sales. For more information, please contact:

Pearson Education Corporate Sales Division
One Lake Street
Upper Saddle River, NJ 07458
(800) 382-3419
corpsales@pearsontechgroup.com

Visit us on the Web at www.awl.com/cseng/

Library of Congress Cataloging-in-Publication Data

Cattell, R. G. G. (Roderic Geoffrey Galton)
    J2EE technology in practice : building business applications with the Java 2 Platform, Enterprise edition / Rick Cattell and Jim Inscore.
        p. cm. -- (The Java series)
    ISBN 0-201-74622-0
    1. Java (Computer program language) 2. Business--Data processing. I. Inscore, Jim. II. Title. III. Series.

QA76.73.J38 C38 2001
005.2'762--dc21   2001022848

ISBN 0-201-74622-0

Text printed on recycled paper.
1 2 3 4 5 6 7 8 9 10—MA—05 04 03 02 01
First printing, June 2001

Contents

5   AT&T Unisource: Cost-Optimized Routing Environment on the Borland AppServer

Foreword

THIS book is for the skeptics. In 1996, the skeptics thought the Java platform would have inadequate performance for Internet and intranet servers. But they were proven wrong: Thousands of scalable Java technology-based servers are now online. In 1997, the skeptics said that Sun's community consensus-building process could not compete with established standards processes to produce a viable platform. But it did—with an overwhelming groundswell. In 1998, the skeptics said the J2EE platform would be too big and complicated to implement, and that Sun would be unable to get others to adopt it. But it was widely adopted, and the design proved very powerful. In 1999, the skeptics said the J2EE platform would come out years late, that it would take too long to complete specifications, a reference implementation, and a compatibility test suite. But the J2EE platform came out right on schedule at the end of the year, with all these deliverables. In 2000, the skeptics said that vendors wouldn't take the compatibility tests seriously and would not implement the J2EE platform in their mainstream products. But they did; all the leading vendors became J2EE licensees, and a dozen vendor products have already passed the extensive J2EE compatibility test suite. In 2001, the skeptics questioned whether real enterprise applications would be implemented and deployed successfully on the J2EE platform. But they have been. This book is the proof.

This book is for the optimists—developers, engineering managers, CTOs, CEOs, and others who will have the foresight to bet their enterprise on a promising state-of-the-art platform that can put them ahead of their competition. In this book, these people will find examples that will help them design their own solutions, and case studies to demonstrate to their colleagues that J2EE is a powerful, proven platform. There have been nearly a million J2EE platform downloads from Sun since its release a year ago, not to mention thousands of customers who use J2EE-compatible products from one of the two dozen vendors that have licensed the J2EE platform to date.

This book is for those who want to better understand the J2EE platform. It demonstrates the most important feature of the platform—that it is an industry-wide initiative, with support and contributions from many companies and many people. The J2EE platform is not one product from one company. It's a standard framework around which the leading enterprise vendors are competing to build innovative, high-performance, distributed enterprise software platforms. In the pages of this book, you will find contributions from BEA, IBM, iPlanet, Oracle, and half a dozen other vendors, as well as their customers: AT&T, Bekins, CERN laboratories, the U.S. Army, and many others.

This book is for all the people who are already involved with the J2EE platform. The success of the platform is the result of outstanding work and vision from a lot of people. I would personally like to thank those people. In this book, you will read about the most important of them—the people who took the J2EE platform into the trenches to solve business problems and reap the benefits of this new technology. Their experience is enlightening. The book's editors, Rick Cattell and Jim Inscore, are ideally suited to bring these experiences to you: Jim has managed all the technical writing for the J2EE platform, and Rick was instrumental to the inception and technical architecture of the J2EE platform. We hope you enjoy reading the book as much as all these people enjoyed working with this technology.

Patricia Sueltz
Executive Vice President
Software Systems Group
Sun Microsystems, Inc.
May 2001

Acknowledgments

WE would like to thank the J2EE licensees for their enthusiasm for this book, and for their spirit of coopetition around the J2EE Platform. Their customers, of course, made this project possible: They were both helpful and encouraging. It has been fun working on a platform with energy and such momentum. Many of these contributors are named as authors of the chapters of this book, but others were just as important in making it happen. In particular, we would like to thank Vince Hunt from Altura; Dave Nyberg from BEA; Eric O'Neill, Ralf Dossman, and Rebecca Cavagnari from Borland; Eric Odell, Elizabeth Dimit, and Anita Osterhaug from Brokat; Mark Herring and Dan Gillaland from Forte; Bob Bickel, Mark Mitchell, and Paige Farsad from HP Bluestone; Jim Reser from IBM; Patrick Dorsey and Michelle Skorka Gauthier from iPlanet; Moe Fardoost from Oracle; Barbara Heffner from Chen PR; Corina Ulescu and Bruce Kerr from Sun; and Brooke Embry and John Selogy from Navajo Company. Patrick Spencer from Sun Professional Services deserves particular recognition for his enthusiastic participation in the project and his ability to always come through with the goods. Ann Betser, Kim Olson, and Ullon Willis have also lent valuable support.

The publishing team deserves credit for getting this book out on time while coordinating over a dozen contributors. Thanks to Mary Darby and Zana Vartanian from Duarte Design for their support on the graphics. And of course, we're particularly grateful to the Java Series publishing team: Lisa Freindly, Series Editor from Sun, and Mike Hendrickson, Julie Dinicola, and Jacquelyn Doucette from Addison-Wesley.

Sun's J2EE platform marketing team were very helpful to us: Rick Saletta, Ralph Galantine, Glen Martin, Milena Volkova, Cory Kaylor, and Bill Roth. Thanks also to Carla Mott, Elizabeth Blair, Vijay Ramachandran and Jill Smith. The J2EE management team deserves extra credit for keeping the J2EE project on track—Karen Tegan, Connie Weiss, Janet Breuer, David Heisser, Kevin Osborn, Jim Driscoll, Vella Raman, Steve Nahm, Bonnie Kellet, Carla Carlson, Vinay Pai,

Kate Stout, Linda Ho, Anita Jindal, Larry Hofman, Peter Walker, Vivek Nagar, and Tricia Jordan.

Finally, special thanks to Jeff Jackson, director of engineering for J2EE, for supporting our "enormous enterprise edition encylopedia" and for understanding that people really do read the manual.

About the Editors

D R. R. G. G. "RICK" CATTELL is a distinguished engineer in Java platform software at Sun Microsystems, and a founding member of the Java Platform Group that produced J2EE. He has worked for 17 years at Sun Microsystems in senior roles, and for 10 years before that in research at Xerox Palo Alto Research Center (PARC) and Carnegie-Mellon University. The author of more than 50 technical papers and five books, Cattell has worked with object technology and database systems since 1980. He is co-creator of JDBC, and was responsible for forming Sun's Database Engineering Group, whose performance tuning helped to make Sun a leading database server provider. He led the Cypress database management system effort at Xerox PARC, was a founder of SQL Access, and was founder and chair of the Object Database Management Group (ODMG). He authored the world's first monograph on object data management, and has received the Association for Computing Machinery Outstanding Dissertation Award.

Jim Inscore manages technical publications for the Java 2 Platform, Enterprise Edition, in the Java Platform Software Group of Sun Microsystems. His roles include overseeing developer documentation, such as the J2EE Tutorial and J2EE Blueprints, providing developer content for the java.sun.com/j2ee Web site, and serving as technical editor on the Java Series, Enterprise Edition, from Addison-Wesley. Inscore has been involved with object-oriented and enterprise-related technologies for more than 15 years, working with developer documentation for organizations that include Oracle, Ingres, NeXT, Kaleida, and Macromedia. Prior to that, he spent 10 years writing marketing communications materials for the technical marketplace.

CHAPTER 1

A Multi-Vendor Standard for Distributed Enterprise Applications

THIS book is about business and computing, and about the success of a new standard for business computing in the networked economy.

At its core, business is about relationships and transactions. Business computing is also about relationships and transactions. While they may seem distinct, the meanings are complementary. Business relationships are about customers, vendors, and the products and services they buy or sell—the kind of information that relationships in a computer database are designed to track. Transactions in business are about the exchange of monetary value, goods, and services. These are the same processes that transactions on a computer database must perform with complete integrity.

The point is that these days, business and business computing are inextricably intertwined. As business evolves, the nature of business computing evolves—and vice versa.

Today, business and business computing are evolving together into a networked economy. This book explores efforts to deal with that evolution, from both the business side and the computing side. It does so with a focus on how the Java 2 Platform, Enterprise Edition (J2EE), provides a new standard for supporting the business and technical needs of companies operating in today's economy.

1.1 The Networked Economy

There are shelves of books that describe the new networked economy, so we won't rehash those here. Simply put, in the networked economy, the exchange of information is as important as the exchange of goods and services. Even companies in traditional businesses find they have to develop new techniques for managing, disseminating, and taking advantage of their information resources. Companies need to network, to reach out to new customers, to interact more effectively with their suppliers, to engage in alliances with new partners.

This economy is largely propelled by the Internet, but it also takes in other networks, such as wireless networks of cellular phones and hand-held devices, corporate intranets, and a variety of other networks, local and wide-area. The networked economy is built on two software entities: data and applications.

Historically, the emphasis of information technology has been data management—that is, large-scale database management systems have allowed organizations to gather, analyze, and interpret data for strategic advantage. In the networked economy, the emphasis of information technology shifts toward applications. Distributed computer applications are the key to reusing existing data and accessing new data. Applications are the key to establishing secure and robust links with customers, suppliers, and partners. Thus, the key to competing effectively is the ability to quickly and efficiently develop and deploy innovative applications as new opportunities arise.

The Java 2 Platform, Enterprise Edition, is designed to provide a standard for developing and deploying the applications required to take advantage of the reach of the networked economy.

1.2   Why Standardize?

The simplest answer to this question is that standards expand markets and reduce the friction that impedes transactions. Standards allow businesses to focus on specific business problems rather than complex technical problems. They provide a *lingua franca*—a common language that allows any business, anywhere, at any time, to take part in the market.

Consistent, widely supported standards in enterprise computing are particularly important now that the Internet plays such a large role in new business development. Many students of the networked economy have noted a wide-scale move from economies of scale to economies of networks, where each new node adds value to the whole. In the past, transportation and communications markets have benefited most from network connections and standards. Today, however, industries across the board are able to tap the benefits of the network, thanks to standards such as the Internet and the World Wide Web. The more a company can use standards to effectively connect with its customers, suppliers, partners—and even competitors—the more effectively it will be able to participate in the market, and the more competitive it will be in the networked economy.

There's ample historical precedent for the role of standards in facilitating the growth of markets. For example, railroads became most effective at moving commercial traffic when they adopted a single gauge across whole continents. Adoption of wide scale AC power standards enabled a far-reaching power grid and created a commodity market for electrical goods, from light bulbs to power tools to household appliances. Development of a single telephone standard enhanced the ability of businesses to operate predictably and reliably both nationally and globally.

All these examples involved standardizing the underlying technology of the network to facilitate competition in goods and services delivered or made possible by the network. The standards exist in the medium of interaction and exchange, not in the specific goods and services exchanged. Standards serve the same purpose as money: They facilitate exchange by providing an agreed-upon medium of exchange by which to conduct business. This points out an interesting standards paradox: The more businesses standardize on network technical standards, the more flexible they can be in pursuing new business opportunities and responding to new business challenges.

For these reasons, wide-scale adoption of e-business standards helps create a large, diverse market for related goods and services. This, in turn, makes it easier for customers to solve business problems in a variety of ways.

1.3   Why Standardize on J2EE?

In one of the books on the networked economy referred to earlier, Kevin Kelly notes, "Whenever you need to make a technical decision, err on the side of choosing the more connected, the more open system, the more widely linked standard."[1]

The purpose of the Java 2 Platform, Enterprise Edition, is to standardize development and deployment of applications required by the networked economy. The J2EE standard has been developed by Sun Microsystems and a variety of partners, many of whom are represented among the success stories in this book. In the year-and-a-half since its introduction, the J2EE standard has achieved significant momentum among vendors of enterprise information technology products. A variety of J2EE licensees have now rolled out commercial products based on this standard, and a number of their customers have developed and deployed applications using those products.

J2EE supports a standard model for developing *distributed transactional* applications. *Distributed* applications are those that run on several computer systems at once, generally as tiered or layered processes. For example, the simplest

---

[1]   Kevin Kelly, *New Rules for the New Economy,* New York, Penguin Putnam, Inc. 1998.

distributed applications generally have a client tier on a desktop, as well as a server tier on a separate machine, accessible by multiple clients. More complex distributed applications can be configured by providing business logic tiers in the middle layers and by adding a database tier on the backend. *Transactional* applications are those that involve modifying and updating data from various sources, operations that must be completed in whole or rolled back in whole (see Figure 1.1).

The *client tier* of a distributed application frequently runs on a browser on the user's personal computer. Clients may also be stand-alone applications or other processes. They may run on other devices, such as cellular phones or personal digital assistants.

The *Web tier* usually runs on a centralized server or servers located within a corporate computing center, which delivers content to various clients at the same

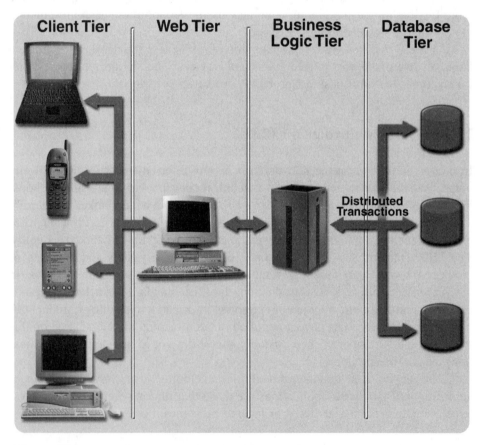

Figure 1.1   A Typical Distributed Transactional Application

time. The Web tier may perform other operations, such as maintaining state information about each user accessing pages on the server, and accessing other tiers of the application.

The *business logic tier* generally comes into play when the Web server needs to access specific behaviors that apply to the business rules for managing an online business or service. For example, an online bookstore uses business logic to perform customer checkout operations. These are transactional because the books purchased must be removed from inventory and the customer's credit card must be billed, in one process. If the card can't be billed for some reason, the books must be left in inventory; if the books aren't available, the card shouldn't be billed. Transaction management in the business logic tier makes sure this happens consistently and with data integrity.

The *database* provides basic storage and access to the organization's data. For example, the data tier accesses the database that allows an online shopper to browse through a catalog of offerings on an e-tailer's site. In many cases, the database management system that enables this may be a legacy system—a system whose use precedes the development of the online application or even the World Wide Web. The data source tier may consist of several systems, acquired at different times for different purposes, but which can interoperate thanks to transaction processing and interprocess communications facilities in the business logic tier.

Organizations doing business in the networked economy have been developing distributed transactional applications like these for some time now, well before the evolution of the J2EE standard. The difference is that previous technologies for developing these applications have generally involved vendor-specific technologies. When a company buys such a solution, it finds itself in vendor-lock. Investments in application development, in training and support, and in legacy application code and data all serve to bind the organization to the vendor of that solution.

While vendor lock may be good for the vendors, it's not always useful to customers. In some ways, it may even be counter-productive for the vendors themselves.

When all the vendors in the marketplace for a technology offer their own unique solutions, they effectively divide the marketplace into lots of little pies. Each may have its own customers locked in, but every other vendor has the same—it's hard for one vendor to sell to another vendor's customers. It's also hard for third parties to offer useful services, since the economies of scale of each small pie market may discourage the investment required. It also slows the rate of change in the marketplace and reduces its overall size, because potential customers who want to avoid vendor lock move into the marketplace cautiously.

The goal of the Java 2 Platform, Enterprise Edition, is to eliminate vendor-lock and create one big pie, a single market in which every vendor can sell to every customer. Vendors can still differentiate their products and compete effectively by providing better performance, better tools, or better customer support. And customers can easily reuse the standards-based resources and skills they acquire using products from the variety of vendors. What's more, third parties can effectively offer ancillary goods and services—training, support, system configuration, custom applications, custom components, and so on. This further enhances the customer's ability to efficiently and effectively develop applications. The J2EE marketplace represents the networked economy at work, where every new node—vendor, customer, third party—enhances the value of all the others.

By breaking vendor-lock, the J2EE standard creates a larger market than exists in a world of proprietary systems, in which each vendor's basic marketing strategy is to lock in customers. A larger marketplace pulls in more players and more types of players, and increases the number and variety of offerings. It allows vendors to concentrate on their strengths, and improves the quality of the resulting applications, since customers can choose the solutions focused on their precise needs.

1.4   Why a Standard Based on Java Technologies?

The market for the Java programming language and its related technologies has grown to nearly two million developers in the years since the Java Development Kit was first released on the Web. Implementations of the Java programming language are now available on desktop systems, servers and mainframes, and in cell phones, personal digital assistants, and other devices.

The Java programming language has gradually morphed from an interesting way to animate static Web pages to a sophisticated platform for producing world-class Web-based applications. While the development of server-side Java technologies may have seemed highly ambitious at one time, server product vendors have shown increasing interest in the technology, and application developers have readily adopted each new server-side Java technology as it was introduced.

Java technology on the server started simply enough with JDBC. This technology allowed clients written in the Java programming language to access server-side databases using standard Application Programming Interfaces (APIs). Java Servlets were the first server-specific technology for the Web, designed to replace Common Gateway Interface (CGI) programs written in a platform-dependent way with a technology that offered the "Write Once, Run Anywhere"™ capabilities of Java technology.

JavaBeans technology paved the way for a component model based on the Java language. Beans provided portable, reusable chunks of functionality, with well-defined interfaces that could play together easily with relatively little additional programming. Java Remote Method Invocation (RMI) enabled applications running in different processes on different machines to communicate with one another in a way that preserved the object-oriented paradigm, thus simplifying the development of distributed applications in the Java language. As the portfolio of Java technologies for supporting enterprise-scale distributed applications grew, so did the interest in presenting them together as a single platform with a unified programming model.

Enterprise JavaBeans (EJB) was the first technology to present the possibility that all these technologies could work together in a unified application model. Designed to simplify the development of transactional business logic, EJB defined a component model in which services such as transaction processing and database access were managed automatically, thus freeing the component developer to focus on the business model of the application. The momentum generated by the EJB model ultimately led to the development of the Java 2 Platform, Enterprise Edition, a complete platform for supporting component-based, distributed enterprise applications.

By providing a component-based solution in which certain services are provided automatically, the J2EE standard commoditizes expertise. The programming expertise required to create sophisticated multitier applications is largely built into the platform, as well as into platform-compatible offerings in the areas of standardized components, automated tools, and other products. This simplifies the programming model, makes expertise available to all, and enables application developers to focus on application-specific technologies.

1.5   Why a Book of Success Stories?

First, this book of success stories exists because it *can* exist. That is, there are a lot of organizations out there today designing and building applications based on J2EE technologies. This book presents just a handful of the applications that we're aware of. Many IT departments are now specifying J2EE compatibility as a requirement in new systems they acquire. A wide range of industry partners are providing J2EE-compatible products. The J2EE platform is a success.

In terms of information about J2EE, there are already a number of publications available, from Sun Microsystems, our J2EE partners, and other publishers and Web sites, describing technical aspects of the J2EE platform in detail.

Sun Microsystems and Java software group provide many resoures. The J2EE platform specification, along with the EJB, JSP, Servlets, and other related specifications, define the core functionality of J2EE. They are available at http://java.sun.com/j2ee/specifications. The J2EE SDK, which allows developers to try this new platform before they buy one of the offerings described in this book, is available at http://java.sun.com/j2ee/downloads. The Java Tutorial, Enterprise Edition, (available at http://java.sun.com/j2ee/tutorial) focuses on how to get started developing enterprise applications with J2EE. The J2EE Blueprints book (*Designing Enterprise Applications with J2EE*) and the Blueprints Web site (http://java.sun.com/j2ee/blueprints) discuss design considerations for architecting applications to take best advantage of the features of J2EE.

The information in this book is different from other resources in a couple of ways. First, it focuses on real-world applications built using J2EE technology. It looks at specific business applications of the J2EE platform and discusses why the technology was appropriate for the problem at hand. It describes architectural configurations that were made possible by J2EE and how they suit certain requirements, such as time to market, robustness, scalability, and other features required by modern distributed applications. Where possible, it describes alternative technology choices that may have been considered in the process of developing the particular system, and explores the reasons why J2EE technology best suited the technical and business requirements of the customer. It also explores alternate architectures using J2EE that may have been considered for a particular application, and explains how the design decisions and tradeoffs that resulted in a real application were made. This book has its own Web site (http://java.sun.com/j2ee/inpractice), where you'll find the customer success stories here plus additional real-world experiences, as adoption of the J2EE platform continues.

In addition to its focus on the real world, this book's development was very much in keeping with the community process for evolving J2EE and other Java technologies. Each of the case studies represents a partnership between Sun J2EE licensees, and their customers—that is, the folks building successful J2EE-based products, and the folks acquiring those products to solve the problems they face day to day. This is very much a community effort. The licensees and customers who have participated in the preparation of this book are all interested in furthering the adoption of the J2EE platform. Each success story in this book represents a pioneering effort to try the technology and to work with it to solve business problems.

Before looking at the business applications of J2EE, the next chapter focuses on its technology. It takes a closer look at both the individual technologies in the platform and at the ways they work together to provide a complete platform for distributed application development.

For more on the J2EE platform, see http://java.sun.com/j2ee. For more on these J2EE case studies, see http://java.sun.com/j2ee/inpractice.

CHAPTER 2

Overview of the J2EE Technology and Architecture

THIS chapter examines the architecture of the J2EE platform, the technologies behind the platform, and the types of components it supports. It looks at some typical application configurations that can be implemented using J2EE, and at the various roles involved in developing and deploying J2EE applications. To keep the discussion grounded, this chapter also points out general benefits that J2EE architecture and technologies provide to IT organizations.

There are a lot of technologies, buzzwords, and acronyms encountered repeatedly as you read the case studies that follow. This chapter should help you with the specifics of the various J2EE application designs presented in those discussions.

2.1 The Evolution of Distributed, Multitier Applications

Applications in the networked economy tend to be multitier, server-based applications, supporting interaction among a variety of systems. These applications are distributed—that is, they run on several different devices, including mainframes for data access on the backend, servers for Web support and transaction monitoring in the middle tier, and various client devices to give users access to applications. Clients can include thick clients—stand-alone applications on the desktop—and thin clients, such as applications running in a browser on the desktop, applications running in personal digital assistants, even cell phones and other personal communications devices. For business-to-business applications, distributed computing involves peer-to-peer connections among dispersed server systems.

The proliferation of systems and devices and the extension of the services provided by the server have increased the complexity of designing, developing, and deploying distributed applications. Distributed applications are increasingly called on to integrate existing infrastructure, including database management systems, enterprise information systems, and legacy applications and data, and to project these resources into an evolving environment of diverse clients in diverse locations.

To help you understand the issues involved in developing these applications, here's a look at some typical multitier application scenarios.

The earliest distributed applications were client-server applications running on time-sharing computing systems (see Figure 2.1). A mainframe computer containing data and data management software was connected to a number of terminals, which could be distributed as widely as the technology allowed. The networks used were slow; the client systems were called dumb terminals for good reason. But these client-server systems were easy to develop and maintain because all applications lived on the mainframe.

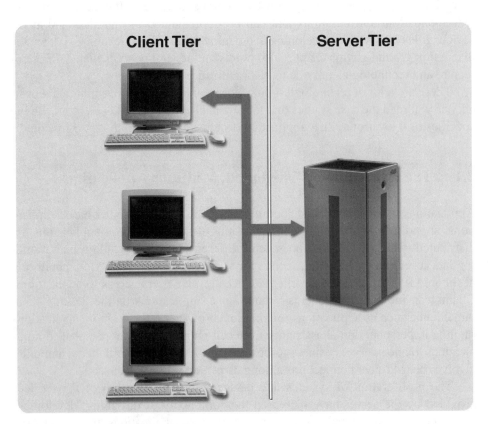

Figure 2.1   Pure Client-Server Application Architecture

With the arrival of high-speed networks and smart PC-based clients with elaborate graphical user interfaces, applications moved from the mainframe to the desktop. This meant more processing power for each user, but less control for IT departments. The application-development process was simplified with a variety of visual tools and other programming aids, but application deployment in this multitiered environment became a problem with so many desktop machines and configurations (see Figure 2.2).

Browser-based applications on the Internet or intranets are a variation on this model. A browser running on a desktop PC provides access to the server. Applications run on Web servers, providing all the business logic and state maintenance. Using this configuration, applications can provide everything from simple page lookup and navigation to more complex processes that perform custom operations and maintain state information. The technologies supporting this application architecture include plug-ins and applets on the client side, and Common Gateway Interface (CGI) scripts and other mechanisms on the server side. The problem

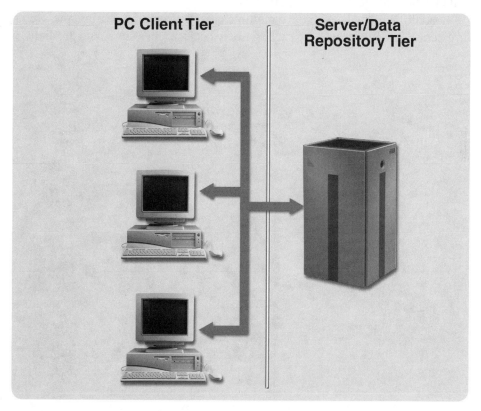

Figure 2.2   PC-Based Client-Server Application Architecture

with adding functionality in this environment is that there is no single standard for clients or servers, and the applications assembled in this way are hard to develop and maintain.

While the architecture of multier applications has evolved, new capabilities have been added to the mix. A pure client-server architecture is viable for a tightly controlled environment, with one type of client and one backend server providing some business logic and access to data. But the real world soon became more complicated. Eventually, organizations wanted to connect multiple backend systems—for example, to connect a warehouse inventory system to a customer billing system. Another example would be companies that merge and need ways to integrate the computing capabilities they inherit.

These requirements led to the evolution of the middle tier in enterprise computing in the nineties. In this configuration, the business logic of an application moves onto a centralized, more tightly controlled system. Transaction monitors in the middle tier are capable of integrating disparate data sources with a single transaction mechanism. With this technology, traditionally disconnected systems could become connected (see Figure 2.3).

In addition to the need to have multiple databases communicating, the need to have multiple applications interacting soon became an issue. With millions of

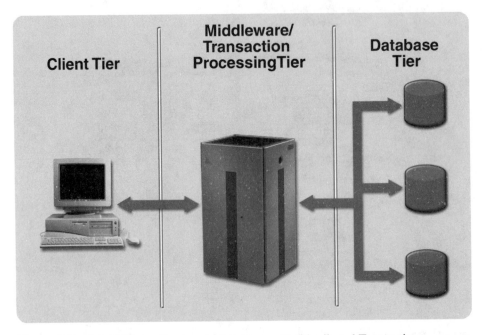

Figure 2.3   Multitier Application Architecture with Distributed Transactions

lines of code and the corresponding development and debugging time investment in legacy applications, organizations wanted ways to reuse the capabilities of existing applications, and to get time-proven systems communicating in new ways. Among the solutions proposed, the CORBA standard achieved success by allowing modules in various programs to communicate with one another. This helped support a new era in distributed computing (See Figure 2.4).

All these configurations have proven useful in the enterprise computing world. However, each has its drawbacks. Primarily, the lack of widely accepted standards means no unified programming model—diverse skills (and often deep skills, at that) are required to do the complex programming required to make

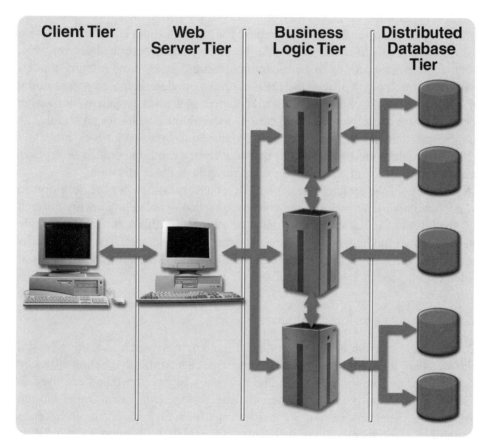

Figure 2.4 Multitier Application Architecture with Multiple Servers and CORBA Interoperability

applications work together. And in many cases, each vendor of the technologies involved—Web servers, transaction processors, database management systems— provides its own proprietary programming models and APIs.

2.2 J2EE Platform Architecture and Technologies

The technologies that make up the Java 2 Platform, Enterprise Edition, have been evolving since the introduction of the Java programming language more than five years ago. Many of them, such as Java Servlets, JDBC, and JavaIDL (providing application interoperability using the CORBA-standard Interface Definition Language), were introduced to simplify the development of the types of applications described in the previous section.

The basic value the J2EE platform adds to the mix is that it combines these technologies into a single, unified standard for building applications in a variety of configurations to suit these needs. Unlike the scenarios described above, which often require applications to be assembled using diverse programming models, APIs, and developer skill sets, the J2EE platform provides a unified programming model and a standard set of APIs. This means greater responsiveness when increasing the capacity of an application: the volume of hits it can handle, the number of transactions it can perform. In addition, with vendor-lock broken by J2EE, the underlying hardware and server software can be upgraded or replaced with minimal effect on the design or configuration of the application.

In addition, the architecture of the J2EE platform simplifies the development of applications by introducing the concept of redeployable components throughout the layers of multitier applications. The support for this architecture is implemented as two fundamental parts: components and containers. These are covered in detail in the next section, followed by a look at the standardized services provided to components by their containers.

2.2.1 Components and Containers

Components represent units of development and deployment, designed to be simpler to build than other models. They provide standardized functionality, have well-defined application interfaces, and can easily be developed and deployed for specific business purposes. Containers that support the components represent reliable, standardized services and a consistent environment from one product vendor to another. Containers are the mechanism by which J2EE supports the "Write Once, Run Anywhere" promise of the Java programming language. Containers provide automatic support for certain aspects of application behavior, such as Hypertext Transfer Protocol (HTTP) interaction, transaction management, and security. They also offer a set of standardized services that components can use to perform useful work.

The concept of components and containers is fundamental to the benefits of the J2EE standard. By enabling developers to focus on creating components to encapsulate application specifics, such as graphic look and feel, navigation, and business logic, the J2EE architecture reduces the amount of coding and debugging required to develop fully functional applications. By providing a model in which applications can be assembled from standardized components, J2EE improves the productivity of organizations and allows organizations to buy standardized behaviors off the shelf—expertise becomes a commodity in the J2EE marketplace. Vertical market components for doing inventory management, checkout services, or medical-records tracking are among the possibilities. Such commoditization means greater productivity, faster time to market, more reliability, and simplified application development. The expertise required to assemble fully functional J2EE applications isn't as skills-intensive as developing the underlying technologies supported by the J2EE platform. Organizations can focus on recruiting and training developers based on their understanding of the business needs of the organization, not just on their ability to solve arcane technical problems.

2.2.2   Containers

J2EE containers support the component-based application programming model in two major ways. First, they automate much of the standard functionality that requires programming expertise in other models, such as transaction management and security. And they provide standardized APIs in the Java programming language for other features of value to components, such as messaging (Java Message Service) and database access (JDBC). These container features unify the J2EE programming model, simplify application development, and support portability of both individual components and full-scale applications.

Because they're based on the Java 2 Platform, Standard Edition, containers provide standard features of the Java runtime environment automatically, including cross-platform development support and memory management to simplify debugging. In addition, the J2EE platform and component specifications define features and enhancements to containers that include security management, transaction management, lifecycle management, and other features.

Containers provide a working environment for their components. They provide a way for services to be "injected" into the operations of the components, without the component developer needing to write specific code. This is especially important in distributed application development, where the complexity of providing such services may be daunting.

One example of container intervention in a component is container-managed transactions in Enterprise JavaBeans. Container-managed transactions let multiple EJBs automatically work together in the same transaction, without the developer of each component needing to know or program any of the transaction details. This facilitates assembling applications from preprogrammed components. For example, when a store-front e-commerce application requires customer checkout operations to update customer and inventory records, an EJB representing a customer can be included in a transaction with inventory EJBs. This can work automatically, even with components developed at various times by different organizations, and even with components purchased from third-party vendors. This simplifies assembling complex J2EE applications from easy-to-develop and readily available components.

As another example of standardized service access, all J2EE components can use security mechanisms built into the platform. Containers can control access to components through these mechanisms, checking a client's access attributes for individual methods or whole interfaces. In addition, security attributes of components can be specified at deployment time, to ensure that the security model of the application maps to the security environment of the deploying organization.

Because J2EE containers were designed with input from a variety of enterprise platform partners, they can easily be implemented on top of existing information systems, and can interact effectively with services provided by those systems. This enables organizations to begin adopting J2EE-related technologies as needed, without having to completely redeploy all existing enterprise applications and data resources.

2.2.3   Java Servlet Technology

Java Servlet technology provides a basic mechanism for generating dynamic Web content. Think of them as Java applets for servers. Servlets were developed as an improvement over CGI scripts, which are generally platform-specific, and are limited in their ability to support rich interaction. Because servlets are based on the Java programming language, they offer several benefits over CGI, including portability, flexibility, and programming ease. In addition, they provide better performance because they are persistent—a servlet needs to be loaded into memory and initialized just once. It's then available to serve any user request. (In contrast, CGI scripts are loaded each time the server receives a user request; this consumes both memory and processor cycles, thus affecting scalability).

Like all J2EE components, servlets run in a container implemented by the J2EE platform provider. The container manages a servlet's interaction with its client and provides a rich environment for the servlet to use to access various services based on Java technology. A servlet container implements all of the Java 2

Platform, Standard Edition APIs. This makes a variety of technologies based on the Java programming language available to servlets, including JDBC, Java Naming and Directory Interface, RMI, JavaBeans, and others. The container can also implement features that allow servlets to share information about a particular client and session, overcoming the obstacles generally presented by the stateless HTTP protocol.

The flexibility of servlets is enabled through the servlet API, which implements a mechanism for more complex interaction with the requesting client than can CGI. Various servlet methods provide information to the servlet and allow it to respond. Because of the object-oriented programming model, items key to servlet behaviors are provided as objects with a well-defined API.

In a typical interaction (see Figure 2.5), the client, normally a Web browser, makes a request to a Web server via HTTP or HTTPS. When the Web server processes the request, it hands it off to the servlet container, which hands the request off to the appropriate servlet. The servlet is given a *request object,* which provides

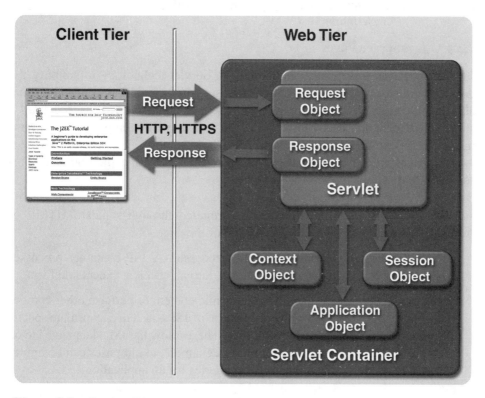

Figure 2.5   Servlet-Client Interaction

it with rich information about the request, including who called it, which HTML form parameters were sent with the request, and other information about the HTTP request. The servlet can send data back to the client via a *response object*. At any time during the processing of a request, the servlet can use a *context object* to log events, obtain Uniform Resource Locator references to resources, and set and store attributes that other servlets in the context can use. Similarly, a servlet may access a *session object* that provides it with information about client state.

In addition to defining servlets and their containers, the servlet specification defines the concept of a *Web application*. A Web application is a collection of servlets, JavaServer Pages, HTML pages, and supporting content, such as images, all intended to be deployed together to provide a complete, interactive experience on an intranet or the Internet. These resources are packaged together in a *Web application archive (war) file* that can easily be deployed on a Web application container—any Web server that supports the Java Servlets specification. For scalability, Web applications can be distributed across multiple Web application containers. Other features that Web application containers support include deploy-time security configuration, which enables an organization to enforce the access rules of the Web components and applications it deploys.

2.2.4   JavaServer Pages

JavaServer Pages technology builds on Java Servlet technology to simplify the development of dynamic Web content. JSP supports a page-based metaphor that conveniently separates dynamic and static Web content; the JSP page defines a static HTML template, with embedded calls to code written in the Java programming language to fill in dynamic portions of the page.

JSP pages contain four kinds of elements, each with a specific role in the presentation of dynamic content.

1. *Text elements* are normally content formatted through standard HTML or XML. These represent the static portion of the page.

2. *Directives* are instructions to the JSP processor. A JSP container processes these directives when compiling the page into an efficient executable form.

3. *Tags* invoke JavaBeans to generate dynamic content or perform other computations. Tag libraries are a powerful feature of JSPs used to encapsulate specific functionality invoked via HTML tags. These allow the JSP "language" to be easily extended in a portable fashion. For example, tag libraries can be implemented to support embedded database queries for an application.

4. *Scripting elements* may be declarations, scriptlets, or expressions. Like tags, scripting elements can be used to perform computations to generate dynamic content. They are useful when standard tags are inappropriate or have not been defined.

The combination of these four elements makes it easy to generate Web pages for client browsers. Because JSP is based on servlets, users benefit from the application support and other features built into Web application containers. These include portability, access to common services, the ability to maintain state and client-access information via common APIs, and other servlet benefits.

The advantage of the JSP model is that Web designers need not be familiar with the Java programming language to create sophisticated JSP pages. JSP is designed to enable Web authoring tools to automatically generate tags, scripting elements, and other HTML, and to enable the incorporation of dynamic elements by means of familiar drag-and-drop authoring techniques. Programmers can focus on providing JavaBeans and custom tags for use by the Web designer; organizations can even acquire custom behaviors from third-party developers.

This supports one of the higher goals of J2EE, separating the skill sets required to develop and assemble complex applications into more logical roles. Using J2EE technology and tools, Web-page designers and content providers can focus on presenting the best look and feel possible, without programming, while application programmers can develop complex behind-the-scenes behavior, without having to be user-interface experts.

2.2.5   Enterprise JavaBeans

In addition to servlets and JSP components for providing a rich user experience, the J2EE platform includes the Enterprise JavaBean component model for transaction-processing support. EJB provides a standard component architecture for building distributed, object-oriented business applications. Like the servlets and JSP component models, the EJB model is powerful because it provides separation of concerns.

- EJBs allow a programmer to focus on business logic without having to manage the details of transaction processing, security, load balancing, connection pooling, and other performance concerns in an application server system. These details are automatically handled by the EJB *container* implemented by the J2EE product provider. The EJB specification is designed to make it easy for container providers to build on legacy systems by "wrapping and embracing" existing technologies.

- The Enterprise JavaBean specification clearly defines the lifecycle of an enterprise bean, from development to deployment to runtime, and clearly divides the responsibility for relieving most concerns about such issues. By interceding between clients and components at the method-call level, containers can manage transactions that propagate across calls and components, and even across containers running on different servers and different machines. This mechanism simplifies development of both components and clients.

- EJBs can be implemented by trusted programmers who encode business logic, guaranteeing the integrity of corporate data. Then different user interfaces can be built on top. EJBs are client-neutral—a single EJB may be accessed from a Web client through JSPs or servlets, or it may be invoked directly by a Java application client in a standard two-tier model. Component developers are free to focus on business logic, since containers provide services automatically by interceding in component method calls. A simple set of callback interfaces are all a developer needs to implement to participate in container-provided services.

- EJBs allow business logic to be developed without regard to the details of a particular installation. A separate *deployment descriptor* is used to customize EJBs at the time they are assembled and deployed. Deployment descriptors are XML-based text files whose elements declaratively describe how transactions, security, and other installation specifics are to be handled in an EJB-based application. A variety of Enterprise JavaBean attributes, including the default component transaction type, can be specified at either development or deployment time and enforced through mechanisms built into the container architecture.

Like other J2EE components, EJBs support the "Write Once, Run Anywhere" paradigm of the Java programming language. An enterprise bean can be developed once, then deployed on multiple platforms, without source-code changes or recompiling. This allows application developers and deployers to purchase third-party components that perform common tasks, and to focus specifically on the custom behaviors required by their organization. In addition, the EJB architecture is designed to enable tools for the rapid development and deployment of enterprise beans. This helps further increase application development productivity, and ensures that appropriate skill sets can be applied to each application development task.

A client's view of an Enterprise JavaBean remains the same regardless of the container it is deployed in. Any container in which an Enterprise JavaBean is deployed presents the same interfaces to the client. This extends to containers from various vendors, running against different servers and databases, on diverse systems on a network. This client transparency ensures wide scalability for multi-tier applications.

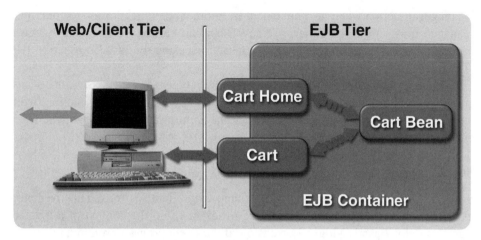

Figure 2.6   EJB Container-Client Interaction

The client view of an EJB is provided through two interfaces—the home interface and the remote interface. These interfaces are provided by classes constructed by the container when a bean is deployed, based on information provided by the bean. As shown in Figure 2.6, the home interface (cart home) provides methods for creating a bean instance, while the remote (cart) interface provides the business logic methods for the component. By implementing these interfaces, the container can intercede in client operations on a bean and offers the client a simplified view of the component (see Figure 2.6).

To the client, there appears to be direct interaction with an Enterprise Java-Bean through the home and remote interfaces. However, the architecture of Enterprise JavaBeans is designed to enable clients and components to exist in different runtimes on various systems on a network. The container intercedes between client and component, completely concealing both the bean instance and its own actions from the client.

Container intervention enables transaction management, security constraints, container-managed persistence, and other important features of the EJB component model. The Enterprise JavaBeans architecture provides automatic support for distributed transactions in component-based applications. Such distributed transactions can atomically update data in multiple databases, possibly even distributed across multiple sites. The EJB model shifts the complexities of managing these transactions from the application developer to the container provider.

A container supports a variety of transaction properties for beans. Beans can be invoked entirely outside the context of a transaction. They can be required to initiate a transaction when they are called. They can be allowed to participate in an existing transaction when they are called by another bean. In addition to container-managed transactions, an Enterprise JavaBean can participate in client-managed transactions, or it can manage its own transactions using the Java Transaction API (JTA).

The EJB component model supports three types of beans: session beans, entity beans, and message-driven beans. Each is designed for specific, well-defined roles, so developers can easily pick the appropriate bean type for each specific architectural requirement.

Session Beans

Session beans represent behaviors associated with client sessions. They're generally implemented to perform a sequence of tasks within the context of a transaction. A session bean is a logical extension of the client program, running processes on the client's behalf remotely on the server.

Session beans are intended to be short-lived, as their name suggests, existing for the duration of a single interaction, or session, with a user. Session beans can provide simple, almost CGI-like behaviors. Stateless session beans are ideal for this role, since they retain no state between calls and are intended simply to perform one task at a time. They're also amorphous, in that any instance of a stateless bean can be used by any client at any time, at the container's discretion. They are the lightest weight and easiest to manage of the various Enterprise JavaBean configurations.

In contrast, stateful session beans can be used to track session data, such as maintaining running information on page hits. The information tracked by a session bean need not be directly represented in a database, although the bean may make JDBC calls to fetch and store data. Stateful session beans maintain state within and between transactions. Each stateful session bean is associated with a specific client. Containers can automatically save and retrieve a bean's state in the process of managing instance pools of stateful session beans.

The session-bean developer defines the home and remote interfaces that represent the client view of the bean. Tools for a container get information from the Enterprise JavaBean at deployment time by introspecting its classes and interfaces. They use this information to dynamically generate classes implementing the home and remote interfaces of the bean.

Entity Beans

Entity beans are intended to represent persistent objects, such as a record or a set of related records in a database. Entity beans could be developed to represent business records, such as a customer (name, address, phone) or purchase order (customer, items purchased, purchase price). Entity-bean methods provide operations for acting on the data represented by the bean.

The entity bean provides a mechanism for multiple users of an application to have shared transactional access to data. Because of their transactional, data-specific nature, entity beans are designed to be persistent and robust—a bean and any references to it are required by the EJB specification to survive the crash of an EJB container. This is enabled by ensuring that the state of each entity bean is transactionally stored in the database.

The entity-bean developer defines the home and remote interfaces that represent the client view of the bean (without actually implementing any code for these interfaces). The developer also defines finder methods to provide a way to access an entity bean by its contents. Finder methods are designed to be introspected and displayed by development and deployment tools. This enables a user to graphically manipulate entity beans in the process of developing applications.

As with session beans, the deployment tools provided by the container vendor generate additional classes for an entity bean at deployment time to implement the home and remote interfaces. These classes enable the container to intercede in all client calls on the same entity bean. They can be implemented to mix in container-specific code for performing customized operations and functionality. In addition to these custom classes, each container provides a class to provide meta data to the client. Finally, where specified by a particular bean, a container manages persistence of selected fields of the entity bean.

In container-managed persistence, entity bean data is automatically maintained by the container using a mechanism of its choosing. For example, a container implemented on top of an relational database management system may manage persistence by storing each bean's data as a row in a table. Or the container may use Java language serialization for persistence. When a bean chooses to have its persistence container managed, it specifies which of its fields are to be retained. In bean-managed persistence, the bean is entirely responsible for storing and retrieving its instance data. The EntityBean interface provides methods for the container to notify an instance when it needs to store or retrieve its data.

An entity bean can be created in two ways: by direct action of the client in which a create method is called on the bean's home interface, or by some other action that adds data to the database that the bean type represents. In fact, in an environment with legacy data, entity objects may "exist" before an Enterprise JavaBean is even deployed.

A client can get a reference to an existing entity bean in several ways. The client can receive the bean as a parameter in a method call. It can look the bean up through a finder method of the home interface. And it can obtain the bean as a handle, a runtime-specific identifier generated for a bean automatically by the container.

Message-Driven Beans

Message-driven beans—new in the EJB 2.0 standard and to be offered with J2EE 1.3 compatible products—provide a mechanism for constructing loosely coupled applications that can communicate indirectly using the queuing and subscription models supported by JMS. Message-driven beans provide a new and more flexible way to support some application configurations.

2.2.6   J2EE Standardized Services

The containers supporting the J2EE components provide a number of standardized services, specific to the needs of distributed, enterprise applications. These include:

- *Communication services,* including RMI-IIOP, Java IDL, the Java Message Service, and JavaMail.

- *Enterprise services,* including JDBC for database access, JTA for the Java transaction API, JNDI for Java naming and directory services, and the new connector API for encapsulating existing enterprise components as EJB.

- *Internet services,* including support for HTTP, Transport Control Protocol/ Internet Protocol, Secure Socket Layer, and Extensible Markup Language via a variety of APIs.

Communications Services

To better support distributed applications with containers running on multiple machines, as well as to enable enterprise applications to communicate with one another more effectively, J2EE supports several standard communication technologies. These include RMI-IIOP, JavaIDL, JMS, and JavaMail as a means to communicate on a network, sending messages or invoking services.

The Object Management Group (OMG) has defined the Common Object Request Broker Architecture (CORBA) to allow object interfaces to be defined and invoked in a variety of programming languages and environments on a network. CORBA objects are defined using OMG's Interface Definition Language (IDL). OMG has standardized JavaIDL, allowing objects written in the Java programming language to participate in a distributed CORBA environment.

JavaIDL is now required as part of both the J2SE and J2EE environments. It allows objects written in the Java programming language to invoke other CORBA objects written in other languages, and vice versa, via OMG's Internet Inter-ORB Protocol. The use of JavaIDL requires that an IDL definition be compiled into Java programming language *stubs* and *skeletons* to support Java technology clients and servers.

RMI-IIOP is a simpler alternative to JavaIDL. It allows interfaces to be defined in the Java programming language instead of in IDL. The remote interface can be converted to IDL and implemented or invoked in another language, since RMI-IIOP uses the same on-the-wire protocol as JavaIDL (IIOP). RMI-IIOP thus provides interoperability with CORBA objects implemented in any programming language. J2EE allows Enterprise JavaBeans to be invoked via RMI-IIOP.

In contrast to JavaIDL and RMI-IIOP, the Java Message Service (JMS) provides an API for asynchronous messaging. Rather than invoke a service and wait for a response, a JMS message is queued for delivery, and control returns to the invoker. In addition to supporting specific message queues—for example, for a specific EJB, JMS supports publish-and-subscribe messaging in which any number of clients can subscribe to (request messages on) well-known *topics* in a hierarchy of topics, and any number of clients can publish to (send messages to subscribers of) a specific topic. JMS supports reliable, guaranteed delivery of messages. JMS support is optional in J2EE 1.2 and required in J2EE 1.3.

The JavaMail API supports a different kind of asynchronous messaging: electronic mail. The JavaMail implementation supports widely used Internet mail protocols, allowing J2EE components to send mail to users—for example, to confirm an on-line order. JavaMail abstract classes may be subclassed to support new protocols and functionality.

Enterprise Services

For access to database management systems and other existing enterprise computing resources, J2EE provides support for JDBC, JTA, JNDI, and connectors.

JDBC provides J2EE's database connectivity. Standard Query Language (SQL) commands or queries can be issued to a relational database, and the results returned to any Java application. The JDBC API supports stored procedures, transactions, connections, and user authentication. JDBC drivers may support connection pooling, distributed transactions, and caching of rows from the database.

JTA is the transaction API for J2EE. It provides the transactional integrity support used by EJB containers. It can also be used directly by Enterprise JavaBeans that choose to implement bean-managed transactions. JTA allows transactions to be started and completed, or aborted and rolled back. JTA also allows coordinated distributed transactions across multiple resources, such as two or more separate database management systems. When EJBs use container-managed transactions, the bean programmer does not have to make JTA calls; they are made automatically via the container.

JNDI provides access to a naming environment. It provides methods for performing directory operations, such as associating attributes with objects and searching for objects using their attributes.

JNDI is used for a variety of purposes. JDBC data sources and JTA transaction objects can be stored in a JNDI naming environment. A container provides an environment to its components via a JNDI naming context. JNDI can be used by components in a distributed application to locate one another and initiate communications. Existing corporate directory services can be accessed via JNDI.

The J2EE connectors architecture defines a standard mechanism for connecting J2EE components to enterprise resource planning systems, mainframe transaction processing systems, and database systems. Connector support is required in the 1.3 release of J2EE, but most earlier J2EE implementations provide some kind of connector functionality.

Connectors are intended to solve the problem of integrating m EJB container implementations with n enterprise information system products without building m x n separate bridges. The connector architecture assists with integration of security and transaction contexts and the flow of control between the two systems. Connectors provide a "wrap-and-embrace" solution to extend your legacy business logic and transaction processing systems with a flexible J2EE layer.

Internet Services

For access to Internet services, J2EE supports the HTTP, TCP/IP, and SSL protocols.

- TCP/IP (Transport Control Protocol over Internet Protocol) provides a mechanism to establish connections and reliably deliver streams of data between Internet hosts.

- HTTP (HyperText Transfer Protocol) is the basis of Internet browsers and Web servers. A client makes an HTTP request to a server, and HTML hypertext is returned via HTTP.

- SSL (Secure Socket Layer) provides a secure mechanism for clients to access hosts on the Internet, without someone eavesdropping or tampering with the messages.

In addition, new eXtensible Markup Language (XML) functionality is supported in J2EE 1.3. XML provides tagged data similar to HTML, but the tags describe the data rather than the way the data is displayed. XML can be used to transfer formatted data between applications or servers on the Internet—for example, for supporting transactions between businesses (B2B). Support for parsing XML and representing XML as objects is implemented and is being standardized at the time of this writing.

2.3   Application Configurations Supported by the J2EE Architecture

This section looks at some of the ways in which the J2EE architecture can be used to configure various multitier applications.

In a typical multitier Web application, a Web server implemented using JSP or servlets sends HTML or XML to a Web browser client. It generates dynamic content by making calls to database systems or existing enterprise services using JNDI, JDBC, JavaIDL, and other J2EE supported technologies (see Figure 2.7).

A multitier J2EE application uses Web components and accesses multiple databases, with Enterprise JavaBeans in between to encapsulate more-complex business logic than could be supported in JSP alone (see Figure 2.8). EJBs also automate the transaction monitoring required to access multiple databases. Alter-

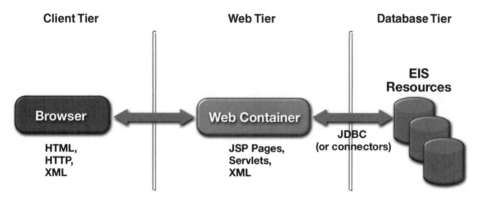

Figure 2.7   Multitier Application with Web Server/JSP Interface

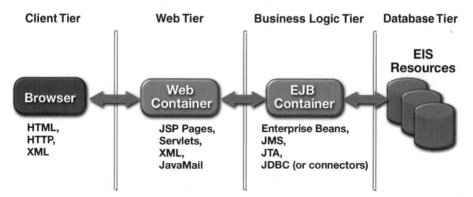

Figure 2.8   Multitier Application with Web Server/JSP Interface and EJB Middle Tier

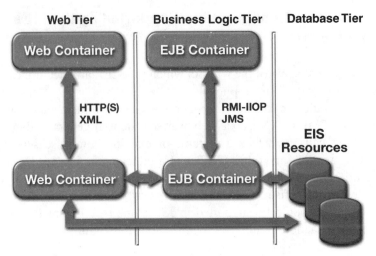

Figure 2.9   Multitier Application with XML B2B Connections

nately, the business logic encapsulated in the enterprise beans may be invoked by a client application written in the Java programming language.

With its inherent flexibility, J2EE can support an endless variety of sophisticated application configurations. For example, business-to-business transactions may be accomplished by XML transfer between J2EE servers, or business-to-consumer confirmations may be sent via JavaMail (see Figure 2.9). Enterprise Java-Beans containers can interact directly using CORBA-based standards, or communicate asynchronously using the newly specified message-driven EJB (see Figure 2.10).

While these application configurations are in many ways similar to those shown earlier for standard multitier applications, the advantage that J2EE offers is a simplified, standards-based programming model. The skill required to implement these configurations are divided into a small set of well-defined roles. In addition, the automation provided by J2EE containers reduces the need to acquire new skills to introduce new functionality. J2EE also supports a cleaner migration path between application configurations. For example, a simple online catalog implemented using JSP and JDBC can be rearchitected as an online shopping service by adding EJB business logic in the middle tier. EJB can perform shopping-cart and user-data updates without changing programming models, servers, or other aspects of the application.

2.4   J2EE Roles

One of the benefits of the Java 2 Platform, Enterprise Edition, is that it breaks the application development and support tasks into well-defined roles. The general

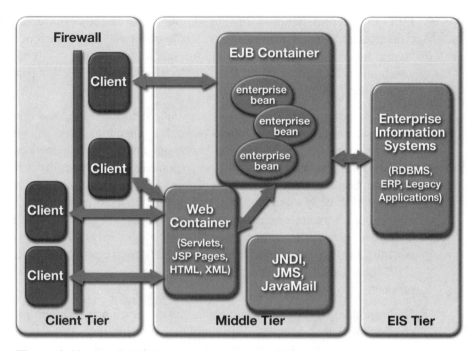

Figure 2.10 General J2EE Application Configuration

goals of this division of labor is to move many of the more complex programming issues to the J2EE platform, reduce the amount of work required by application developers to support new application requirements, and allow a clear separation of tasks based on specific skill sets and qualifications. This separation also helps to commoditize expertise—fully functional J2EE applications can potentially be assembled from off-the-shelf components that conform to well-defined interfaces, with a minimum of programming or other customization.

- J2EE *product providers,* many of whom have contributed chapters to this book, have implemented J2EE-compatible platform products. For example, a database system vendor may extend its database management system to support EJBs and the other J2EE functionality. An application-server or Web-server vendor may extend and modify its product to provide J2EE compliance. The J2EE product provider runs the J2EE Compatibility Test Suite (CTS) to ensure compliance.

- J2EE *tool providers* sell tools for developing and packaging J2EE applications. Generally, J2EE product providers are also the tool providers, supplying tools that work with their J2EE platform product. However, a number of independent tool providers are already working on tools that can be used with multiple

J2EE product provider platforms. In addition, tools can be customized for specific tasks and roles. For example, one tool vendor may focus on cool tools for laying out JSP-based Web pages, while another may focus on coding and development tools that support Unified Modeling Language design patterns for J2EE object modelling.

- J2EE *application component providers* implement EJB, JSP, and other components that are the building blocks of J2EE applications. J2EE allows an application component provider to build components that are independent of the J2EE product provider they deploy on. When custom functionality is required, application component providers will most likely be in-house developers or consultants directly employed by a company. When more-generic or vertical-market behaviors are needed, component providers may be independent software vendors or systems integrators. Given the popularity of J2EE and its component models, it's possible to predict a lively marketplace for off-the-shelf J2EE components, and even application frameworks including JSPs, EJBs, and servlets.

- J2EE *application assemblers* assemble the application component providers' components into a complete J2EE application, using tools from the tool provider. The application assembler need not have the source code for the components. Instead, he or she focuses on assembling the various components (both custom and off the shelf) into complete, working J2EE applications.

- J2EE *deployers* are responsible for the installation of an application at a site, again using graphical user interface tools from the tool provider. The deployer resolves external references created by the application assembler and component providers in order to deploy the application into its operational environment and to make it available to users.

- J2EE *system administrators* use the product provider's runtime monitoring and management tools to oversee J2EE applications.

As you will see, all these roles come into play in the specific application case studies in this book.

2.5   Things to Come

With some understanding of the in's and out's of the J2EE platform, the remainder of this book shows how J2EE technologies have been used to solve specific customer problems in a wide variety of domains.

Chapter 3 describes how JCrew enhanced its traditional catalog sales operation by revamping its Web presence with a full-featured e-commerce site built using Art Technology Group's Dynamo Suite, which implements J2EE technologies. The new multitier architecture and added personalization features of jcrew.com have more than doubled annual revenues every year since its launch. While its previous architecture had inherent scalability problems that caused site crashes during peak usage times, the current J2EE-based infrastructure can support up to 8,000 concurrent users generating more than 85 dynamic page views per second.

Chapter 4 outlines how one of the country's largest mortgage companies, HomeSide Lending, produced an innovative end-to-end online lending service on the Internet. The company used the BEA WebLogic application server and Oracle database for its application, and provided XML integration with Fannie Mae's underwriting system. Homeside used both session and entity EJBs, object/relational mapping, and servlets and JSPs for the Web front end. All the other J2EE technologies (JNDI, JMS, and JDBC) were utilized as well. Homeside saw a substantial increase in sales after implementing this online system.

Chapter 5 explores the Borland Application Server and the AT&T Unisource CORE project. Highlighting an application successfully developed and deployed in four months, this chapter explores the benefits of J2EE both for delivering specific application functionality and for creating application frameworks that can easily be enhanced, extended, and modified. With the CORE project, AT&T Unisource was looking for ways to respond more quickly to changes in the marketplace for long-distance voice traffic routing. CORE uses EJB business logic, including container-managed persistence, as well as RMI-IIOP/CORBA compatibility to communicate with legacy systems, and JSP and Java Servlets technology to provide rapid prototyping and deployment of user-interface features. By using J2EE technology, AT&T Unisource was able to move from an isolated, department-specific application development process to an enterprise-wide approach that maximizes resources and reduces costs.

Chapter 6 shows how Codexa Corporation used Brokat's GemStone/J platform as the basis for Codexa Data Services, an Internet application that delivers and filters information for professionals in the financial services industry. The application uses JSPs, EJBs, XML, JTS, JNDI, and JDBC, along with other Java programming language APIs for authentication, security, and other services. GemStone's object-oriented database, multiple virtual machine architecture, multilevel failover, and load balancing provide fast access, reliability, and scalability. The Codexa application stores about 4 gigabytes of new data every day, with a quarter terabyte of existing data online.

Chapter 7 describes eTapestry.com, which delivers applications to assist in nonprofit fundraising. Like Codexa, eTapestry uses the GemStone/J application server, along with Sun Microsystem's Forte for Java integrated development environment. eTapestry's application uses Java Servlets, JSPs, JavaMail, JNDI, and Java secure sockets technology. As in most of the other chapters of this book, the application is architected with a thin client, a Web server layer, an application server layer, and a database layer. There are more than a million nonprofit organizations in the U.S. alone, with more than $600 billion in proceeds, so eTapestry's software addresses a huge market.

Chapter 8 describes the experience of Altura International using the HP Blue-Stone J2EE-based platform to implement online business-to-consumer (B2C) catalog shopping. Altura is responsible for the Web's first catalog shopping portal, CatalogCity.com, as well as many other sites. The Altura Merchant Operating System application currently uses Java Servlets, JDBC, and JavaMail, and Altura plans to add an EJB layer in the near future. Altura reports, "Going from our original environment to Java and J2EE was like being in hell and going to heaven!"

J2EE applications from two IBM customers, Bekins and Honeywell, are described in Chapter 9. The Honeywell application is used to track defects and corrective actions on a manufacturing floor. The client tier of this application is written in the Java programming language on Internet client machines that support a powerful user interface. The middle tier is written as EJB business logic components running on IBM's WebSphere application server. The EJB components invoke third-tier IMS/CICS applications on a mainframe via the MQSeries JMS implementation. The Bekins HomeDirectUSA application supports inventory and shipping for large items delivered business-to-consumer. Using an architecture similar to Honeywell, the company implemented EJB business logic components on top of third-tier legacy IMS applications on a mainframe. They used SQL Server for the warehouse database and DB2 for the inventory database, accessed via EJB JDBC calls to stored procedures. Former 3270 user interfaces were replaced with HTML generated by servlets. Both Honeywell and Bekins used Visual Age for Java for development, and despite their limited experience with the technology, were favorably impressed with their time to market and the performance of their J2EE applications.

Chapter 10 highlights International Data Post (IDP), a Copenhagen, Denmark-based postal technology solutions company. A pioneer in "hybrid mail," IDP's ePOST application enables electronic delivery of letters from the sender to the post office, where they are processed and physically delivered. Using Java 2 Platform, Enterprise Edition (J2EE) technology, Sun Professional Services helped IDP architect and design a Web access channel for ePOST, called WEB ePOST. They utilized J2EE-compliant iPlanet Application Server and iPlanet Web Server. WEB ePOST users save significantly on printing, administration, and postage costs, and traditional postal operators have a Web-based means to exploit new market opportunities. J2EE technology has given IDP a rapid application development environment that can easily be leveraged for future projects.

While the European physics research institute CERN may best be known as the original home of the World Wide Web, it is also the hub of the world's largest scientific collaboration with over 500 institutes and universities taking part in CERN's programs. Chapter 11 focuses on CERN's work with Oracle to provide an enterprise-wide Electronic Document Handling workflow system. Using J2EE and related technologies, CERN embarked upon migration of a system capable of handling everything from Web catalogs to purchase requests to import/export regulation compliance to vacation and overtime requests. The system is available globally 24 x 7, serving a base of 6,500 users. It tracks more than 16,000 standard inventory items, and connects to more than 20,000 suppliers. CERN's EDH uses a combination of technologies, including EJB components for business logic, Java Servlets for user interface presentation, Oracle9*i* Application Server Workflow engine for business process integration and SQLJ for data access. This chapter also describes CERN's hands on experiences with the Oracle8*i* database, Oracle Internet Developer Suite, Oracle9*i* Application Server and other products.

Finally, Chapter 12 takes a look at a system that helps the US Military Traffic Management Command, Freight Systems Office (FSO) to manage the shipping of small packages worldwide. Designed with support from Sun Professional Services, the Small Package Application is intended to reduce the per-package cost of shipping parts and supplies, and help the US military increase its field readiness by ensuring adequate resources wherever units are deployed. The Small Package Application provides the FSO with a reverse-auction site that enables shippers to openly bid for shipping orders. As a proof of concept for J2EE, the FSO found that the application design approach helped standardize the development process to increase productivity, and provided an application framework that could easily be enhanced and maintained. By providing a clear separation of development responsibilities, the JSP, Servlets, and EJB component models enabled the developers to focus specialized skills on various tasks.

For more on the J2EE platform, see http://java.sun.com/j2ee. For more on these J2EE case studies, see http://java.sun.com/j2ee/inpractice.

ATG/JCrew

About the Author

Dao Ren is a practice manager at SunPS e-Business Architecture Practice, Sun Microsystems. He has six years of industry experience, focusing on financial services, retail, and the media industry. Ren has a track record in managing and architecting large-scale e-business projects for such clients as J. Crew Group, Merill Lynch, FleetBoston Securities, and Cablevision. Prior to his current role, Ren was a senior Java architect at Sun Java Center, the leading consulting arm of Sun Java Software. Ren received his MSEE degree from the University of Michigan, Ann Arbor, in 1995.

CHAPTER 3

J.Crew Rebuilds its Web Presence with the ATG Dynamo Suite

NEW York City-based J.Crew was first launched in 1983 as a mail-order company offering a line of men's and women's clothing, shoes, and accessories. The products sold by J.Crew are designed by an in-house staff and produced by third-party manufacturers in more than 30 countries.

The J.Crew brand quickly gained popularity for its subdued, classic style, along with the high quality of the clothes. J.Crew has proceeded to leave its mark on American casual dress by designing the first stone-washed chino pants, the roll-neck sweater, and the solid cotton pocket tee shirt in a wide range of nontraditional colors. These designs—revolutionary when introduced to consumers—have become staples of American sportswear, and J.Crew's colorful catalog, with its magazine-style photos, has become a mainstay among shoppers interested in fashion that withstands fluctuating fads and current trends.

Over the years, growth has been staggering for the company. It now distributes more than 80 million catalogs a year worldwide and has also developed into a major player in the brick-and-mortar space, with more than 150 retail and outlet stores. Sales are driven even further by its highly successful online store—jcrew.com. Today, with more than $800 million in annual sales, the company attributes its success to its customer-focused business model that fortifies customer loyalty through various integrated sales channels. Under its vision of One Crew, the company strives to bring value through a synergy between its brick-and-mortar locales, its paper catalogs, and now to the Web, with its jcrew.com Web site (Figure 3.1).

Figure 3.1   The jcrew.com Web site Sets New Standards in the
Business-to-Consumer e-Commerce Market.

3.1   Technology Evolution

In 1996, jcrew.com was launched, allowing customers to browse through the
pages of the J.Crew catalog and place orders from the convenience of their computers. The online store became one of the first apparel Web sites, paving the way
for the transformation of traditional brick-and-mortar retailers into e-tailers.
Although ahead of its time in 1996, the site's architecture eventually hampered
J.Crew from fully realizing the potential of online sales.

The original jcrew.com was developed under a Common Gateway Interface
(CGI) framework using C++ as the language that provided the basic functionality
and interactive capabilities of the site. The online catalog was largely static, with
each product and category of products having its own HTML pages. Since the
application was designed on a closed, proprietary architecture, it was prohibitively
difficult to extend the existing functionality.

The site did, however, provide real-time inventory verification when customers
purchased items, along with a shopping cart, basic check-out services, and one billing and ship-to address. These capabilities were innovative at the time, but grew
less so as newer, more robust e-business technologies became available. This,
coupled with the exponential growth in the business-to-consumer e-commerce sector, prompted J.Crew to revamp its underlying Web infrastructure.

3.2   Why J2EE Technology?

The decision to redeploy jcrew.com using a multitier architecture and server-side Java technologies was based on the need for a highly scalable, extensible, and flexible infrastructure. J.Crew reviewed about a half-dozen proposed solutions from various vendors before deciding on the architecture proposed by the combined team of Sun Professional Services, Fort Point Partners, and ATG. Fort Point Partners, an e-integrator with consultants, developers, and programmers, collaborates with Sun to deploy e-commerce solutions for the retail, manufacturing, and financial services sectors. ATG is a leading provider of Java technology–based e-business solutions for large enterprises. Its flagship offering, ATG Dynamo, is highly regarded as a robust solution for enterprise-scale e-business applications.

J.Crew needed an infrastructure that could take its Web site to the next level in e-commerce—namely, a more personalized presentation of the catalog, enhanced scalability as more and more customers purchased clothes online, and the flexibility to modify, add to, or integrate the site's functionality. A services-driven architectural assessment performed by Sun Professional Services showed that separation of the application into three tiers—presentation tier, business logic tier, and database tier—would dramatically increase the ability of the jcrew.com site to handle concurrent user sessions. In addition, the granular, object-oriented design of Java technology-based applications provided a flexible environment for developing complex functionality. Finally, the interoperability of Java components could easily be used in conjunction with nearly all of today's e-business technologies—freeing J.Crew from being locked to one vendor for future development.

Much of the Java technology used to implement the J.Crew Web site became the underpinnings of the J2EE platform. At the time, J2EE technology and the Java language itself were in limited use for server-side, enterprise-scale applications. The Java programming language was primarily used for the development of portable desktop applications. Its "Write Once, Run Anywhere" capabilities were revolutionizing a market typically dominated by the Microsoft Windows operating system.

J.Crew was one of the first deployments of J2EE technology, breaking new ground in J2EE evolution. The success that J.Crew is realizing now, along with lessons learned at the engagement, have helped push J2EE technology into the mainstream market.

"J.Crew showed the IT world how powerful Java technologies can be for enterprise-scale, server-side applications," says Dao Ren, technical manager and chief architect for the jcrew.com project, Sun Professional Services. "The widespread adoption of the J2EE framework is a very important step toward creating best practices in application development. The interoperability of the technology and the commonality of the APIs allow seamless communication among any applications, running on any platforms. This decreases the amount of time and the cost needed to integrate different application components, as well as to meld applications to the systems of partners, suppliers, and customers."

Table 3.1   Technology Environment of jcrew.com

Technology Environment	
Java Technology	• Java 2 Platform, Enterprise Edition
	– JDBC
	– Java Servlets
	– Java Naming and Directory Interface (JNDI)
	– Extensible Markup Language (XML)
	– JavaMail API (JMAPI)
	• Other Java Technology
	– JavaBeans
	– Java Virtual Machine
	– Country Quirks Service
Hardware	• Sun Enterprise 4500 and 5500 servers
	• Sun StorEdge disk arrays
Software	• Solaris Operating Environment 2.7
	• Sun Cluster 2.1
	• VERITAS Volume Manager
	• Oracle8i Database
	• Oracle Parallel Server
	• ATG Dynamo
	• ATG Dynamo Application Server
	• ATG Dynamo Personalization Server
	• ATG Dynamo Commerce Server
	• iPlanet Web Server
	• iPlanet Certificate Server
	• iPlanet Directory Server
Services	• Sun Professional Services
	– Java Center
	– e-business Architecture Practice
	• Fort Point Partners
	• ATG Global Services
	• SunPlatinum Support

3.3 Problem/Opportunity Profile

During the planning stages of the jcrew.com redeployment, Sun Professional Services, Fort Point Partners, and ATG focused on four core goals that needed to be met.

3.3.1 Scalability Limitations

The first goal was to overcome a scalability limitation inherent in the existing architecture. During peak usage times, such as the annual holiday rush. when much of its revenue was generated, the site often came to a complete stop, leaving J.Crew in danger of losing the customers it had worked so hard to acquire. The architecture did not leverage any type of connection pooling to the database, which meant that for each customer session, a new connection was opened up to the database. This put tremendous strain on the database, and as jcrew.com attracted more and more customers, the site simply could not handle the load.

3.3.2 Personalization and Segmentation

J.Crew sought to leverage customer behavior and transactional data to help target merchandise more effectively. It hoped to do so through understanding the impact of the products, pricing, promotions, and inventory management on the actual interests and habits of customer. On the original site, customers could browse through a static, online version of the catalog. J.Crew knew that this was only a small part of what its site could be, however. It wanted to enhance the relationship with its customers by segmenting registered users based on purchasing behavior and by presenting dynamic, personalized content to users based on the products they tended to prefer. Segmenting would also allow anonymous customers to find products more easily by presenting more segments to search. Customers would be able to shop by season, gender, product type, or clothing style (such as casual or business attire).

3.3.3 Cross-Channel Integration Opportunity

J.Crew developed a concept called One Crew, which was designed to leverage its personalization capabilities to create a seamless, cross-channel communications layer that links its brick-and-mortar stores, mail-order house, and online store. Under the One Crew approach to sales, customers could purchase a product online or through the catalog and, if needed, return it to any of J.Crew's retail stores. The products purchased through any of the three channels had a direct impact on the type of special promotions made available to a customer. For example, if a customer logged on to jcrew.com a week after purchasing a pair of khaki pants at a J.Crew store, this information could be used to promote an item that would complement that purchase. This level of integration supports more extensive cross-selling opportunities, providing a robust and convenient shopping environment that can drive sales and revenues. For such channel integration, J.Crew required a flexible IT infrastructure.

In addition, J.Crew knew it needed to enhance the functionality of its site to keep it ahead of increasing competition in the clothing world. Companies were slowly beginning to gain market share by offering customers added convenience through their own sites. J.Crew wanted its site to offer these features and more, including:

- Multiple ship-to addresses

- Address books for sending gifts

- Gift wrapping and messaging

- Multilingual support for expansion into foreign markets

Table 3.2   Implementation Timetable for jcrew.com

	1995	1999	2000	2001
Initial launch of static Web site	✓			
Launch of dynamic, rearchitected Web site by Sun Professional Services		✓		
Deployment of multitier Web site with personalization features		✓		
Internationalization of Web site with Japanese version			✓	
Further internationalization and customization of Web site				✓

3.4   Collaboration with Sun Professional Services

The success of the J.Crew engagement was made possible by the contributions of myriad companies, all working together under the project management of Sun Professional Services. The delivery of the project was a joint effort, with Sun providing architecture leadership in application development and infrastructure and Fort Point Partners providing business analysis and application development expertise. ATG Global Services was also on site to help with the integration of its ATG Dynamo software and to assist in the development of business logic.

After the initial assessment, the architects and consultants from Sun Professional Services outlined a functional description of the technologies required to meet all of J.Crew's business objectives. Based on this outline, the team would construct the architecture, test it for readiness, and assist with the transition from pilot to production environment.

"Sun Professional Services really pushed the implementation of its architecture plans, and their knowledge and expertise has paid off," says Paul Fusco, senior vice president and chief information officer at J.Crew. "Our site is reliable and scalable, both vertically and horizontally. And it supports our business plan to make click-and-order sales as easy and enjoyable as possible for our repeat customers."

Indeed, as millions of dollars rested on the success of the new launch, the presence of Sun Professional Services proved to be a tremendous asset to both J.Crew and the development team. The evolving J2EE platform was very new, but J.Crew's confidence in both the technology and the knowledge that Sun Professional Services brought to the engagement paid off in the end. The site was developed in less than four months.

"Everything went smoothly. It was a boring development cycle. Boring is good: it means there were no snags," Paul Fusco notes. "We developed a plan and executed it flawlessly. Sites fail because of bad architectural design. When you look at the architecture of jcrew.com, it is strong and scalable. Sun Professional Services played a key leadership role in designing this architecture and managing our Web site rollout."

A small problem that did arise during the engagement, however, has actually helped in the rollout of subsequent J2EE-based applications. Server-side Java applications run on Java virtual machines, which allow developers to implement numerous instances of an application on the same server. At J.Crew, the Java virtual machine is responsible for hosting each instance of the application server and translating the byte code into native machine language for each user session. To do this, it must keep a log of all the objects used by the application server.

While in the testing phase, the Java virtual machine's ability to handle the massive load that J.Crew expected was pushed to its limit. Inside the virtual machine there is a class-reference hash-table, which keeps a list of all the classes that are loaded into an application's memory. There was a fixed size to this table, and up until the J.Crew engagement, this size was more than sufficient for most Java applications. But the scope of jcrew.com and the fact that every JHTML page was being compiled into one or more distinct classes caused the hash-table size to be exceeded, resulting in the crash of the virtual machine. Developers from the Java Center were called in to find a quick resolution, since it was obvious that future projects of this scope would encounter similar issues. The architects solved the problem by doubling the size of the table, changing the number representing the hash-table's size from a signed integer to an unsigned integer.

"This was something most Java architects have never seen happen," says Vinod Mathew, technical architect with Fort Point Partners. "But it took a real business situation like jcrew.com and its massive volume of traffic to show us how the technology could be better developed. We were lucky to have Sun Professional Services behind us; the Java architects were instrumental in coming up with a solution and ensuring continued, as well as future, reliability and scalability of the jcrew.com infrastructure."

Although Sun Microsystems essentially invented the original client-side Java technology, the evolution of the server-side use of the Java language and eventually the J2EE platform relied on contributions from other companies that adopted the core technology and extended its capabilities. One such company is ATG, which developed what is known as JHTML, the direct predecessor to Java Server-Pages (JSP).

JHTML is very similar to JSP technology in that it allows content developers to specialize in writing code for the logical presentation of HTML content, while component developers can focus on writing back-end business logic.

Sun licensed the JHTML technology from ATG, expanded its capabilities, and then released the JSP specification. JHTML is a pivotal component at J.Crew and was itself an important step in the establishment of the J2EE framework. Sun and ATG thus have a long-standing relationship, having worked extensively together developing J2EE-based solutions for some of today's largest companies, of which J.Crew is the only one.

Table 3.3   jcrew.com Platform as a Precursor to J2EE: Components in Use

Java Server-Side Components	How the Components Are Used
JHTML (precursor to JSP technology)	Provides dynamic, personalized presentation of content
JDBC	Provides a means of connection pooling to data-bases to ensure scalability
Java Servlets	Assist JHTML presentation and interface with back-end business logic
JNDI	Provides naming and directory functionality
JMAPI	Allows J.Crew to automatically confirm orders with customers
XML	Provides a data schema for e-commerce and personalization

"The experience we gained at J.Crew has been carried over to many subsequent installations of J2EE-based applications," says Tareef Kawaf, commerce product lead at ATG. "Launching the enhanced jcrew.com application helped establish the maturity of the platform and stands as proof that the J2EE platform provides highly scalable, flexible, and extensible applications."

3.5   Solution Analysis

Updating jcrew.com using server-side Java technologies involved several steps: analyzing the user scenario, determining a general architecture, then deciding how to apply specific Java technologies to the architecture.

3.5.1   User Scenario

Customers visiting jcrew.com navigate the site from three different status levels: anonymous users; registered users that have not logged on, or registered; and logged-on users. Market segments are created by collecting and analyzing customers' site behavior for all status levels and evaluating transaction data from catalog and online purchases. Each customer can be classified into defined market segments. This attribute is stored as part of the customer's profile. For example, if a customer repeatedly browses men's business casual pants and cashmere sweaters, segmentation analysis can derive a "men's classic" segmentation. This enables merchandisers to personalize online content such that product recommendations, promotions, and product placements can be tailored to that customer's interests. "This enables J.Crew to measure the effectiveness of various merchandising strategies and react quickly to high-performing and under-performing campaigns," says Laura Bertarelli, a senior manager at Fort Point Partners.

The underlying JavaBean and JHTML technology enable this dynamic presentation. A JHTML page begins as a plain text file with elements of HTML in it. The elements, called droplets, can be passed on to parameters presented to the JHTML file by the JavaBean logic. The JavaBeans in Dynamo Application Server (part of the ATG Dynamo solution) pull out request-specific content, manipulate it as dictated, and pass the parameters to the JHTML page. The JHTML page is then compiled into a Java Servlet, which renders the content into a dynamic page according to user attributes. "The beauty of this technology is that you can completely control the level of dynamic presentation," says Tareef Kawaf. "And from a developer's perspective, JTHML and consequently JSP technology allow content developers and component developers to focus on what they do best, without having to worry about whether the logic and the Web components will be compatible."

Tying products in the database to market segments provides J.Crew with many benefits. The application server is configured to track online sales and measure which items in the market segments are selling best. When a user logs on, he or she is presented with a dynamic "what's hot" page that promotes the highest-selling items for that segment. This process, called "dynamic merchandising," runs automatically and cuts down by more than 50 percent on the time and resources that are usually required for such extensive market reporting.

Fort Point Partners designed and developed a complex promotions engine within Dynamo Commerce Server that enables J.Crew to offer catalog and in-store promotions online. This ensures a more consistent buying experience for the customer; the same promotions are now available to customers across various channels. The promotions engine has four levels.

1. *Item-specific level promotions* allow customers to enter a coupon code to receive discounts on an item or a set of items.

2. *Global-item level promotions* give customers discounts across item segments such as men's pants or women's shoes.

3. *Session-specific order level* provides customers with specials that are only valid for a particular user session.

4. *Global order level* gives customers discounts off the total cost of any purchase.

Dynamo Commerce Server receives the request for discounted pricing information from Dynamo Application Server. A JavaBean is created to process and store the discount, and the bean is sent back to Dynamo Application Server to be presented to the customer via JHTML.

Using the personalization engine, these coupons can be tailored to individual preferences, as well. For example, an anonymous customer may have been looking at a cashmere sweater during the last few visits to the site. It appears the user is interested, but perhaps the item is too expensive for him or her. The application recognizes that and flashes a discount coupon to the customer.

The architects were able to quickly and easily define the meta data within the Oracle database using Extensible Markup Language (XML). XML files reside within Dynamo Application Server and describe the objects for the personalization and commerce servers. Using this model, the commerce and personalization server can perform database access operations using JDBC connections.

"The Java programming language allowed us to pool our resources together and develop these complex discount processes very quickly and easily because of the developer-friendly nature of the language," says Ben Kearns, senior technical architect at Fort Point Partners. "Other object-oriented languages aren't as intuitive and consequently make it difficult for multiple developers to gauge the code written by previous programmers. The Java programming language is very clean and easy to work with and allows for very fast time to market."

J.Crew also offers its customers gift cards through either its stores or its catalogs. Each gift card is assigned a number that can be entered onto the Web site when a user logs on. The JavaBeans in Dynamo Application Server pull out the user profile object, and update the user's account by crediting the value of the gift card to the user's available balance.

Customers can now create address books on jcrew.com that allow them to enter and store multiple ship-to addresses. For example, customers can store the addresses of their friends and family members and instantly purchase and ship items to them.

"What we see at J.Crew is an excellent example of the power of the J2EE platform. The J2SE platform—which the J2EE platform is built on—is one that emphasizes open standards for communication among objects and application programming interfaces. This allows developers to build anything that they want, quickly and easily," says Angelo Quagliata, director of strategic alliances at Fort Point Partners. "All the functionality you see there is the result of the intuitive nature of the language. All you need to do now is write the logic within the application server. This was not such a simple task before the framework was established."

3.5.2   Connection Pooling

Each Java virtual machine hosts an instance of the Dynamo Application Server. Within the Dynamo Application Server, the development team created pools of JDBC connections between the application server and the database. This pool can be configured to handle any number of concurrent connections, though its primary function is to serve as a controlling layer that limits hits to the database. If the number of concurrent user requests at any time exceeds the number of connections that has been configured into the database layer, the new requests will be placed in a holding pool until connections are made available. The previous architecture had no controlling layer, so it allowed infinite hits to the database, which overloaded the database and caused stoppages. By taking advantage of JDBC technology, the solution provides better management of the amount of work that can be active in the database in any moment.

3.5.3   Caching Database Requests

Within the Dynamo Application Server and Dynamo Commerce Server, there is a database layer called relational views, which is built entirely on JDBC. This layer performs intelligent caching of the most heavily used SQL queries to the database, storing the query results in a cache table within the application server. iPlanet Web Server is configured to pass requests for data to Dynamo Application Server. When the Web server routes database queries to the application server, Dynamo Application Server verifies the request against the cache table before sending the request out to the database. In this way, further work is offloaded from the database. "We wrote all our own cache tables in Java," says Tareef Kawaf. "This cuts down on the hits to the database considerably. There are many repeating requests coming in from the customers, and caching is a brilliant way of cutting the load on the database."

3.5.4   Dynamic, Personalized Presentation

Each customer registered with jcrew.com has a profile object within the Oracle database, which includes not only the information provided by the customer, but also a log of the customer's browsing and purchasing behavior during visits to the site. This allows J.Crew to target promotions to each customer, based on the customer's expressed interest.

Whenever a user interacts with the site, an event can be generated—for example, adding a product to a shopping cart or browsing a specific item in the online catalog. Dynamo Personalization Server contains logging services that allow application developers to record these events in any number of formats. Any set of events can be configured to change aspects of the user profile object, which resides in the server's memory. The user profile information is usually configured to persist in the database.

When the user logs back onto the site (Figure 3.2), the JavaBeans in ATG Dynamo pull out the user profile object and previous user behavior data, all of which determine which special promotions the user will be offered. The JHTML page, which is compiled into a Java Servlet, can use the profile information to determine the presentation form that is desired. A user who had a saved shopping cart can be shown the cart, which would load the various JavaBeans representing the items in the order.

For example, a "person object" will have "name" as a parameter. A JHTML page can be programmed to present the name parameter of a person object. A JHTML page can be written with various elements, such as dynamic targeters, which could be written to pull out the products matching the segment to which a user belongs and present the pages to the user, thereby tailoring the experience to

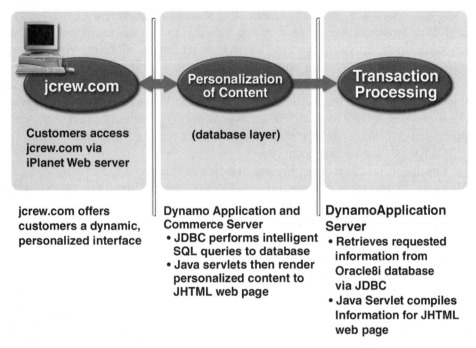

Figure 3.2   Following a Typical Transaction Through the Infrastructure Tiers

the user's needs. The entire JHTML can be a dynamic presentation, or it can be used as a template with small parts of the page pulling out dynamic content.

3.5.5   Multilingual Support for Expansion into New Markets

With a strong multinational brand presence, J.Crew knew it was missing some key sales opportunities by not having support for other languages and countries. The company asked the Sun Professional Services Java Center to modify the Web site's business logic to support other languages and to satisfy country-specific business rules. It was decided that the first expansion would be support for Japanese customers.

The Java team was called onto the project in July 1999. The launch date was set for October of that year, which left the team with only two months to modify the platform. "Luckily, we've done this kind of localization project before," says Michael Dykes, practice manager at the Tokyo Java Center. "We knew that the Java-based architecture would be easily modified to support different languages. We didn't have to create much new code at all. We just modified the existing logic to branch off if a user needed a different language. All the components were there, so we were able to make this a multilingual site very quickly by reusing all the existing JavaBeans and other objects."

When a customer first visits jcrew.com, the language preference is set—either English or Japanese. Jcrew.com then sets a cookie in the customer's browser that announces to the application which language to present for all future visits. When users visit the site, a session object is created with a local object set within the session object. The local object contains the language information. The local object works with the messaging service within the Dynamo Application Server. The messaging service identifies which type of message should be sent to the customer—an error message, for example—and pulls out the pages that contain the right language based on the local object.

But the presentation was only the first step in this project. Shipping items to other countries requires different tax calculations, and local laws can make certain items difficult to deliver. For example, shipping items containing alcohol, such as a body spray, can be complicated. J.Crew wanted to ensure compliance with all local laws and taxes if a customer purchased from another country.

The challenge for the Java Center architects was to write the conditional properties into the business logic that would determine the origin of the order. The business logic within ATG Dynamo Application Server is structured as pipelines of objects. When an order is submitted, the request is relayed to the order pipeline, which can have anywhere from 40 to 50 objects performing different services. These services include the handing off of order information to back-end fulfillment processes or the validating of inventory availability. Writing conditional logic into each of these objects would have been too difficult a task, and as the site expanded, there would have been an explosion in the number of required objects—each of which would have to be updated with country-specific criteria.

The architects therefore developed what are called Country Quirks Services within the application server, which encapsulate all the business logic for a country. The logic in these services calculates local taxes and fulfill any local requirements for shipping items. When a customer places an order, the Country Quirks Service is activated for the country to which the customer is shipping. In this way, J.Crew needs only to add a different service for each country it plans to support. With this new capability, J.Crew has prepared to further expand its international presence.

"J.Crew's first prerogative was to support the Japanese language," says Michael Dykes. "But in no time, we developed a framework that will support any language. Any request that comes into Dynamo goes through a pipeline of 40 to 50 different objects, such as JavaBeans, Java Servlets, entity beans, and so on. Each of these objects fulfills a certain duty, whether checking inventory or serving up content from the database. By using these existing components and writing some logic that allows them to branch off to the language service, we quickly developed a plug-and-play environment that will support any language that J.Crew wants to market to."

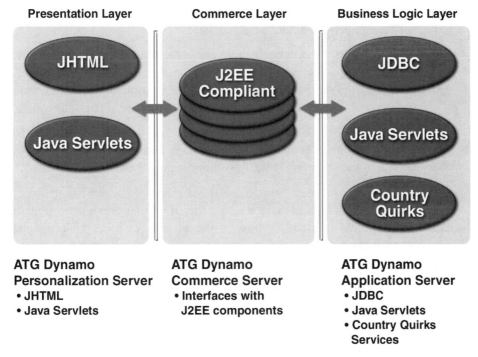

| Presentation Layer | Commerce Layer | Business Logic Layer |

Figure 3.3   Layers in the Application Tier

3.5.6   Transaction Scenario

The following provides a brief description of how the J.Crew application processes a typical transaction with a registered customer who has decided to log on to the site.

1. When a user accesses jcrew.com, iPlanet Web Server routes the requests to Dynamo Application Server, enabling the user to log in. Once the user provides a login name and a password, profile information is loaded from the database and stored in memory for further use by the session.

2. When browsing the catalog, the request for category, product, or SKU information is passed to Dynamo Commerce Server, which checks a local cache for the information. If the items are found, they are returned to the page immediately. Otherwise, the database is queried and the entries are placed in the cache and sent back to the page.

3. Dynamo Application Server manages the JDBC connection pooling. If a request for a connection does not find an available connection, the pool will

block access until a connection is made available, thereby controlling the number of active connections made to the database.

4. ATG Dynamo identifies which page the user is requesting. It then calls a Java Servlet to pull out specific parameters of the requested product object and renders the information on the screen by sending the information back to iPlanet Web server according to the presentation defined by the HTML tags in the JHTML document.

5. When a user clicks on an item to make a purchase, Dynamo Commerce Server adds the item to the shopping cart. If no shopping cart exists, one is created.

6. Dynamo Commerce Server transforms this object into a persistent object, stores it in the database, and maps it to the user ID. Whenever a user wants to check the order, this information can easily be retrieved on request, since it persists in the database.

7. JMAPI within Dynamo Application Server generates an automated email response and sends it to the customer, confirming that the order has been placed.

8. This order object is routed to back-end IBM CICS fulfillment and inventory systems, where the order is pulled, packed, and prepared for shipping. The back-end integration is accomplished by a direct connection between legacy applications and Dynamo Application Server using Transport Control Protocol/Internet Protocol (TCP/IP) socket-based communication.

9. Dynamo Personalization Server logs each of these events and merges them with the user profile for market segment categorization.

3.5.7   Architecture

Jcrew.com is hosted by Digex Inc., a leading application service provider located in the Washington, D.C., area.

1. The first tier is the front-end Web interface that was developed with iPlanet Web Server, iPlanet Directory Server, and iPlanet Certificate Server.

2. The next tier is the application tier, which is powered by ATG Dynamo. The application tier is actually layered into three servers and resides on four Sun Enterprise 4500 servers. Each server has four CPUs and four instances of the application running simultaneously for failover and load balancing.

3. Dynamo Commerce Server provides a means of transforming orders into persistent objects that are then stored in the back-end database. Dynamo Commerce Server also provides shopping cart functionality, the electronic catalog, and the caching of the most heavily used SQL requests to the database.

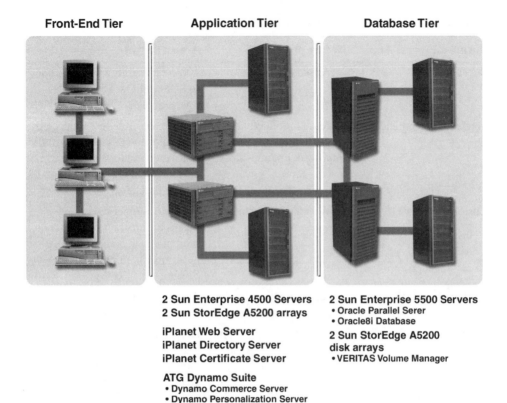

Front-End Tier	Application Tier	Database Tier

2 Sun Enterprise 4500 Servers
2 Sun StorEdge A5200 arrays

iPlanet Web Server
iPlanet Directory Server
iPlanet Certificate Server

ATG Dynamo Suite
• **Dynamo Commerce Server**
• **Dynamo Personalization Server**
• **Dynamo Application Server**

2 Sun Enterprise 5500 Servers
• Oracle Parallel Serer
• Oracle8i Database

2 Sun StorEdge A5200
disk arrays
• VERITAS Volume Manager

Figure 3.4 Multitier Architecture in Place at J.Crew

4. After the commerce tier, Dynamo Personalization Server contains JavaBean and Java Servlet logic for tracking user behavior and integrating it with the user's profile object in the database.

5. Finally, Dynamo Application Server contains all the JavaBean and Java Servlet–based business logic as well as the database connection services. Dynamo Application Server works as a series of Java-based pipelines. The pipelines can have from 40 to 50 separate JavaBeans and servlets that control everything from database queries to validation and multilingual support.

6. The database tier consists of two Sun Enterprise 5500 servers and four Sun StorEdge A5200 disk arrays, with nearly 200GB of storage space, running an Oracle8i database, with Oracle Parallel Server, Sun Cluster 2.1, and VERITAS Volume Manager software.

Table 3.4 Overview of Business Results Achieved by jcrew.com

Business Process Area	Nature of Benefit	Actual Result
Revenue	Increased sales	100% annual growth in revenues to $120 million; 15% of total revenue
Marketing/merchandising	Increased productivity, dynamic merchandising, improved relationships	Market research time reduced by 50%, higher sales per Web traffic ratio, increase in Web sales via customer catalog and brick-and-mortar purchases
Customer service	Improved relationships	Higher customer retention by means of integrating brick-and-mortar, catalog, and Internet channels; more than 650,000 product SKUs
Market expansion	Solidification of relationships, new customers	Ability to offer products online to international customers
Time to market	Quickly deploy new applications, new functionality	Deployment of rearchitected, multitier infrastructure in four months; deployment of multilingual capabilities in two months

3.6   Benefits

With its new infrastructure in place, jcrew.com is continuing its extraordinary success as a lucrative sales channel for J.Crew. The new site has increased J.Crew's annual revenues by 100 percent. This can be attributed to jcrew.com's ability to handle more than 8,000 concurrent user sessions, as well as its ability to generate 85 dynamic page views a second for each of its 250,000 unique daily visitors. The eight million hits it can handle in a given day also contribute to the bottom line. The best-practices methodology designed by Sun Professional Services and Fort Point Partners allowed the site to be launched in just four months. As shown in Table 3.4 the results of this successful deployment has been spiraling revenue growth for the Web site.

Chris Roberts, lead Java architect at the Sun Professional Services Java Center, explains the benefit of developing in a J2EE environment: "J2EE allows you to maintain separate roles and responsibilities so that a lot of work can be done concurrently among groups. For instance, a content team could work completely independently of the application team. It's all standard interfaces and everyone knows how it connects in the end. This best-practices approach to development is what sets applications built in the J2EE standard apart from those built with other methods."

Chris Roberts continues, "JDBC allows you to build your application without concerning yourself with the kind of database you will use in the future. When we go in to ramp up jcrew.com in the next year or so, portability will be of minimal concern. The application doesn't need to know which kind of database it's running on, and that will prove to be a key advantage in the future."

Indeed, since ATG has recently released its fully J2EE-compliant application server in ATG Dynamo version 5.0, J.Crew will be migrating its application to this platform by the middle of 2001.

Michael Dykes elaborates: "We will be seeing a total reduction in development effort as far as accessing the database. The new J2EE-based ATG Dynamo will add another database layer that automatically transforms query results into objects. Before J2EE technology, developers would have to translate between the relational views of the database and the objects. For example, in a database you would have a column for credit card information, a column for the expiration date, and one for the individual's name. Someone has to write the code to tie all these together as an object. The credit card is just one of a myriad of examples of tying data together as an object. The new platform will do this automatically, cutting development time exponentially."

Table 3.5   Overview of Technical Results Achieved by jcrew.com

Technical Process Area	Nature of Benefit	Actual Result
Application development	Enhanced productivity	Reuse of almost 100% of business logic, cutting development cycle for multilingual support
Site performance	Higher availability, scalability, reliability	Support for more than 8,000 concurrent users generating 85 dynamic page views per second; capable of handling 8 million hits a day; 1 to 2 second average response time; average of 250,000 daily visitors
IT operations	Reduced costs, improved productivity	Fewer programmers required to develop and maintain coding, resulting in reduced IT costs
Back-end integrations	Cost avoidance, leverage of existing system	Able to seamlessly connect front-end Web transactions with disparate back-end legacy systems

3.6.1   Looking Forward

Thanks to the Java architects from Sun Professional Services and the teams from Fort Point Partners and ATG, jcrew.com is now a proof-of-concept for consequent rollouts of J2EE-based applications. The number of companies using server-side Java technologies and the J2EE platform is increasing dramatically, and more and more companies are releasing J2EE-compliant solutions that take advantage of the interoperable, reusable components the J2EE platform provides.

J.Crew has plans to migrate the Web site to Dynamo 5 in the near future, to fully realize the benefits of the J2EE platform. "We firmly believe that J2EE is the future for large projects like this. J.Crew was just the beginning. The rapid acceptance of our latest release of Dynamo speaks to this, as companies are clamoring for a more robust and scalable infrastructure," says Tareef Kawaf. "We're firmly committed to Java technology and specifically the J2EE platform. Our work with Sun Professional Services and Fort Point Partners on this project solidified this belief as the true merits of the platform were finally realized."

"We're excited about the new release of ATG Dynamo and are looking forward to taking full advantage of the J2EE platform," says Paul Fusco. "We're proud to have been a part of bringing J2EE into the mainstream corporate market. Our current infrastructure took us to the next level, and we're confident that by migrating to a fully J2EE-compliant platform, we'll be ready for any challenges that come our way."

But for now, J.Crew and its masses of faithful customers are enjoying the benefits of a highly advanced e-commerce channel that exhibits as much style and class as the clothes it provides to consumers.

For more on ATG, see http://www.atg.com. For more on Fort Point Partners, see http://www.fortpoint.com. For the J.Crew Web site, see http://www.jcrew.com.

BEA/Homeside Lending

About the Author

Tony Baer is a well-published IT analyst with more than 15 years experience in application development and enterprise systems. As president of Demand Strategies, Baer studies implementation issues in distributed data management, application development, data warehousing, and leading enterprise applications. He is also a columnist for *Application Development Trends*, frequent contributor to *Computerworld*, and chief analyst of *Computer Finance,* a journal covering IT economics. Baer authored this chapter as a consultant to Bea Systems.

CHAPTER 4

HomeSide Deploys Electronic Lending on BEA's WebLogic J2EE Server

4.1　The Project

Home-mortgage lending has proven to be one of the most difficult processes to adapt to e-commerce. Many banking and finance sites have only partially automated the process, requiring the customer to complete an application, then wait for a telephone representative to call back to complete the transaction. The primary hurdle has been the complexity of the process, which required credit checks and verifications of the customer's assets, liabilities, employment status, and other information.

HomeSide Lending, Inc., headquartered in Jacksonville, Florida, is the sixth largest servicer and the twelfth largest originator of residential mortgages in the nation. HomeSide is also one of the few lenders that has mastered the entire mortgage application and approval process online. Although best known for its secondary mortgage business, over the past few years HomeSide has built a direct sales channel for customers seeking to refinance or purchase their homes.

Based on the lessons of an earlier Web foray, HomeSide developed a unique automated mortgage approval process that can be completed by applicants in as little as 10 minutes. This process required HomeSide to dramatically reengineer and simplify traditional loan underwriting and approval procedures. The new system uses a Java 2 Platform, Enterprise Edition (J2EE)-compliant application using the BEA WebLogic Server built with an existing Oracle 8.1.5 database and an internally developed loan approval application, with XML integration to an underwriting system powered by Fannie Mae technology. The Web application and existing system are deployed on HP UX 11 platforms.

The resulting application not only powers a new online mortgage sales channel, but has been used to streamline call-center sales as well. The new application actually went live on the call center three months before the new Web channel debuted in December 2000. During the first few months, conversion rates for phone sales alone have increased by 75 percent. HomeSide's current plans are to continue offering the new streamlined process itself, and to co-brand it with channel partners to reach wider customer bases.

4.1.1   The Company

HomeSide has grown dramatically in recent years. Formerly a Bank of Boston subsidiary, the company grew by acquisition over the past five years, and was subsequently acquired by National Australia Bank in late 1997. The company's roots came from secondary mortgage lending, in which mortgages are purchased from primary issuers, such as banks, mortgage brokers, and other retail lending institutions.

Today, the company services nearly $175 billion worth of mortgages for nearly two million homeowners. To its customers, HomeSide is the agent that sends mortgage bills and related statements, while handling escrow payments for taxes and insurance.

Among HomeSide's competitive advantages is its efficient cost structure. Because the company is not a traditional "brick-and-mortar" lender, HomeSide has not had to maintain a high-overhead branch network. Another critical differentiator is that, unlike many lenders, HomeSide relies on its own technology platform. This bootstrap strategy helped HomeSide reengineer the home loan underwriting and sales process. HomeSide's Mortgage Desktop, a client-server program that uses an advanced, rules-based workflow engine, provides a fast, automated, intelligent workflow application that delivers home-mortgage approvals quickly.

While the company's core business is focused on secondary markets, once HomeSide assumes the loan, it also assumes the relationship with the homeowner. Thanks to its exposure to nearly two million customers, its efficient, direct business model, and its sophisticated technology base, HomeSide is well-positioned to offer a wide array of home financing products to its customer base.

According to Robert Davis, senior vice president of global e-business development, up to 20 percent of HomeSide's customers consider refinancing in any given year. "When our customers want to refinance, we want to keep them as customers," he explains.

Consequently, HomeSide has developed an active business selling mortgages to customers looking to purchase homes or refinance their homes to get better rates. Three years ago, after opening a call center to handle refinances, HomeSide also began looking at developing a Web-based marketing channel, and developed an early partnership with Intuit and Microsoft. Those early experiences provided valuable lessons on how to effectively sell refinancing over the Web.

4.1.2 Technology Adoption

HomeSide's IT organization was already highly experienced in developing complex applications. The IT group, which was built up through HomeSide's acquisitions, had an extensive background developing mainframe and UNIX-based retail and secondary home financing applications.

The existing back-office application was used originally for the call center. Based on a two-tier client–server architecture, it was written in C++ to run on Windows NT clients and an HP-UX server. It ran against an Oracle database, and operated using a sophisticated, rules-based workflow engine that was custom developed using BrightWare's ART*Enterprise expert system development framework. The application was written modularly, largely in C++. It features separate "engines" dedicated to individual loan processes such as rate comparisons and closing costs. Each of the engines is integrated via point-to-point socket interfaces.

The application's rule-based workflow guided the call-center representative through the process. Once the data collection was completed, a block file was submitted for the underwriting decisions. When underwriting gave the go-ahead, the HomeSide application generated rate quotations and terms (including all closing costs).

"We had good existing call-center technology, but we needed new technology and a streamlined business process to bring this solution to the Web," explains Bill Reed, director of technology, who notes that the success drove HomeSide to develop a fully automated Web sales channel that could scale even further.

A diverse project team which included both technology and business domain specialists guided the new effort, dubbed Project Tango. The project drew on many of the developers who initially created the call-center application, plus consultants from Modis Inc., a global systems integration firm, as well as other integrators.

4.2 Business Problem

Until recently, the online mortgage process was anything but quick and seamless. Getting information on loan availability and rates was fairly straightforward. However, the next part of the process—qualifying applicants for mortgages—proved to be the big stumbling block. This step requires credit reports, verifications of employment and bank deposits, property appraisals, and other information.

Traditionally, the banks handled this legwork. However, on the Web, the process had to be simple enough so that the customer could complete all the steps online during the same session.

In 1997, HomeSide entered into partnerships with Microsoft and Intuit to provide home mortgages online. Although the system could easily generate rates, the rest of the process was not automated. "It was a great shopping vehicle for consumers, but it couldn't easily take customers through the last steps toward approval," recalls Davis. Most customers ended up using the service for comparison shopping, printing out the prices and taking them to their local bank or mortgage broker to match. "Getting an online mortgage approval was far more difficult than trading a stock or buying a book online," Davis says. "The process required interaction with several third parties and was far too complicated."

Following that experience, HomeSide conducted focus groups over a four-month period to learn what information consumers would be willing to share with a mortgage lender, and under what conditions they would be willing to complete the mortgage transaction online.

Not surprisingly, the chief findings showed the process had to be fast and simple. Davis referred to data indicating that more than 80 percent of Web shopping carts were abandoned because the merchant never told the buyer how long it would take to complete the transaction, or because the process was too complicated. In addition, their research demonstrated that customers had to feel in control of the transaction and trust the merchant. The latter condition was a challenge since, not being a retail lender, HomeSide had relatively modest brand awareness.

For HomeSide, the research pointed to the need to reengineer the mortgage qualification process. As a result of detailed analysis, HomeSide was able to eliminate about half the normal questions by identifying information overlaps. "We created a brand new line of business," notes Davis. For instance, the analysis determined that the consumer's track record of making his or her house payment was a better determinant of credit worthiness than credit card payment history. The research also concluded that it was no longer necessary to require credit reports from three credit bureaus for every prospective customer. Instead, a single credit agency report would suffice, a major step that saved time and money in the mortgage process. Furthermore, the reengineered process eliminated the need for the consumer to furnish current employer, employment history, and automobile ownership information.

By working to streamline the process, HomeSide was able to develop a more friendly Web site that enables the customer to get an online mortgage approval decision in one sitting, with very little "data gathering" on his or her part.

4.2.1 Challenges

HomeSide's recent growth was made possible in large part due to its unique technology platform, which was already in use at its call center prior to the development of the Web application. Based on a custom-developed C++ application, as well as a rules-based engine from BrightWare, the company could grant approvals to loan applications in real time, although with considerable human hand-holding.

However, the Web application had to be designed so that prospective customers could have the choice of completing the process without human assistance. In large part, this requirement was due to the growing perception that self-service e-commerce is quicker, more convenient, and often more precise than ordering/applying by phone or mail, or buying at a store. Obviously, the site had to allow customers to request live customer assistance if necessary. Toward that end, the system had to permit *concurrent* access to the same record for Web customers whose actions would be guided by call-center assistance. And HomeSide's solution also had to leverage the existing back-office application, which generates terms and conditions, and handles offline functions, such as document printing. It also had to leverage the existing Oracle database.

Therefore, the Web application had to be designed with a logical navigational flow. In addition, it had to integrate with several existing systems, including HomeSide's mortgage workflow application, which includes the core business logic, and the underwriting system powered by Fannie Mae technology, which guides HomeSide's loan acceptance decisions.

Furthermore, the integration had to be flexible. The existing approach—using socket-based interfaces that allow the different application "engines" (or components) to communicate with each other—was custom developed, and therefore not supported by any vendors. The proprietary design presented a long-term maintenance burden. When the application was modified or redeployed, the protocols used for passing messages through the socket interfaces would often have to be modified because of the point-to-point nature of the socket interfaces. The team required a standard, vendor-supported alternative to separate the application logic from the deployment and integration mechanism.

Although the new Web application involved the replacement of custom socket interfaces, one of the interfaces was kept in place for use with an existing, Windows NT-based third-party product for calculating annual percentage rates, or APRs. Because the government regulates this calculation, HomeSide chose to utilize the services of an outside vendor rather than develop its own calculation engine. The custom socket interface remained necessary because the vendor does not offer a version of its product for UNIX or Java technology.

Other major challenges included designing for scalability. The architecture of the application and the technology base had to support growth, without the need to rewrite the application each time a new server was added. Furthermore, because the Internet rewards companies that are quickest to market, the application had to be designed using a highly productive platform that would enable HomeSide to add or modify functionality rapidly as necessary. The result was that the application had to have a multitier architecture that would keep HomeSide's deployment options as open as possible.

4.3   Technology Choices

Developing the HomeSide application involved selecting the appropriate technologies for their specific functionality and benefits.

4.3.1   Java Technology

Industry standards played a central role in HomeSide's decision to design the new application using a J2EE architecture. "We could have taken a more modest approach by simply writing HyperText Markup Language clients with Common Gateway Interface scripts," Reed says. "We saw this as one of our targeted growth businesses for the company. So we decided to design around an industry-standard platform that was stable and forward-looking."

Therefore, HomeSide chose to develop its new online mortgage application based on the J2EE platform. "Java technology had a lot of momentum going for it in the e-commerce arena," says Reed. "The J2EE platform was based on proven technology, and it was gaining critical mass adoption. We saw it becoming an industry standard."

Most important, the emerging J2EE platform standard provided a framework of services, which eliminated the burden of custom development. For instance, the J2EE platform provided ready-made alternatives to the custom, point-to-point socket interfaces that HomeSide had written in its earlier client–server application. With the new application, HomeSide wanted to redirect its development efforts to business functionality rather than infrastructure. "We don't want to be in the business of writing interfaces, component structures, or transaction management. With the J2EE platform, we can focus our efforts where they deliver the best value," says Brian Higdon, the system architect and a consultant with Enterprise Logic.

4.3.2   XML

XML transactions are used to make the entire application transparent. They encompass many internal interactions, such as checking the rules base to retrieve legal requirements and applicable fee structures that are valid for the state in which the transaction is taking place. XML is also used for all business-to-business transactions in the system, such as interactions with the loan investors or with credit card issuers (for payment of mortgage application fees). HomeSide used the Xerces Project parser for all XML document processing and made use of both the DOM and SAX APIs.

The HomeSide Web application interacted with third-party proprietary underwriting technology using numerous XML transactions. HomeSide worked to define the document type definition (DTD) used by all of the XML documents.

For instance, loan processing includes the following XML transactions.

- **Pull-Indicative-Rates Request.** This transaction returns current or historical pricing information. The data can be thought of as the "wholesale" pricing that is provided. HomeSide adds its fees to this data to come up with the final rates it offers to the general public.

- **Casefile ID Request.** This transaction gathers a group of "casefile IDs," or unique identifiers that HomeSide uses to uniquely refer to a loan throughout its life in the system. One of these numbers is assigned to each loan the system processes.

- **Credit Report Request.** This transaction initiates a request to retrieve a credit report for one or more borrowers from a third-party consumer reporting agency, which provides the data back to HomeSide for processing.

- **Underwriting and Price Request.** The outcome of this transaction is the decision to approve the loan for a set of products at specified rate/point combinations, subject to the consumer submitting an application to HomeSide; verification of income, employment, and assets; and providing HomeSide with an acceptable property. If the loan is not approved for any number of reasons, including too much debt, insufficient funds, and so forth, consumers are asked to contact the call center. This provides the call-center representative the opportunity to correct any errors the consumer may have made during data entry and to submit a loan application that would satisfy the requirements of HomeSide and the applicable investor.

- **Rate Option/Lock Notification Request.** This transaction notifies underwriting that a consumer has chosen to "lock" his or her loan at a given interest rate and point combination. From the Web perspective, this is the last transaction the consumer performs with underwriting.

The following is an example of the XML document used for the Credit Report Request.

```xml
<?xml version="1.0" encoding="UTF-8"?>
<!DOCTYPE ECommerce_Message SYSTEM "E_Commerce_Interfaces_v1.01.dtd">
<ECommerce_Message>
    <CreditReportRequestInput>
    <RequestHeader BusinessSourceID="HSL" LenderID="2329282-A2"
RequestorSubmissionDateTimeStamp="20010110 08:56:34"
RequestorTypeCode="LT"/>
    <Casefile CasefileID="2232410998"/>
    <ApplicantSummaries>
    <ApplicantSummary ApplicantSSN="999889215" ApplicantTypeCode="0"
CoAppSSN="999889210" FirstName="PENELOPE" LastName="PUBLIC"
MiddleName="A">
    <Location City="LOUISVILLE" State="KY" StreetAddress="2935 AUGUSTA
ST" ZipCode="40219"/>
    </ApplicantSummary>
    <ApplicantSummary ApplicantSSN="999889210" ApplicantTypeCode="1"
CoAppSSN="999889215" FirstName="PETER" LastName="PUBLIC"
MiddleName="E">
    <Location City="LOUISVILLE" State="KY" StreetAddress="2935 AUGUSTA
ST" ZipCode="40219"/>
    </ApplicantSummary>
    </ApplicantSummaries>
    <CreditAgencyInstructions AgencyAccountNumber="239921"
AgencyPassword="292113" MergeTypeCode="1" ReportFormatTypeCode="1"
ServiceProviderName="ir"/>
    </CreditReportRequestInput>
</ECommerce_Message>
```

In most cases, these XML transactions are triggered as customers enter data to the Web-page forms. However, the Pull-Indicative-Rates and Casefile ID Requests are batch transactions in nature and are not initiated by any consumer action. To perform these automated transactions, HomeSide used the time services API of BEA WebLogic.

4.4   Vendor Selection

HomeSide's IT infrastructure was already open systems-based, consisting of HP UX servers and Windows NT clients. Therefore, the Java application had to support these platforms. In addition, because the application involved complex interactions with the Oracle database, an application platform with proven transaction management functionality was required. Given its decision to embrace J2EE standards, HomeSide's platform required an application server that would support technologies such as Enterprise JavaBeans (EJBs), Java ServerPages (JSPs), and Java Servlets.

HomeSide chose BEA WebLogic Server for both the application server and the Web-server tiers. "We liked BEA's close conformance to the J2EE specifications, and that WebLogic has been one of the earliest products to support them," says Higdon. At the time, BEA WebLogic was also one of the only J2EE products that ran on the HP UX platform. He adds that BEA's transaction management technology also helped clinch the deal. With BEA WebLogic Server, HomeSide could build an application that was flexible enough to support database concurrency, allowing Web customers and call-center staff to access the same records and process during the same session.

Having worked with the BEA Tuxedo transaction monitor while with a previous company, Higdon was already quite familiar with the technology. "BEA has a history of knowing transaction management," he says.

In addition, HomeSide felt that while there was competition from other vendors, BEA has both the market share and mindshare to ensure that BEA WebLogic Server would not become an orphaned product.

4.5   Application Architecture

The architecture for the Homside Lending application consisted of four tiers: client, Webserver, application server, and database.

4.5.1   Client Tier

The Web client uses a standard browser with HTML to make it as accessible and efficient as possible.

4.5.2   Web-Server Tier

A proxy server, which currently runs on a four-processor, HP L-class midrange UNIX server, caches the static home page and some graphics to deliver fast response, as well as to provide an additional layer of security in front of the Web server. All other Web pages that are served are generated through the use of JSPs that are deployed by the Web server.

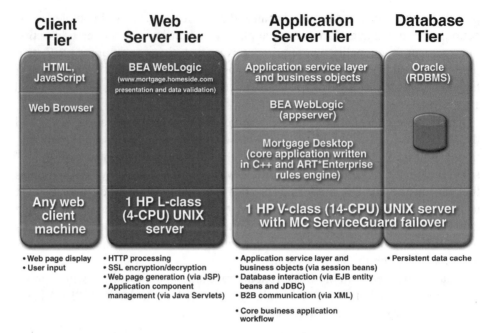

Figure 4.1 HomeSide Application Current Architecture

Performance was a key design criterion. Therefore, with the exception of the home page (which is cached), most pages carry relatively simple graphics to minimize download times. Future plans call for redeploying the Web server on a cluster of smaller HP A-class servers.

The Web tier handles data presentation and validation. It also contains a servlet that manages the JSP pages that are displayed as the consumer moves from page to page on the Web site.

4.5.3 Application-Server Tier

BEA WebLogic Server is deployed on a 14-processor HP V-class server, which accesses a dedicated EMC storage array. In addition, there is an HP T600 server configured as a failover box using the HP high availability product, MC Service-Guard. (Currently, the database and existing back-office application also run on the same servers. In the future, HomeSide plans to redeploy the Web application on a separate array of servers.)

The application-server tier provides a service layer for the Web-server tier. These services invoke the back-end processing, where the real mortgage processing work is performed. On this tier, the functions of the mortgage application process are handled, including user authentication, all database interaction via JDBC, along with interaction with the underwriting system, powered by Fannie Mae technology.

The application tier divides labors as follows.

- A service layer is provided to the Web tier, which encompasses the ability to order credit reports, underwriting, data persistence, closing cost calculations, and credit card charging. Additional services provide the data that is used to fill in the drop-downs on the data-entry forms on the Web tier.

- The underwriting system makes the loan acceptance decisions.

Currently deployed on the same server as the existing application and database, future plans call for migrating the Java application to its own clustered servers.

4.5.4   Database Tier

The back end includes the twin foundation components: the existing mortgage-loan approval system, which serves as the core business logic, and the Oracle database.

4.5.5   Data Integration

Session beans coordinate the actions of entity beans for all interactions with the back-end Oracle database. These session beans provide a service layer that the Web-server tier uses for all interactions with the database, the underwriting system, and the "legacy" rules-based decision-making applications.

To promote ease of use, the application provides several options for customers to save their data and continue their sessions at a more convenient time. For instance, at several critical points during the data entry process, the Web server calls a service on the application server, requesting that it persist the data the user has entered to that point. By doing this, the customer does not have to reenter data should the browser or Internet connection fail. In addition, the customer has the ability to click a Save and Continue Later button. This option allows the customer to save his or her data at that point and log out. The customer is then free either to return to the Web site at a later time and complete the loan application, or, phone the call center and continue the loan process with the assistance of a loan officer.

All communications initiated by the Web tier involve the creation of Java serializable objects. These objects are used as parameters to the back-end service tier when one of the services is invoked. When responding to the request, the application tier sends back the appropriate information either in the form of a Java serializable object or an XML document. XML documents passed between the Web and application tiers are considerably different in both form and content from XML documents passed between the application server and the underwriting system.

These documents have considerable "value added," provided by other application-tier services, and as such cannot be simply translated using a technology such as XSLT.

The services that communicate with the underwriting system retrieve data either from objects written in the Java language which are passed to them or from the previously persisted data in the database. Using the Apache Xerces XML API, HomeSide builds the XML documents to be transmitted for underwriting. The Document Object Model (DOM) Level 1 API is used for constructing the XML documents sent to underwriting. However when parsing the XML documents, because of their size (sometimes as much as 70K), the Simple API for XML or SAX, version 1.0, is used for parsing the data into compound Java objects. This approach proves more efficient than using DOM for parsing and allows the data to be "grouped" into vectors of objects that can be easily persisted or sent to other services for additional processing. Similarly, XML is also used for other business-to-business transactions, such as getting credit card authorizations for customers paying the standard mortgage application fee.

Based on the underwriting decision, the HomeSide system generates the response—whether the customer can get a mortgage, and under what terms. In most cases, customers may qualify for a choice of mortgage options, with varying terms, rates, and documentation requirements. In many cases, customers may qualify for several dozen options.

Each of the rate and point combinations that underwriting supports for that customer must be augmented with HomeSide's pricing adjustments. These adjustments are made with the assistance of the Art*Enterprise rule engines originally developed for HomeSide's previous origination system.

Once these adjustments are made, the data is converted for a final time into an XML document that is sent back to the Web-server tier to display to the consumer. The Web-tier servlet extracts the relevant data from the XML document using DOM. It then displays to the customer a table of the most attractive loan options, based on the criteria they defined when the request was submitted. If the consumer qualifies, additional loan options may be viewed by clicking buttons that lead to more pages with tables of other loan options.

Consumers are never rejected on the Web site. Should the consumer not meet established underwriting guidelines, they are presented with a page that refers them to HomeSide's call center. Here an experienced loan officer may be able to identify alternative loan solutions to meet the customers' needs.

4.6   Solution Analysis

In order to solve specific technical issues, a mix of technologies needed to be used, including Enterprise JavaBeans, Servlets and Java ServerPages, XML, JNDI, and others.

4.6.1   Enterprise JavaBeans (EJBs)

Session beans encapsulate all interactions with the back-office mortgage application first developed with C++ and Art*Enterprise as part of HomeSide's previous origination system. Session beans, via the service layer, also control the entity beans that access the Oracle database.

4.6.2   Session Maintenance

A session is established when a customer registers on the site or logs back in, using a previously entered user name and password. Like many e-commerce sites, transactions are grouped on a page basis (when the customer presses the Continue button) to minimize database interactions. This feature also allows customers to pick up where they left off if the Web connection is disrupted, or for transactions to be rolled back and resumed if the entry somehow becomes corrupted.

HomeSide developers wrote approximately 40 session beans and roughly 150 entity beans. By comparison the database numbered over 200 individual tables.

4.6.3   Entity Beans

While session beans provide a service layer for the Web server, entity beans are used for persisting and retrieving data from Oracle tables. The entity beans were based on the database's table structure, with one entity bean per table. "At the time we designed this, we thought this was the most straightforward solution, and it was the approach recommended by many professionals," says Jeff Griffith, the consultant who was the primary entity-bean developer. He adds, "In retrospect, it would have been more efficient for us to have designed the entity beans as true objects representing concepts rather than a simple one-to-one mapping to the table. That would have made the objects less granular." Instead of being table-specific, the entity beans would have corresponded to common application objects such as property, borrower, or loan.

In fact, designing object-based entity beans might have been more complex at the outset, because it would have required the object/relational mappings to be designed into the bean itself, rather than the application. However, in the long run, using object-based beans would have incurred less maintenance, since there would have been fewer of them to manage.

Nonetheless, most of the time, the application invokes a small fraction of the beans, such as those relating to contact information and basic information about the loan, such as loan amount and property location.

4.6.4   Persistence

HomeSide used Bean-Managed Persistence (BMP) to manage object/relational database mappings, and to maintain state. The team decided to have each bean manage persistence individually because the alternative—Container-Managed Persistence (CMP)—would have required more performance overhead for its more-generalized settings.

In order to provide for scalability, the application would need to deploy BEA WebLogic on a clustered configuration. Due to concurrency issues, CMP entity beans in a clustered installation must assume that the database is shared with other instances of the bean. This limitation means that an entity bean built to mimic the database structure would have caused two round trips to the database any time a getter or setter method was called on the bean. First the bean would execute a select on the database to fill the bean with current information. After the get or set was complete, the bean would then execute an update to ensure that the database matched the current state of the bean.

According to Griffith, this level of database activity proved impractical for the application because of the sheer volume of data that could come from the underwriting system for each transaction. BMP allows the developer to control when the database is accessed. The primary hurdle in this case is, again, concurrency. There is a tradeoff between developer effort when writing code that uses BMP entity beans, and performance of the BMP beans. "We chose to require our developers to pay close attention to all BMP access, and to manage concurrency ourselves in order to gain the tremendous performance benefits provided by BMP entity beans" notes Griffith. The use of BMP beans resulted in a fivefold increase in database access efficiency, a welcome performance benefit for a Web-based application.

4.6.5   Interaction with Existing Applications

A key function performed by Session Beans is the interface with HomeSide's existing loan origination application. As noted below, the existing application is activated after the loan approval process. At this stage of the process, the workflows vary by customer, dictating the use of the existing system.

4.6.6 Servlets and Java ServerPages

Servlets are used in conjunction with JSPs to coordinate the front end. Specifically, a "master" servlet is used for activating the JSPs that, in turn, dynamically generate the Web pages.

Significantly, servlets, rather than HomeSide's existing loan origination application, are used for managing all the basic steps required for getting loan approvals. Servlets could handle this task because, on the Web, the process for all customers is the same.

Relationship with Existing Application

Although servlets handle the standard workflows for the loan approval process, once the underwriting decision is delivered, the workflows vary by consumer. Instead of reinventing the wheel, HomeSide leveraged its existing loan origination application based on C++, and used Session Beans to encapsulate interaction with the system.

This part of the process involves extensive data gathering that is conducted on the back end, isolating the consumer from all the complexity. At this stage, the existing application choreographs all workflows, including the gathering of all remaining information (such as income and asset verifications) and the completion of all necessary tasks (such as ordering appraisals or flood certifications) in the proper sequence, all the way through the final printing of the actual closing documents.

4.6.7 JNDI

The Java Naming and Directory Interface (JNDI) provides location transparency when locating services. This transparency helps to make the migration to a clustered environment a relatively trivial exercise.

4.6.8 JMS

Java Message Service (JMS) was employed in the service layer for some of the long-running beans. Those beans include the underwriting and credit report ordering beans. A pool of servers was set up to read the messages written to the JMS queue and process the transaction. By doing this, HomeSide was able to put a governor on the number of simultaneous underwriting or credit report transactions that can occur. This allows them to better manage system resources, since the underwriting process can sometimes be long and resource-intensive. Significantly, this mechanism is very similar to the new Message Driven Bean component introduced in the EJB 2.0 specification.

4.6.9   Oracle Database

The existing database and table structure was, for the most part, maintained with the new application. However, the changes in the business process and workflow dictated some minor modifications and the addition of new tables.

4.6.10   XML

This standard data format is used for most interactions, except to and from the Oracle database, in order to keep the data as transparent as possible. Using XML is critical, especially to HomeSide's OEM marketing strategy, which involves having retail partners co-brand the process to sell mortgages to their customers. The use of XML simplifies the task of adapting this process for OEM deployment, because data can be converted using off-the-shelf XML parsing tools.

4.7   Current Results

The HomeSide on-line mortgage system has been phased in, going live for the call-center staff in September 2000, followed by the release of the new external Web site, in December. "Our goal was a system that would be truly self-reliant," says Higdon. By taking the phased approach, the HomeSide development team was able to evaluate ease of use, scalability, and performance, before opening it to direct customer access on the Web.

By all measures, the initial shakedown was successful. Since going live, the application based on BEA WebLogic Server has successfully handled a daily average of one million to two million database hits, and 6,000 to 7,000 XML business-to-business transactions. When this account was written, the public Web site had not been open long enough to provide meaningful figures. However, based on three months of results from the call-center, the new application has improved call-center productivity by 60 percent alone, an indication of the site's potential ease of user for customers accessing directly over the Web.

Significantly, the system has plenty of room for growth. The development team embraced component-based development approaches, based on J2EE-compliant technology. This enables HomeSide's application to expand, through redeployment, into more-scalable distributed configurations, without rewriting the application. Aside from modifying deployment targets, the only noticeable changes will involve migration to BEA WebLogic 6.0, which supports the EJB 2.0 draft standard. The team expects those changes to be minor.

4.8   Future Directions

According to Higdon, players such as HomeSide have to embrace change as part of their competitive strategy. For instance, the company in its current form is the product of merger and acquisition. "Mergers and acquisitions are facts of life in our industry," says Higdon. "Our use of component-based design principles means that we can modify or replace parts of the application without disrupting the business." For instance, changes could be made to business logic in a service layer EJB without affecting the Web layer. Conversely, JSPs that generate graphics, logos, or other presentation details could easily be swapped out and recompiled, without any disruption to the Web site.

He adds that BEA's support of J2EE standards helps HomeSide keep its future deployment options open. First, there is the fact that both Java technology and BEA support open systems standards. "We are assured that WebLogic will run on whatever server platform we choose," notes Higdon, who adds, "Since BEA WebLogic Server is scalable to any kind of hardware platform we may need, our business can grow well beyond our current projections and we will be able to handle the additional load."

Then there is the issue of staying current with technology. "With the J2EE platform and BEA WebLogic Server, we believe we will stay up-to-date with the latest trends in the marketplace. That gives us a pathway to the new and emerging standards that Sun and its partners are developing, and helps us to retain developers who are interested in working on the cutting-edge, and keeping their skills marketable." Higdon is confident that BEA's strategy to support new J2EE platform standards as early as possible will give HomeSide an important technical competitive edge over other lenders.

4.8.1   Distributed Deployment

HomeSide plans to redeploy the application and Web server tiers into a more equitably distributed configuration that takes advantage of clustering to provide high availability. Specifically, the application server (which contains the EJBs) will be moved off the large HP V-class server, which currently houses the database and back-end application. "We had to prove the viability of the new system before we could buy the right hardware for the application," notes Higdon.

Under the new deployment plan, BEA WebLogic Server will be based on a cluster of HP L-class servers (the same systems currently used for the Web-server tier). The Web server layer will be moved onto smaller, rack-mounted HP A500 machines that are more appropriately sized for the task (they will be based on a

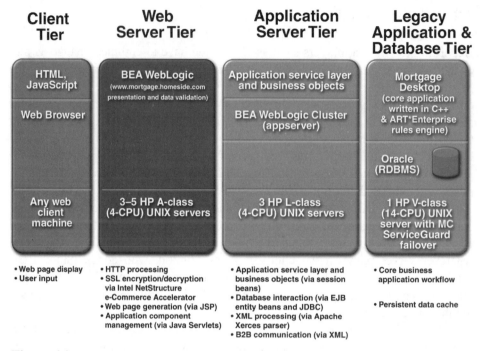

Figure 4.2   HomeSide Application Proposed Future Architecture

cluster of multiple, four-processor systems). In addition, accelerators for performing compute-intensive secure socket layer (SSL) encryption/decryption processes will be used to increase performance.

The database will remain on the V-class machine, along with the legacy applications, which should experience a significant performance improvement once the application server is moved off onto the cluster.

4.8.2   Upgrades

When the project began in late 1999, HomeSide implemented the Web application using BEA WebLogic Server 4.5.2, which supported version 1.0 of the EJB spec. The development team has already begun migrating to BEA WebLogic Server version 6.0, adopting the emerging EJB 2.0 specification.

However, the transition to a newer version of the EJB spec may affect the current development schedule somewhat. That will require such changes as:

- Conversion of the deployment descriptors from text to XML

- Code modifications, such as the use of the RMI-IIOP compatible narrow method instead of the look-up method that was used in the EJB 1.0 spec

According to Higdon, the changes should be somewhat minor, but will require a thorough regression test of the system.

HomeSide is also looking at approaches to speed the download of Web pages from its site. Toward that end, it is reducing the size and number of graphics on the site, favoring a textual Next anchor rather than a graphic. In these cases, the differences won't affect the use of JSPs; they will still be used to generate Web pages that happen to contain fewer images. However, another alternative being considered would, in some cases, substitute the use of JSPs with Dynamic HTML for features such as task bars. The team has yet to decide what its Web-page tune-up strategy will be.

HomeSide also plans to add additional services to make the data-entry process less error-prone. An address validation service will be provided in the near future. This will standardize and correct the data the user enters for home address, as well as property address, and make sure the ZIP code matches the entry. HomeSide will also add checks to ensure the city, county, and area codes match to ensure the user is entering correct data. Correcting the data at this point will help speed the processing of the loan later and will ensure a timely close of the loan.

4.9 Lessons Learned

HomeSide has applied valuable lessons learned during its initial foray into Web commerce by redesigning the business process to make online home mortgage lending more attractive to consumers. In so doing, it has adopted a strategy to maximize reuse of core business logic, while building a Web-commerce infrastructure that emphasizes flexibility, scalability, and adherence to open standards.

Specifically, HomeSide has made extensive use of J2EE technologies to design an application that is modular and easy to maintain. A master servlet coordinates the standard workflows used for data entry during the initial loan approval step, allowing this process to be maintained without affecting other back-end functions. Interaction between the Web application and the existing back-end loan origination systems is similarly modularized through encapsulation inside a session bean. In addition, the use of JNDI will facilitate application redeployment because it modularizes all user access to application services. Because of the transaction-intensive nature of home-mortgage lending processes, and the huge potential market for online mortgages, the modularity of the design based on the J2EE platform will allow HomeSide considerable flexibility when it comes to redeploying the application to support incoming traffic levels.

The use of standard XML transactions with the underwriting system results in an open process that can be applied by any of HomeSide's prospective business partners, who may wish to brand the process with their customers.

HomeSide looked to BEA WebLogic Server, both for its strong support of J2EE standards and because of BEA's expertise with transaction processing. "With WebLogic, we are assured of working with a tool that fully supports our transaction-intensive processes," says Higdon.

For more on BEA, see http://www.bea.com. For the HomeSide Lending Web site, see http://www.homeside.com.

Borland

Borland/AT&T Unisource

About the Author

William Louth is a J2EE/CORBA solutions architect for Borland Europe. He has extensive experience in building large-scale distributed systems in the banking and telecom industries. Currently, he is working on performance tuning of J2EE systems built on top of Borland products, and on the development of ancillary products. Louth is the architect of the CORE system at AT&T Unisource and the developer of CORE's innovative Object-Oriented User Interface (OOUI) framework.

Rod Peacock is a senior systems consultant currently working in the telecommunications industry. He has considerable experience in object-oriented systems within the telecom, financial, and broadcasting industries. Currently, he is at work on large-scale distributed systems built using the J2EE and CORBA architectures. Peacock was a senior developer for the AT&T Unisource corporate development team, working under William Louth specifically for the Core project.

CHAPTER 5

AT&T Unisource: Cost-Optimized Routing Environment on the Borland AppServer

RELEASED in beta form in December 1999, after four months of development, the CORE (Cost Optimized Routing Environment) project is a set of integrated tools to help deliver significant cost savings within the voice network business of AT&T Unisource.

CORE tools were integrated through a Java application called the CORE Desktop Environment (CDE). They were built around a component model that reflected both the structure and behavior of the voice network. The tools and their visual representations provided a pleasing, highly interactive user experience that offered speed of execution, consistent display, and sophisticated, extensible features. The main client, a Java application, provided advanced usage and functionality; a browser-based front end provided the advantages of a thin-client interface.

The tools used to build the solution included Borland AppServer, built on top of Visibroker 4, JBuilder Enterprise Edition, and Unified Modeling Language (UML) design tools. The technologies used in the CORE project included CORBA 2.3, XML, and Java 2 Platform, Enterprise Edition (J2EE) features, such as Enterprise JavaBeans (EJB), JDBC data access, Java Naming Directory Interface (JNDI), Java Servlets, and JavaServer Pages (JSP).

5.1 Technology Adoption

Before undertaking the CORE project, AT&T Unisource hadn't used the Java programming language on a full-scale production system. Most system development had relied on Microsoft and Delphi component technologies on the back end with Visual Basic for client-tier development. Typical architectures used either simple client-server or three-tier models. Business logic was concentrated heavily in either the client or the database tier, with little or no logic in the component tier.

Though projects had been successfully completed, management felt that the existing development model wasn't working well. Code reuse, scalability, failover support, and development productivity all needed to be improved to keep pace with telecommunication developments and trends. In short, the company felt it needed to improve its ability to deliver robust solutions in "Internet time." At the same time, the IT department was spending increasing time building and maintaining frameworks, an undertaking often complicated when initial creators of the frameworks moved on to new projects. Among the technologies that were repeatedly built into such frameworks were naming services, session-tracking mechanisms, persistence management, and transaction management. At the time, such services were just beginning to be made available through application servers implementing the J2EE specification. The specialized nature of these technologies often meant that the quality of the framework implementations wasn't always optimal, since infrastructure building was not the main business of the development team.

When the CORE project was proposed to the IT department, the first thought was that this would be the time to look for a general solution to these issues. The initial proposal was to build the CORE system using proprietary technologies. However, this didn't seem workable, since it would make it difficult to meet the various system requirements. There was also significant skepticism about the ambitious project timing—which, in any case, wouldn't deliver the application in time to meet the business requirements of the organization.

To address these concerns, the organization brought in a specialist in enterprise component development to assist in making a transition to newer technologies, and to act as architect and mentor to the development teams. The architect hired was a contractor, with no connection to either the company or to any specific tools vendor. On joining the team, the architect set down some ground rules for developing the solution. Though some of these rules may seem simplistic, contradictory, or amusing, they proved very useful to the team. The ground rules were:

- **Standardize.** The architect proposed basing the system on established and emerging industry standards with the support and backing of more than one vendor. The standards at that time included the Java programming language;

C++ and other languages; component technologies, such as CORBA and Enterprise JavaBeans; and other technical standards, such as XML. When selecting an implementation, the architect recommended giving preference to vendors that provided compliance to specifications and broad support of as many related standards as possible.

- **Use Best-of-Breed Tools.** Tool selection would be based on the technical merit and effective integration with other tools. Some total-package solutions provided by vendors were seen to have significant weaknesses as end-to-end solutions. The alternative approach was to select the best available tools for each task, and to be sure that their conformance to standards enabled them to be used together effectively. Tool selection also took into account potential vendor lock-in that could result from tools that used proprietary application frameworks or produced proprietary code tags.

- **Take a User-Centric Approach.** The system needed to be easily tailored to user needs, not shaped by the requirements of some hyped-up technology. The required systems had to be delivered to end users on time and had to effectively integrate into their workflow. The user interface technology also had to allow for new workflows that hadn't been possible with earlier technologies, due to their inherent restrictions.

These user interface design requirements suggested the need for an object-oriented approach that would be intuitive, simple, consistent, complete, extensible, and responsive. Every effort would be made to balance system processing between the client and server, while concealing the distributed nature of the system from the end user. It was also clear that the user interface needed to accommodate different user backgrounds and levels of experience. To meet all these goals, users were to be involved in the design process from the outset, not subjected to prolonged, painful, and frustrating usability issues that result from not gathering user feedback early and often.

- **Aim to Do Nothing.** For system infrastructure, the goal was to avoid any development work at all. Delivering the CORE system was the main goal, rather than building a naming service, transaction service, persistence-mapping engine, or any other system infrastructure.

To this end, all development efforts were to be focused on delivering added value to end users. The reference architecture from the CORE system was a deliverable to the IT department. The architecture and its implementation had to provide inherent scalability, reliability, robustness, and performance. The view of the company and team echoed that of industry analyst Anne Thomas, who referred to IT departments that attempt to build their own application servers as "those who practice self-abuse."

- **Partner with Vendors.** The vendor for each tool involved in developing the CORE application had to demonstrate that it understood the need to be partners in the undertaking. The project was very ambitious, with no time to wait on slow communications regarding support. Where new technologies were being applied, senior members from the vendor's development team needed to be available on short notice to discuss usage, standards compliance, potential features and enhancements, product direction, bug fixes, and other critical path issues.

5.2   Business and Technological Challenges

The CORE application development team was faced with a number of critical challenges, from both business and technical standpoints. Its ability to handle these challenges was key to the success of the solution.

5.2.1   Business Problem

Major legislative and competitive changes in the telecommunications industry led AT&T Unisource to seek significant reductions in off-net voice traffic costs. To do this, it needed the ability to reconfigure network switched routing tables regularly—monthly or even daily. The CORE system was proposed to provide a real-time routing configuration environment supporting both least-cost routing (LCR) and optimal-cost routing (OCR). LCR is to the voice network routing what Hotspot is to Java technology process execution, an effort to improve the performance of an existing design without altering it. LCR provides improvements, but it is limited by current network design and contractual obligations. OCR provides an approach based on optimizing the design of the network to allow even further improvements by LCR.

5.2.2   Obstacles

In designing and developing the solution, the team was presented with many obstacles, including automation of routing configuration for all switches on the network simultaneously. At the time development began, these operations were performed by highly trained switch engineers and even the smallest changes could take considerable time. Automating the process had the potential to reduce this effort, but would require a solution that could span multiple machines with different operating systems. This made the use of system proprietary technologies untenable.

To meet its design goals, the system needed to provide a software model representing the structure and configuration of the network at any point in time, for both accounting and auditing purposes. Some devices on the network used existing C libraries and interfaces, so CORBA technology (included in the J2EE platform) became a requirement for enabling objects implemented in different languages to interact. While Java Native Interface was also considered for this purpose, the team preferred an object interface around existing libraries for easy, transparent process distribution.

The CORE system also needed to let carriers submit pricing details efficiently, with less human intervention. XML technology was used to supporting this business-to-business communication. A carrier could submit pricing details by posting an XML document to a Web server. A document type definition (DTD) would be provided to all carriers to ensure the validity of the data. This simplified communication mechanism made it possible to speed up data entry of pricing information and turnaround of the routing process. Through its built-in validation mechanism, XML helped ensure high quality of the pricing data entering the system at either end. It also removed dependence on application macros formerly used for this task. These had previously been written and maintained in office productivity applications by the staff, so the CORE system helped to improve efficiency by eliminating this user burden.

5.2.3 Requirements

Because the CORE system was intended to offer a high level of automation, issues of scalability, reliability, failover support, and performance needed to be addressed early in the design process. Though the CORE system didn't initially have a large user population, scalability was important for other reasons, including the high level of user interaction, the required responsiveness of the user interface, and the complex nature of the transactions.

Another requirement was that the system adapt to the needs of several departments, each requiring access to certain information from all areas of the system. At the same time, it had to provide a robust security model to protect sensitive information that might be exposed as a result of this wide accessibility.

To maximize the potential savings and to meet contractual obligations, the system needed to be highly reliable and available. It needed to ensure that pricing data submitted by carriers could be acted on quickly and securely. Actions had to either execute completely or be rolled back completely in the event of system failure. With less dependency on switch engineers, the interface to the network needed to be available around the clock. This was required to allow business managers to monitor network configuration and to ensure that the system was meeting various operational goals, such as quality of service and cost effectiveness.

As in any distributed system, performance was an important factor, requiring early and constant attention. The CORE system needed to quickly create a software model of the network for any user and within any time frame. Along with batch updates to synchronize the database with routing tables in the network switches, transactions needed to be sufficiently fast to provide a "real-time" view of the current configuration. The routing models involve complex calculations, spanning large sections of network elements that needed to be represented persistently for modeling purposes. Optimized persistence would prove to be an important factor in meeting performance objectives.

The level of automation introduced to the network configuration process made it critical that the underlying architecture be robust and reliable. If any of the requirements specified here had not been met, the result would have been reduced confidence in the system, from both business and network engineering perspectives. This would have meant reduced reliance on the system and an end to future development. With this critical factor in mind, mature technology implementations were assessed.

5.3   Approaching the Challenges

Key to resolving the business and technical challenges was to develop a system that was flexible anough to accomodate existing systems while providing the means to do business in completely new ways. It was also key to find a vendor capable of delivering the latest technology while working closely with the CORE team to ensure its success.

5.3.1   Architecture Choice

The choice of an architecture was based on careful consideration of these issues and other factors, including available skill levels within the organization and discussions with senior representatives from leading development tool vendors. As a result, it was decided that the J2EE platform, which had just been publicly released in draft specification form, would be evaluated, along with CORBA, for the server-side component model used by the CORE system. Some important architectural services requirements, along with their J2EE and CORBA implementations, are summarized in Table 5.1.

A comparison of the features of these technologies with the system requirements covered earlier led to the decision to move to J2EE as the architecture of choice, with CORBA integration mandatory. CORBA was seen as very mature but still requiring substantial effort to use for building highly scalable, fault-tolerant business systems. At the same time, the CORBA component specification was in very early development, and there were no vendor implementations. In contrast, Enterprise JavaBeans, JDBC, servlets, and JavaServer Pages APIs (all incorporated into the J2EE specification) were proving to offer a simplified but powerful programming model. J2EE also promised to extend these technologies with a full list of enterprise services, as well as integration with CORBA 2.3.

Table 5.1   Architectural services requirements, with their J2EE and CORBA implementations

Service	J2EE Implementation	CORBA Implementation
Naming	**JNDI**	**CosNaming**
A naming service enables the development of powerful and portable directory-enabled applications	The Java Naming and Directory Interface (JNDI) provides a unified interface to multiple naming and directory services in the enterprise. As part of the Java Enterprise API set, JNDI enables seamless connectivity to heterogeneous enterprise naming and directory services.	The CosNaming service is a generic directory service. The naming service provides the principal mechanism through which most clients of an ORB-based system locate objects they intend to make requests of.
Database Connectivity	**JDBC 2.0**	**Not Specified**
Databases are nearly always an important feature of any large-scale enterprise application.	JDBC provides cross-DBMS connectivity to a wide range of SQL databases. With a JDBC technology-enabled driver, a developer can easily connect all corporate data, even in a heterogeneous environment.	CORBA doesn't specify database connectivity as a distinct service. Different database APIs, including JDBC, are expected to be used within each language mapping. Connecting transactional applications to databases is specified in CosTransactions service via resources and resource managers.
Transaction Management	**JTA/JTS**	**CosTransaction**
Transaction management is required to enforce the ACID transaction properties of atomicity, consistency, isolation, and durability.	J2EE includes support for distributed transactions through two specifications, Java Transaction API (JTA) and Java Transaction Service (JTS).	The Transaction service is a set of interfaces used to encapsulate a variety of existing transaction and resource-management technologies. It provides a standard interface across different implementations of transaction monitors.

continues

Table 5.1   Architectural services requirements, with their J2EE and CORBA implementations *(Continued)*

Service	J2EE Implementation	CORBA Implementation
Transaction Management	**JTA/JTS**	**CosTransaction**
	JTA is a high-level, implementation- and protocol-independent API that allows applications and application servers to access transactions. JTS specifies the implementation of a transaction manager, which supports JTA and implements the Java mapping of the OMG Object Transaction Service (OTS) 1.1 specification at the level below the API. JTS propagates transactions using the Internet Inter-ORB Protocol (IIOP).	The transaction service though, is used extensively with databases; it is not solely designed for this and has a wide range of applicability. The transactions service works in several modes, including direct and indirect context management and explicit and implicit propagation.
Component Model A component model should address the challenges in enterprise application development, which include concurrency, transactions, security, and data access. The distribution of such components over a network should also be transparent. Since many business components are inherently persistent, it is important that a component model address this in a powerful, portable, and configurable way, transparent to the component provider.	**EJB** Enterprise JavaBeans (EJB) servers reduce the complexity of developing middleware by providing automatic support for middleware services, such as transactions, security, database connectivity, and more. The EJB 1.1 specification requires that the EJB container provider implement persistence for entity beans with container-managed persistence. The advantage is that the entity bean can be largely independent from the data source in which the entity is stored.	**CORBA components** At the time of the CORE project's inception, the CORBA component model was still undergoing the OMG's submission stage, so there were no implementations. The three major parts of CORBA components are: 1. A container environment that packages transaction management, security, and persistence, and provides interface and event resolution 2. Integration with EJBs 3. A software distribution format

Table 5.1 Architectural services requirements, with their J2EE and CORBA implementations *(Continued)*

Service	J2EE Implementation	CORBA Implementation
Messaging Messaging provides a reliable, flexible service for the asynchronous exchange of critical business data and events throughout an enterprise. Messaging allows businesses to communicate asynchronously and across numerous decoupled processes. Messaging supports one-to-many and many-to-many communication.	**JMS** The Java Messaging Service (JMS) API improves programmer productivity by defining a common set of messaging concepts and programming strategies that will be supported by all JMS technology-compliant messaging systems. JMS is a set of interfaces and associated semantics that define how a JMS client accesses the facilities of an enterprise-messaging product.	**CosEvents and CosNotification** The Event service provides a generic model for push- and pull-based message passing. It allows for transmitting messages among components in a decoupled mode. Events are communicated using IIOP. The Notification service provides a way to filter events and allows for the quality of service to be specified. The CORBA Messaging Specification was under development at the time the CORE project was initiated.
Web Integration With increasing reliance on both the Internet and intranets for application distribution, close integration of Web services was key to developing the thin-client front ends included in the CORE system specification.	**Java Servlets/Java Server Pages** Java Servlets and Java Server Pages (JSP) are platform-independent, 100% pure Java server-side modules that fit seamlessly into a Web-server framework and can be used to extend the capabilities of a Web server with minimal overhead, maintenance, and support.	**Java Applets** The Firewall Specification defines a bi-directional General Inter-ORB Protocol connection useful for callbacks and event notifications. The Interoperable Name Service defines one URL-format object reference.

continues

Table 5.1   Architectural services requirements, with their J2EE and CORBA implementations *(Continued)*

Service	J2EE Implementation	CORBA Implementation
EIS Integration	**Connector**	**Not Specified**
As more businesses move toward an e-business strategy, integration with existing enterprise information systems (EIS) becomes the key to success. Enterprises with successful e-businesses need to integrate their existing enterprise information systems with new thin-client, Web-based applications.	The J2EE Connector architecture defines a standard architecture for connecting the J2EE platform to heterogeneous enterprise information systems. The J2EE Connector architecture enables an enterprise information system vendor to provide a standard resource adapter for its enterprise information system. The resource adapter plugs into an application server, providing connectivity among the system, the application server, and the enterprise application. If an application server vendor has extended its system to support the J2EE Connector architecture, it is assured of seamless connectivity to multiple EISs.	The CORBA components container does not address this directly. But through the transaction service and CORBA inherent cross-language support, it is possible to integrate into many enterprise information systems. Most vendors of such systems provide a CORBA interface (IDL) for some parts of their offering.

Note that the above descriptions refer to specifications and not implementations. In fact, an implementation of a service within one specification may be used as the basis for another. As one example, JTS/JTA can be built on top of implementations of the CosTransaction Service

Because the J2EE architecture is based on RMI-IIOP inter-object communications, it offered to combine the ease of the RMI programming model with the robustness and maturity of CORBA implementations. The CORBA-compliant IIOP protocol made it possible to interoperate with clients and servers implemented in other languages. In turn, this allowed planning for future migration and integration of the CORE system with other AT&T Unisource applications and systems.

5.3.2   Vendor Selection

After the desired technologies were identified, the next step involved contacting leading application server vendors to evaluate their offerings. The evaluation included prototyping, determining the level of standards compliance, and determining the level of technical quality of support provided. Vendors contacted included WebLogic, IBM (Websphere), Persistence, and Borland. The technical criteria for selection included

- Compliance with the J2EE specification, in particular with the EJB 1.1 specification

- CORBA 2.3 support, including RMI-IIOP as the communication protocol

- Support for container-managed persistence in entity beans

- Support for the Java 2 Platform, Standard Edition

- Support for JDBC 2.0, Servlets, and JavaServer Pages technologies

- Development tool integration

- Flexibility in partitioning systems across nodes and processes

- Ease of use in deployment, management, and clustering configuration

- Integration with application management tools

- Maturity of implementation and its underlying foundations

- Performance measurements through the use of a test program

Customer service criteria included

- Speed of vendor response to initial inquiries

- Level and quality of vendor technical support

- Feedback regarding concerns and queries coming from the vendor development team

- Vendor recognition of partnership as the basis for working together

Based on these criteria, the team decided to go with the Borland AppServer. Support from the local Borland office was very good and the Borland AppServer development team seemed very responsive and positive to questions and suggestions. While the Borland solution was still in early development—moving from Alpha to Beta status—it was quite robust and offered high performance in the areas of main concern to the CORE project team. In early benchmark tests specifically tailored to the problem domain, Borland AppServer appeared to outperform other offerings. An additional benefit of choosing Borland AppServer was that the technology was built on top of Visibroker, which some of the team members had previously worked with.

5.4   The Solution

The proposed solution, the CORE system, used a fairly standard multitier distributed architecture. One interesting twist is that the network switches, essentially dedicated mainframes specifically deployed to perform voice-network routing, were modeled through an additional back-end tier, the process tier. Rather than represent data storage, this tier represented the actual physical network modeled in the CORE system.

5.4.1   Architecture Overview

Figure 5.1 illustrates the architecture of the CORE system.

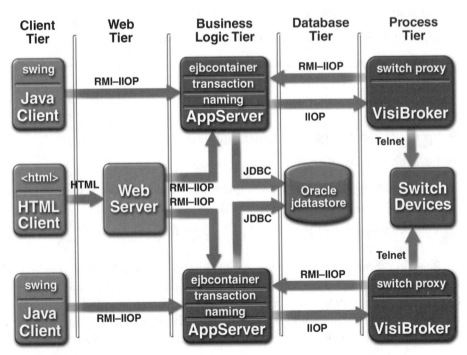

Figure 5.1   CORE System Architecture

The tiers of this architecture consist of client tier, Web-server tier, application-server tier, database tier, and process tier.

- Client Tier

The CORE system was provided to clients through two user interfaces. One was a stand-alone Java application called the CORE desktop, which provided full application functionality. The other provided a subset of the desktop functionality through a Web-based thin client generated using Java Servlet technology. Both are discussed in more detail later in this section.

- Web-Server Tier

The Web-server tier was used to serve up the Web-based thin-client application and to run the servlets that provided dynamic interaction in the Web client.

- Application-Server Tier

The application-server tier consists of heterogeneous and homogeneous clusters of application servers and services, supporting load balancing and failover safety. One application server is installed on each node. Each node potentially has a different configuration. For example, the Borland AppServer allows some services to be run on a single machine to reduce interprocess communication in which one service is heavily utilized by another. Some services run outside the server process, allowing them to be quickly started and stopped without disruption to the rest of the system.

Some nodes run multiple instances of services, such as the EJB container service. This allows load balancing and failover support through clustering, which could be turned on or off, without code or design changes—the implementation is totally transparent. This feature is also unaffected by physical changes to the network.

- Database Tier

The database tier consists of an Oracle database, running on the Sun Solaris platform. Since this was a new project, and no information system was present, there were no constraints in the design of the system, which allowed us to design and tune the database around the access and update mechanisms in the object model.

- Process Tier

The process tier consists of CORBA servers that can be activated on demand in a couple of ways: through an Object Activation Daemon or through active processes. CORBA servers are used to communicate with the switch devices, extracting network routing information and executing instructions for rerouting voice traffic.

CORBA interaction was used extensively in the process tier because of the unusual device interface requirements and the need for a design feature like Active Objects. CORBA servers allowed the implementation of singletons, which could interface to I/O systems using different protocols, and which could live past a client invocation through thread management. This responsibility is placed in the CORBA server tier because of EJB restrictions in the application-server tier with respect to I/O and thread management.

5.5   Client Tier

The CORE desktop and its client-side framework are among the many innovations coming out of the CORE project. The success of the project can largely be attributed to the performance of the application, its ease of use, and the physical appeal of its user interface. These features are the result of a framework that enables objects and their properties, as well as actions and sub-parts to be displayed consistently throughout the whole desktop. This means that users can quickly become familiar and comfortable in the desktop surroundings. Architectural choices on the server side made more time available for developing a desktop of world-class quality. Because the CORE system improved the speed of developing new business components and their integration into the desktop, the system started to take on a bigger role within the company. As a result, the meaning of CORE was changed to Common Object Repository Environment, representing this new, expanded role of the framework. The architecture and the CORE desktop were considered to be redeployable as solutions in their own right and as references for other projects in the development pipeline.

The CORE desktop was built to bring the benefits of object-oriented technology to the user interface. The design goal was to build a framework similar to the JavaBeans technology used to build windows and components for user objects. The desktop application would need to interface with only one type of object, although there would be many types of objects in the system. Every user object would provide a mechanism to inspect its *properties*—how to display it in terms of *name*, *icon* and *type*, what *actions* could be executed, and any other objects (*children*) it contained. On top of this, each object would integrate into a client-side security framework. One goal of the framework was to reduce the amount of code needed to build these aspects into objects. Another goal was to avoid altering the user objects to reflect this requirement. The programming benefits of this framework include

- Reduction in code

- Faster and easier creation of frames

- Greater maintainability

- Focus on user-objects interaction

- Increased extensibility and clean integration

- Self-documentation of user objects

In terms of user interface design, the benefits include

- Consistent appearance of user objects across windows

- Inherent support for direct manipulation techniques

- Integration of a fine-grain security model

The following example shows the typical code previously used for a user interface with a window containing a table. For every user object type displayed in the table, similar code is written. The result is a lot of type-specific, repetitive code. This code maybe be duplicated for the same class in different frames, which potentially leads to more bugs.

```
public Object getValueAt(int row, int col) {
CustomerDetails c = (CustomerDetails)_list.get(row);
switch(col) {
   case 0: return c.getFirstName();
   case 1: return c.getLastName();
   case 2: return c.getCompany();
   ...
 }
}
```

One solution to this problem to have all user objects support methods that let visual components access specific properties without having to know the method for each. This may be done by placing all the methods directly into each user-type object through inheritance from a base abstract object or from an interface. Either way, the user object is required to implement all the defined methods. This clutters up the user object with methods related to the windows environment, and forces development of more code.

The better approach taken in the client-side framework uses an interface developed specifically for maker purposes. This technique is similar to the `java.io.Serializable` interface. The interface `Describeable` indicates objects with a corresponding `Descriptor` object. On the client side, a `DescriptorManager` object, when given an object implementing the `Describeable` interface, returns an instance of a `Descriptor`. The descriptors are serialized from the server side, for reasons that become evident in looking at the `Descriptor` object and how it is created.

Here's a listing of the `Descriptor` interface as defined in the framework

```
public interface Descriptor extends java.io.Serializable, Securable {
 public String getName(Object obj);
 public String getType(Object obj);
 public String getIcon(Object obj);
 public List getActionDescriptors();
 public Visitor getActionDescriptors(Visitor v);
 public List getPropertyDescriptors();
 public Visitor getPropertyDescriptors(Visitor v);
 public PropertyDescriptor getPropertyDescriptor(String name);
 public SecurityDescriptor getSecurityDescriptor();
 public boolean allowsChildren();
 public List getChildren(Object obj);
 public Key getKey();
}
```

The aim of the descriptors is to provide a bridge between the graphical representation requirements and the user object, without the need to alter the user object's interface. Each class has an instance of a `Descriptor`, and when a user object needs to be displayed, the appropriate `Descriptor` is looked up. The client application uses the `Descriptor`, along with the user object, to effectively render the object-oriented user interface. For example, the client can request the icon and name for an object by passing the object to the `Descriptor`. The `Descriptor` can then determine the icon and name by examining the state of the object. In the case of the icon property, the `Descriptor` might just return a value for all instances of this type, or it might inspect the object's state for further refinement of the icon. This is the case with the trunk object in the CORE system, which can have state indicating whether it is leased or owned, each represented by a distinct icon in the user interface. User interface descriptors are mostly used by Swing user interface renderers, such as `TableCellRenderer`, `TreeCellRenderer` and `ListCellRenderer`.

To enforce security, the client also uses sub-components of a `Descriptor`, such as `ObjectDescriptor`, `PropertyDescriptor`, `ActionDescriptor`, and `Folder-Descriptor`. One important requirement for this system is to provide a fine-grained security system, which does not get in the way of the user experience. While the current EJB specification deals with authorization at the server-side, it does not give any guidance about how to integrate this into a client application that relies heavily on context-sensitive menus. Security is enforced when a method is sent across the wire and reaches an object. The container that holds the object can then check if the user is authorized for this method call before dispatching. If the user is not authorized to execute the method, an exception is thrown. This reactive design allows the user to initiate operations that can't be completed. This can lead to frustration and violates good design principles, since a user interface should always try to protect the user from making such mistakes. To get around this problem, the CORE system implements a proactive security system on top of the reactive EJB security system.

Descriptors can enforce security at the object, property, and action levels. The level of access can be set to restricted, read-only, read-write. With restricted access, the user does not see the user object, property, folder, or action in the interface. With read-only access, the user is able to read a user object but not alter it, view an action but not execute it, view a property but not edit it. With read-write, the user can alter the state of a user object, execute an action from some menu-like control, or edit a property using some visual control.

This leaves one problem: how to generate the descriptors. If we created a separate class for each user type of object, the implementation still requires a lot of repetitive code. This repetition was key to the solution, since the reason for the repetition is to interface with a particular user object type and other associated objects, such as actions. By generalizing the code for a `Descriptor` and extracting the methods, classes, and caption names into an XML document, the CORE system can create a single implementation with different instances and different states relating to different user objects in the system.

Descriptors are created and initialized with values extracted from a single XML file. A `DescriptorLookup` session bean uses the XML file stored in a JDataStore database (Borland Java technology object-relational database) or some specified directory system to build objects that reflect the XML element contents. These objects use initialized values extracted from the XML file and the Java reflection API to work their magic. When the client logs on, these objects are streamed in bulk to the client side for caching and local execution.

Here is an extract from the XML for the user object `ContactPersonDetails`.

```xml
<object-descriptor>
  <class-name>ContactPersonDetails</class-name>
  <name>class:ContactPersonName</name>
```

```
        <type>string:Contact Person</type>
        <icon>string:contactperson</icon>
        <property-descriptor width="200">
          <name>Company</name>
          <method>getCompany</method>
        </property-descriptor>
        <property-descriptor>
           <name>First Name</name>
           <method>getFirstName</method>
        </property-descriptor>
        ...
        <action-descriptor>
          <name>Properties</name>
          <icon>property.editor</icon>
          <class-name>PropertyAction</class-name>
          <parameter>
            <name>home</name>
            <value>core/contactpersonmaintenance</value>
          </parameter>
        </action-descriptor>
        <security-descriptor>
          <security-role>
            <name>Traffic-Manager</name>
          </security-role>
        </security-descriptor>
      </object-descriptor>
```

5.5.1   Web-Server Tier

The Web server tier provides a mechanism that simplifies application deployment while enabling a more flexible application update mechanism.

Version Control

The CORE desktop uses the Web server to access application versioning information. An XML file stored on the Web server contains information regarding the latest version of the desktop application. The application checks versioning information on startup and periodically thereafter. If versioning differences are detected, it triggers installation of new and modified jar files across the network. Jar file locations are specified in the XML file, which also contains information about the new components in the release stored on the server. The user is informed of the update through visual feedback listing each component added or changed.

Because most of the desktop application is configured through XML properties files, it was easy during the development phases to issue new releases that migrated applications to different CORBA domains, naming service instances, or different entry points in the naming service. Even JNDI names for bean homes could be configured in this way. By reducing the amount of time for checking a new version, the development team could react quickly to network and software changes during the early beta program.

The software included functionality to inform the development team of errors as they were detected. The information was immediately available to the development team, allowing "Internet time" modification and release of software. Turnaround was fast because of the programming language, architecture, client and server design, and application-server technology. This automatic update feature, similar to Sun's recently announced Java WebStart technology, was the only real infrastructure functionality built by the development team. The rest of the implementation used the J2EE architecture and the implementation provided by the Borland AppServer.

5.5.2 Application-Server Tier

The Borland AppServer provided a quality implementation of the J2EE architecture. The implementation excelled in the areas of persistence, container scalability, data integration, transactions, session management, load balancing, fault tolerance, and management.

Persistence

Persistence is an important part of any business system today and has great importance to the CORE system. Many object-relational mapping systems have been implemented, with different levels of success, by other vendors and within corporate IT departments. Most such systems don't allow easy object mapping across different database systems or between a system's different database tables. Sometimes, the integration of the mapping goes counter to the component technology used for the business object—resulting in an "impedance mismatch" within a system.

The container-managed persistence feature in the Enterprise JavaBeans 1.1 specification provides a greater level of independence between bean implementations and the persistence mechanism. Choosing container-managed persistence for all entity beans in the system was in keeping with the rule "aim to do nothing." In this context, no SQL code needed to be implemented in entity beans—all persistence requirements are delegated to the container's persistence engine. This leads to fewer maintenance issues, easier migration, database knowledge encapsulation, and faster development, and also provides major performance improvements. In addition, it means that not every bean developer has to become an expert in SQL or the JDBC 2.0 API.

Runtime performance improvements come from many optimizations specific to the Borland AppServer's persistence engine. In fact, the EJB 2.0 specification includes similar features, to ensure greater portability across vendor implementations.

The optimizations and features provided by the Borland AppServer persistence engine include

- **Automatic Read-Only Detection.** Within a transaction, the container can detect read-only access to an entity bean by inspecting its state using the Java reflection API. When no bean state changes, expensive SQL UPDATE calls aren't necessary. This improves performance in typical business systems, where read-only access volumes are much higher than read-writes or writes. With increasing sophistication, execution optimizations, and resource utilization management built into applications servers, the limiting factor on scalability is the amount of I/O performed. By reducing the amount of traffic to and from the database, read-only detection helps overcome this remaining scalability limitation.

- **Tuned Writes.** When a container detects modifications to data, only modified fields need to be written to the database. This is especially important when entity beans have large numbers of fields or fields containing large amounts of data that aren't modified frequently.

- **Bulk Loading of Finder Methods.** As implemented by some containers, Container-Managed Persistence can adversely affect the performance of the system when it's handling large numbers of SQL calls. For example, executing a finder method initially involves one SQL SELECT statement. This returns the primary keys of beans meeting the criteria, and generates a separate SELECT statement for each of these beans. If there are N primary keys returned, the container generates $1 + N$ SELECT statements. The Borland AppServer optimizes performance by loading all state for the selected beans on the initial query, reducing the number of SQL calls to 1.

- **Caching Prepared Statement and Connection Pooling.** Application servers typically provide JDBC connection pooling in one of two ways, either through an internal adaptor mechanism that wraps around a JDBC connection, or through direct support within the JDBC driver. Creating connections is very expensive and needs to be offset over many invocations to maximize performance. Borland AppServer pools JDBC connections and further optimizes performance by reusing prepared statements across transactions.

- **Batch Updates.** Sending multiple updates to a database for batch execution is generally more efficient than sending separate update statements. Significant performance improvements come from reducing the number of remote calls through batch-data transfer. The Borland AppServer performs batch updates if the underlying JDBC driver supports this feature.

- **Object-Relational Mapping.** The Borland AppServer's persistence engine facilitates a variety of object relational mapping strategies. The most basic mapping is one entity bean to one database table. The engine also handles mapping of one-to-many and many-to-many relationships. It doesn't limit primary and foreign key values to single column values; instead, they can be composites of more than one column value. The engine also supports the use of composite keys in the finder methods. The persistence engine even supports mapping from one entity bean to multiple tables, with tables in either a single database or in separate databases.

- **Primary-Key Generation.** Many databases have built-in mechanisms to provide an appropriate primary-key value. Unfortunately, the way entity beans are typically used, it is hard to use these built-in mechanisms without introducing a fair amount of complexity into either the beans or the calling client implementations. Borland AppServer's container-managed persistence engine provides a set of facilities that can be used to automatically fill some or all of the primary-key values. There are two ways to configure a primary-key generator. One relies on a primary-key generating class, which the user implements. The other, which relies on database facilities, is built into the CMP engine.

To support primary-key generation using database-specific features, three entity properties are provided: `getPrimaryKeyBeforeInsertSql`, `getPrimaryKeyAfterInsertSql`, and `ignoreColumnsOnInsert`. The first property would typically be used in conjunction with Oracle Sequences, the second and third would both be needed to support SQL Server's Identity columns. These capabilities are general enough so that it should be straightforward to support key-generation techniques provided by any DBMS (see Section 4.6).

Container Scalability

Careful management of resources is key to increasing scalability of a system.

- **Memory Management.** The choice of the Java programming language makes memory management easier from the outset. Finding memory leaks in other languages consumes an enormous amount of development time. With the garbage collection mechanism in the Java programming language, the development team could concentrate on the real issues involved in the writing of business logic.

  For a system to scale, it must manage memory to avoid leaks and reduce process size. The CORE system needs to provide configuration information on the whole voice network. This involves thousands of objects at any point, and it is typical for many users to be looking at different periods of network use at the same time. This complexity requires efficient resource management in the server to avoid performance effects. The EJB specification allows memory management on this scale through its well-defined sequence of bean lifecycle events. By separating the client interface to a bean from the actual bean implementation, the EJB specification makes it possible to implement sophisticated object pooling, object activation (late binding), and bean state management mechanisms.

  In the Borland AppServer, session beans can scale to a very large number of objects through instance pool management and careful activation and passivation of beans. As volume fluctuates, the server can periodically evict instances from memory and write their state to secondary storage. When a request comes in for an instance not in memory, it can be resurrected from storage. The server also continuously removes instances from secondary storage that have reached a specified expiration time.

  Design investigations revealed that the pool size setting for each bean type had an impact on performance figures. For some beans, the default pool size of 1,000 was too low, so the figure was adjusted to reflect peak usage. This reduced the amount of work for the garbage collector, the overhead of object creation, and the cache miss rate for beans with state cache across transactions.

  In addition to memory management for a single container, other approaches include replicating services across servers and load balancing to achieve better scalability and performance. This approach was also used by the CORE system.

- **Thread Management.** Developing multithreaded servers is a complex, challenging task. The Enterprise JavaBeans architecture makes it easy to write business applications that benefit from multithreading, without the complexity.

The bean provider isn't required to understand or write code to handle low-level thread management. Since most business applications are I/O bound with regard to database access, there are considerable performance gains from multithreading. With automatic thread pooling, incoming requests can be delivered to waiting threads via a queue or a notification. By limiting the EJB developer's ability to do thread management directly, the specification's thread management constraints actually enable implementation of sophisticated thread management features in EJB servers and containers.

While restrictions on creating threads within the EJB container have frustrated other developers, the CORE team found this a useful decision by the EJB architects. Many design approaches that initially looked like they needed to manage threads directly turned out not to. The two design issues in which direct thread management was useful in CORE included messaging with JMS and interaction with CORBA servers. Enterprise JavaBeans aren't designed for active processes or objects that control their own execution. Beans are driven by external invocations, while a server is constantly responding to both internal and external events, which requires the ability to adjust their execution based on internal criteria.

- **Connection Management.** Connection management was important to the CORE system, not because of a large user population, but because of the highly multithreaded nature of the client application. Multiple client requests needed to be sent across the same connection, rather than consume one connection each. The Borland AppServer is built on top of VisiBroker, which minimizes the number of client connections by using one connection per server. All client requests to the server are multiplexed over this single connection.

Data Integration

The JDBC 2.0 API is an important part of any system based on the J2EE architecture. JDBC aids container-managed persistence by providing a uniform data access API to all database management systems. Because of the architecture and extensive vendor support for JDBC, the core team was able to build and run the system on different database systems with different driver implementations, without any change in code. This was very important during the development phase, when demonstrations were done for users in remote locations. It was relatively easy for the team to switch the data sources pointed to by entity beans from Oracle production database to a local JDataStore demo database. Configuration mechanisms in the EJB specification for managing data sources as resource references made it easy to move among instances of different systems.

One feature in the Borland AppServer the development team liked was the ability to run the entity beans against a database without the need to predefine the corresponding tables. Where it doesn't detect the appropriate tables in the database, the container generates an SQL CREATE TABLE statement in the appropriate dialect for the target database. The Borland AppServer also supports generating entity beans from an existing database schema. By taking advantage of these benefits of container managed entity beans, the development team was able to achieve significant development time savings.

Resource management is also provided in the J2EE architecture through container resource pooling. This allows database connections to be shared across many transactions. Some vendors, including Borland, have added enhancements to this JDBC connection management, such as prepared-statement caching.

Transactions

Transaction management is a key technology in most business computing, central to building reliable large-scale systems. Transaction management is still an area of intensive research, and successfully understanding and implementing transactional systems requires significant experience. The Enterprise JavaBeans architecture effectively conceals the complexities of transaction management, allowing mere mortals to build such transactional systems quickly. The EJB architecture fully supports distributed transactions—that is, transactions involving access and update of data in multiple databases running on disparate computing nodes. The Enterprise JavaBeans architecture's declarative transaction feature greatly simplifies programming the CORE system, giving bean providers on the team freedom from dealing with the complexities of multiuser access and failure recovery.

Though automated transaction support in the J2EE architecture greatly assisted the development of this system, the one area in which developers felt they needed to take particular care was in transaction demarcation. Incorrect use of transaction attributes can lead to inconsistent application logic and can dramatically affect system performance. Transactions are simpler with component-based transaction management, but still require some careful choices by the developer.

Session Management

The J2EE architecture allows session management to be distributed across many tiers, including the Web tier using the Servlet Session Tracking API and the Application Server tier using Session Beans.

In most cases, the design of the session-management features for the CORE system placed responsibility in the application server tier. This decision was based on the desire to reuse business logic as much as possible. In order to best support both the Java application and browser-based HTML clients, it seemed obvious to place as much session management in session beans. This allowed various types of clients to be simplified and reduced in footprint as much as possible. Another factor in this decision was that clients typically needed to display only small sections of a complex object graph. In some cases, the graph didn't need to be refreshed frequently because data didn't need to be updated often, and users didn't need a real-time view of the model.

While small amounts of data passed between server and client, there were large calculation costs spanning many entity beans due to the resulting changes. By providing session management through session beans rather than in the client or Web-server tiers, it was possible to perform some hidden caching optimizations. The two clients were implemented to perform a small amount of session management specific to their behavior and environment.

Load Balancing

Load balancing is the mechanism for distributing client requests over a number of nodes and processes. Many implementations of the J2EE architecture provide this added value though clustering technology. Typically, load balancing is implemented at the point of binding to a JNDI service or a lookup on a JNDI entry. These two techniques are used in the deployed CORE system.

Load balancing across naming service instances enables the team to implement client-container affinity. This improved performance in cases in which caching takes place across transactions. It also makes it possible to bind clients to a particular naming service for various reasons, such as providing preferential treatment for better performance and enabling updates to the system in a controlled manner to selective users before complete rollout to the whole user base. Load balancing at the point of name lookup in the JNDI service allows easy configuration of workload distribution across similar nodes. One important result of this is that it is possible to have a test model to help correctly evaluate certain partition configurations.

Fault Tolerance (Availability)

Load balancing and fault tolerance go hand in hand, since both are implemented through clustering technology. The general approach to fault tolerance is to use redundancy and data replication, and to move processing from one node to another. To achieve a high degree of availability required of the system, multiple application servers and containers are run on the network. The Enterprise Java-Beans packaged jar files are grouped based on usage and intercommunication and deployed simultaneously to different nodes within the running container. If a bean's container fails during client invocation, the underlying infrastructure transparently fails over to another container containing the same bean deployment.

Failover support is provided for session beans (both stateful and stateless) and entity beans. The failover of a stateful object requires moving data between containers. The techniques generally used are *replication* and *switchover*. *Replication* means that several containers keep copies of data. *Switchover* involves containers having shared access to some stateful storage. Borland AppServer provides a switchover technique based on a stateful session storage service. Entity beans use their underlying persistence database. For failover of stateful session beans, containers use the callback methods `ejbActivate` and `ejbPassivate` in the bean implementation. This mechanism is defined in the EJB specification and the J2EE vendor's implementation of distributed shared session storage. It is important to note that during code development, these concerns didn't need to be considered by the bean provider. Instead, they were left to the configurations department to tune transparently to the CORE system.

Note that this support was useful for both unplanned outages and planned outages during and after development. Servers could be brought down without knowing which clients were connected or asking users to restart their desktop and attach to another process once service was restored.

Management

Maintaining any distributed system can be incredibly hard. System management is a critical element in enterprise systems. As distributed processing becomes more prevalent in systems, the need for tools to manage this complexity becomes increasingly important. In keeping with the focus here on software rather than hardware, the objective of application management is to enhance performance and availability of the whole system. The system management tools include the Borland AppServer console and AppCenter.

The console included with the Borland AppServer allows viewing of all application servers and services throughout a CORBA domain or particular naming service. From this console, it is possible to start, stop, restart, and ping all services, including containers, JNDI services, and JMS services. It is also possible to edit the configuration properties of each service within each server. These features, along with the ability to view event and error logs within one tool, allows for easy management of the system by both development and IT operations staff.

Such tools became very significant as the team moved the system between the different server environments for development and production. Because the EJB specification defines roles in the development and deployment process and the J2EE platform enables tool support for such distinctions, it was easy to hand over the final development build to operations, with no need to change the code to reflect the new environment. Differences between deployment environments could include different database instances, different database structures, different naming service structures, and so on. Since each could potentially be configured without requiring code changes, the team and the company have come to highly value the flexibility of the J2EE architecture.

Design Patterns and Guidelines

In designing the beans tier, a number of design patterns and guidelines were identified. The patterns aren't unique to Enterprise Java Beans; some of them have their origins in general high-performance distributed computing applications.

- **Business Components.** An important point during early development was that bean development didn't mean that one single bean class would service all the functionality required by a specific business interface. A bean can delegate all or part of a request to helper classes. A component can be made up of other components and classes. For example, one session bean can use the services of other session beans and helper classes to service a request.

- **Policy-Based Design.** In keeping with the first point, any logic likely to require future changes or cause complexity in bean development can be moved to a helper class. An interface can then be defined, which the default bean class implements. During deployment, an environment property for the bean can be specified to provide the name of an alternate class implementing the interface. When servicing requests, the bean looks in its environment context ("java:comp/env/") for the name of the alternate class. If the context specifies an alternate class, the alternate is dynamically loaded.

- **Logical and Physical Design.** Conceptual issues tend to dominate design analysis. However, ignoring physical implementation issues can lead to performance problems that aren't easy to fix. Performance should always be considered when factoring components for granularity and for interface consistency and clarity.

- **Puts Abstractions in Code, Details in Metadata.** Another important pattern is to write code that executes the general case, then place specifics of each execution outside the code base. The CORE desktop uses this approach in the descriptors framework. It also uses it in loading reference data objects from database tables. Reference objects in the system consist of at least two fields: an identifier and a description. A reference object might be a Country type, with an identifier and description. The description is used in the user interface. Other fields in the Country type could include the International Standards Organization code. Because these objects are fine grained, the team decided to map them to a Java helper class rather than to an entity bean. Because of the large number of reference type objects in the system, the code for loading particular instances is isolated from the specifics, such as table and column names.

- **Objects that Play Together Should Stay Together.** Many application servers built for Enterprise JavaBeans contain optimizations related to local invocations. Deploying beans that communicate frequently in a single jar improves performance by minimizing network latency and marshalling cost through remote invocations. This design principal minimizes traffic in the business logic tier.

- **Perform Useful Work.** The overhead costs of remote invocations are high, so it is important to maximize the ratio of useful work to each invocation. A typical invocation on an Enterprise JavaBean involves at least two remotes calls: client-to-server and server-to-database. It is important that the overhead is offset by a large amount of server work before returning to the client.

  The general design guideline is to hide entity beans behind a session bean. The session bean provides lightweight Java objects to the client. The Java objects can contain state from one or more entity beans, including the results of calculations performed on other data. Data from multiple sources can be executed in one transaction.

- **Caching.** When data is repeatedly requested remotely, a dynamic cache should retain a copy closer to the client. Caching can greatly improve system performance at all levels. Caching is easy to implement for reference data. It is provided in the CORE system through a CORBA server behind a stateless session bean. When data is updated, a simple timeout mechanism or a cache coherence protocol can be used.

- **Data Reduction.** What is the quickest way to send 5,000 objects to a client? Not to send them at all. Sending large numbers of objects from database to the middle tier to the client creates performance problems at all levels. The database has to perform more work with regard to transactions spanning such a large number of objects, then transfer them to the middle tier. The container has to extract the data and place it into a similar large number of beans. Another bean then has to extract the data from those beans and transport it to the client. Finally, the client has to display all this data to a user, whose brain (short-term memory) isn't equipped to deal with such volumes. This kind of design is typical of business applications in which proper task analysis hasn't been performed. The design time and effort is instead spent on solving the problem from an engineering perspective. The real solution lay in a user-centered approach—that is, consider that users do not generally ask for 5,000 objects at once.

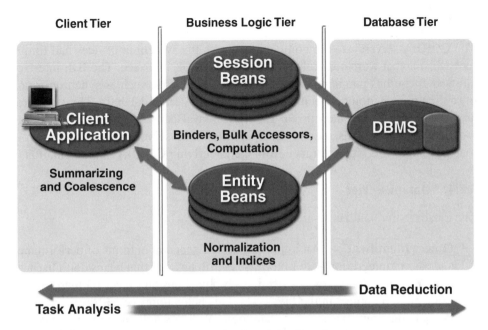

Figure 5.2   Expected Data-Traffic Behavior of the Core System

At the outset of the design work on the CORE system, a task analysis and data reduction diagram was produced, showing the expected data-traffic behavior (Figure 5.2).

This diagram shows some of the techniques used in data reduction. For example, task analysis might have determined that for the user to perform his function, he requires the system to isolate some objects based on some standard criteria, such as bank accounts overdrawn for two months, in which the amount is greater then 1,000 Euro. A session bean is provided that accepts two parameters: the number of months and the amount. The Account home has a finder method that retrieves a collection of Accounts based on months overdrawn and overdrawn amount. This would have resulted in the following SQL statement executed against the database.

```
SELECT * FROM ACCOUNT WHERE (MONTHS_OVERDRAWN >= ?) AND (AMOUNT <= (-1*?))
```

Knowing this, the database administrator would have created indices to support such queries. Further reduction is possible by designing the session bean so that it provides only the fields from the Account entity bean that the user requires at that time.

5.5.3   Process Tier

The CORBA servers used to communicate with the switching devices had timing mechanisms that were controllable through their IDL interface. The IDL interface allowed operations people to change the timing of events, such as synchronization of routing information between the switch and an external database. These features aren't provided for in the current Enterprise JavaBeans specification. However, most enterprise systems require these abilities. The servers also benefited from load balancing and fault tolerance from the underlying CORBA implementation.

5.5.4   Database Tier

The database tier handles a variety of tasks.

- **Object Identification.** An important design decision in terms of performance and ease of integration with Enterprise JavaBeans was that beans don't use natural keys as primary keys. Instead, each object has an object ID mapped to a Long numeric object in the Java code. This helps improve performance of the system and simplifies some update logic. With a single numeric primary key representing every bean, it is easier to implement a general caching mechanism at each tier in the system, and to generalize other parts of the code.

- **Finders and Query Tuning.** The design choice to use container-managed persistence for all entity beans made it possible to extract all SQL select statements in the system and present them to the database performance tuning experts for review and possible improvements. This could be done without searching through reams of printed code. During the early development phase, suggestions were easily incorporated because persistence configuration was separated from the bean implementation and placed in an XML file. It also made it easy to edit the SQL statements, redeploy bean jars into containers, then monitor performance through EJB test clients. Because persistence was an important aspect of the system, improvements in the query performance through query rewriting, providing hints, and creating indices was very noticeable. Best of all, these performance improvements came about with the need to change code and possibly introduce a bug.

- **Optimistic Concurrency.** Optimistic concurrency means executing transactions without setting a lock, and checking transaction validity at commit time (note that most systems do not provide true isolation). Optimistic concurrency overcomes the performance impact of having a high degree of isolation. Lower levels of transaction isolation reduce the amount of data that is locked and the duration of each lock, increasing the chances for concurrent execution of different transactions. This comes at the cost of possible inconsistent reads and writes.

The Borland AppServer provides some mechanisms to counter potential inconsistencies, without greatly affecting performance. The container persistence engine provides an entity bean flag, `ejb.cmp.optimisticConcurrencyBehavior`, with the following values:

1. `UpdateModifiedFields` issues an update only on the fields that were modified, or suppresses the update altogether if the bean was not modified. This can give a significant performance boost.

2. `UpdateAllFields` issues an update on all fields, regardless of whether they were modified or not.

3. `VerifyModifiedFields` issues a tuned update, while verifying that the fields it is updating are consistent with the values that were previously read in.

4. `VerifyAllFields` similar to `VerifyModifiedFields`, except that all fields are verified.

- **State Versioning.** The optimistic concurrency mechanisms provided by the Borland AppServer are only relevant to concurrent transactions. The mechanism is implemented by comparing the state loaded from the database with the state in the database at the time of update. Though very useful, this design falls short when we look at the current way of designing of business processes and user interfaces. What it doesn't address is the fact that an entity bean's state can be displayed to a user using one transaction and updated by the same user in another transaction. During the time between the read and write transaction, another user could have committed an update. The optimistic concurrency mechanism does not work in this situation, since the state loaded at the start of the write transaction already reflects the update done by another user. A mechanism is needed to track the versioning of an entity bean's state across transactions. There are a number of ways to approach this, including:

1. Use a stateful session bean to keep a copy of the image sent to the user for editing. When the session bean performs the update, it compares the state of the entity bean with the state it stored in the previous transaction. In the event of conflicts, it throws an exception back to the client.

2. Use a stateless session bean that has two parameters: the state read and the state edited. The comparison process is exactly the same for the stateful session bean. Here the client is required to keep track of the state read in the first transaction.

3. Similar to the previous technique, a version field in the entity bean can be used to track changes. When executing the update, the client sends the edited state object with the version number initially read. Before the session bean performs the update, the version number in the entity bean is compared with the version read in the first transaction. If the version number is older then the current one, an exception is thrown. This has better performance than the previous technique, but still allows for sophisticated resolution where the state is subsequently compared. The only drawback is that the database schema must support this new persistent field.

4. Use a client-demarcated transaction that spans the read, edit, and update steps. This has the potential to hold expensive and precious resources for a considerable amount of time, during which the resources are under-utilized.

The approach taken for the entity beans requiring such support in the CORE system was the third option.

5.6   Life after CORE

The impact of the CORE system within AT&T Unisource was significant in a couple of ways. First, the business benefit resulting from automating the call-routing processes was substantial. Second, the architectural reference provided by the system clearly demonstrated the abundance of "out-of-the-box" services the J2EE platform provides for complex heterogeneous environments.

5.6.1   Business

The CORE project delivered on its promise as a robust, user-friendly, and scaleable system. It met fairly sophisticated business requirements, yet proved both responsive and stable. It provided ease of use, yet still delivered information that contributed to the cost optimization of network traffic.

The fact that the use of technology in this area of the business was relatively new increased the importance of the CORE system becoming widely accepted by its users. This success has been substantiated by the high level of user demand for additional functionality enhancements to future releases of the system.

5.6.2   Development

The CORE application, the J2EE platform, and the Borland AppServer allowed the development efforts at AT&T Unisource to shift focus from primarily isolated departmental projects with a "one application, one solution" approach to a more enterprise-wide approach.

In addition, where other component models were available that provided some reusability, they also required a considerable amount of proprietary code to deliver features that are part of a standardized J2EE architecture. Thus J2EE technology reduced the resource burden in building new systems and maintaining existing ones. The new architecture also exhibited a cleaner separation between presentation, business, system, and database tiers, which structure allowed a considerable increase in the levels of parallel development.

The J2EE platform also provided the ability to distribute the tiers of the system to their appropriate places, irrespective of platform or vendor. This ensures true scalability and vendor independence. Using these technologies within the systems department has provided teams with proof that the J2EE platform delivers an architecture that displays the "write once, run anywhere" approach to development.

CORE provided the following benefits

- A clear, structured demarcation among all application tiers, improving accuracy and reducing research time for impact analysis in the light of change requests.

- Reusability, with more than 75 percent of the programming effort reusable across similar projects.

- Reduced time to market through a more usable and structured business object model that requires enhancements to focus only on extensibility, not on code rewrites or system rearchitecture.

- Greatly reduced maintenance costs and reduced dependence on vendor-specific tiers, such as the RDBMS or operating system.

- Architecture that has proved more scaleable, reusable, and future-proof than ever before. An architecture that has not been written from the ground up, but compliments a feature set and suite of services that has been tried and tested in the marketplace, providing a natural and logical extension to the problem domain.

- A repository of components that can be clearly identified for all future developments.

- A new, robust, and scalable entity object model that reduces costs and development time, automatically including connection pooling, object pooling, security, and transactional services.

- Significant reduction in development source code, allowing greater refinement and concentration of development effort.

- Clearer understanding of business logic for developers, thanks to an architecture that focuses much more on the business requirements.

Development with the J2EE platform for both the CORE application and other systems within AT&T Unisource will continue to evolve as enhancements to EJB and other technologies are released. These enhancements will aid the pursuit of reduced dependence on hardware vendors, database vendors, and proprietary development practices, further improving development productivity and application performance.

Brokat/Codexa

About the Authors

Dr. Lougie Anderson is vice president of the Java Server Unit at Brokat Inc, and an adjunct faculty member at the Oregon Graduate Institute. Currently responsible for product development of Brokat's J2EE platform, Anderson has more than 20 years experience in the computer industry, managing Internet technology, object technology, databases, and interactive multimedia. She has published more than 20 research papers in database technologies. Anderson has been active in object technology and database conferences for many years, including serving as the general chairperson for the OOPSLA '96 Conference, in San Jose California. She received a BS in physics, a BS in mathematics, and an MS and PhD in computer science, all from the University of Washington.

Thomas Geer has worked with large Java technology-based enterprise-class applications for the past four years. While at Visa International, he was the chief architect on applications that displayed the power of Java technology in the enterprise (see http://java.sun.com/events/jbe/98/features/security.html and http://java.sun.com/features/1999/11/security.visa.html). He has also worked on a number of industry counsels to assist in the definition of Java platform specifications, as well as with vendors to define product roadmaps. Today Geer is the chief architect at Codexa, working again on a large distributed system written using Java technology. The current production system for Codexa has received a great deal of industry recognition (see *JavaPro Magazine Solutions Awards* and CORBA Success Stories). Geer has contributed to such magazines as *Component Strategies, Application Development Trends, Computer World,* and *Information Week.*

CHAPTER 6

Codexa: Building a Big Bang Architecture with Brokat's GemStore J2EE Server

Cᴏᴅᴇxᴀ Corporation is an Internet information service provider whose mission is to solve the information overload experienced by professionals in a wide range of markets including finance, business, government, and academia. Codexa aims first to help financial professionals synthesize the avalanche of financial information available through any digital information source, including the Internet, e-mails, wire services, market data feeds, and so forth. To do this, the company has built an infrastructure based on the J2EE platform that is architected to manage explosive growth in usage, information volume, and variety of applications. The J2EE platform's layered, distributed architecture is crucial to the performance, scaling, and reliability of Codexa's always-on, always-growing solution.

6.1 Codexa "Big Bang" Architecture Explodes onto the Scene

Codexa Corporation is an Internet information application service provider (ASP), founded in 1999 to help professional investors and traders to cope effectively with the avalanche of available financial information. Codexa's customers include top investment and trading institutions with worldwide reach. Like the industry that it serves, Codexa moves fast. Release 1.0 of Codexa's product, known as the Codexa Service, was first deployed for selected customers in January 2000, less than a year after the company's founding. The far more sophisticated version 2.0, based on J2EE technology, was released in beta in October 2000.

Codexa's patent-pending infrastructure uses autonomous software agents to analyze traditional and nontraditional digital data sources. These include information sources on the Web, such as message boards and financial and corporate Web sites, plus conventional market data, wire services, and SEC/Edgar feeds. The Codexa Service gathers and aggregates this raw data for Codexa's clients. Using artificial intelligence and intelligence-augmentation techniques, combined with natural-language processing, the Codexa Service filters, parses, and prioritizes information to match clients' selection criteria before alerting them via the Web, process-to-process communications, or mobile device alerts.

6.2   Charting Galaxies of Financial Information

Opportunity abounds for Codexa's financial information applications. The world financial securities markets are huge, and participants have a voracious appetite for information that might give them an edge. In 1999, for example, almost 500 billion shares were traded on all U.S. exchanges, and the U.S. represented more than half of equity trading value globally, according to the *Securities Industry Association 2000 Factbook*. Underlying this trading activity is the analysis of a huge volume of information affecting companies' securities around the world. Gathering, integrating and synthesizing this information can overwhelm even the most-seasoned financial experts.

Accurate, current information is the ally of the professional trader, analyst, and investor. Financial institutions realize tremendous benefits by being the first to see and understand information regarding such factors as mergers and acquisitions, major events in related industries, hiring/firing of executives, and important product announcements. Prevalidating this information relative to source, relevancy, or other criteria adds even greater value. As of this publication, Codexa covers the Wilshire 5,000, an index that tracks approximately the top 7,200 traded companies in the United States and provides an online "first-alert" service about factors affecting these equities. Codexa intends to synthesize information in various languages from sources around the globe and to expand its coverage to companies on exchanges around the world.

To meet these opportunities, the Codexa Service's architecture has to support "big bang" demand. The application must start with explosive growth and keep expanding in multiple directions. Codexa must gather and analyze data from a diverse array of sources, extracting the useful information from the noise, and alerting clients to its existence in real time—delivering it via many channels, including Web browsers, Wireless Access Protocol (WAP), Java applications, and bulk data delivery. The architecture has to be robust enough to process huge amounts of financial data and flexible enough to support the heterogeneous mix of data sources and delivery channels.

Financial information derives its value from its immediacy. The greater the volatility in financial markets, the greater the demand for information to keep pace. The Codexa Service must be always available, always current, and fully performant even under peak loads. Finally, the Codexa Service must integrate with a wide and growing base of Web-based applications for investing and trading.

6.3   J2EE Helped Codexa Bring Order to Its Universe

Despite daunting requirements, the Codexa Service was built and deployed in only 18 months. Codexa believes that the J2EE platform helped to make that possible. It is naturally channel-neutral, because it is layered, distributed, and network savvy. The architecture has everything in place for client-side delivery of data. It allows data to be rendered dynamically in many different ways, and it gives a rich, multidimensional interface capable of rendering sophisticated views of how market sectors decompose, how information within sectors decomposes, and so forth. As an ASP, Codexa felt that development time with any other technology would have been prohibitive.

On the server side, the J2EE component architecture lends itself to building extensible application frameworks, and it leverages the Java 2 platform to provide for security and scalability. To be vendor-independent, the J2EE platform does not dictate how lifecycle services will be delivered. Rather, it is centered around CORBA, which Codexa used to provide the lifecycle-management services defined in the OMG's Object Management Architecture (OMA). CORBA relationship services enable componentization of the entire system, which makes for ease of deployment and profiling.

Codexa chose GemStone/J as its J2EE application server in part because of a successful shared history. Tom Geer, Codexa's chief architect, had worked with GemStone Systems (now Brokat AG's Java Server Unit) starting back in 1997, while building a network management system for Visa International, currently in production. At that time, the Java-technology-based application server market was not well-defined, but Geer felt that GemStone had and continues to have the best vision among application server vendors about the direction of J2EE technology. When he joined Codexa, Geer turned to the J2EE platform and GemStone/J to build the channel-neutral and highly expansive architecture of the Codexa Service.

6.4 System Architecture: Layers Upon Layers

To ensure that its applications are channel-neutral, Codexa has layered its application architecture and centered business logic in the application server. This allows the applications to interface with new devices and standards without affecting the core business logic. Of course, the J2EE platform provides a natural fit for this kind of architecture because it is inherently layered.

Figure 6.1 illustrates the layering and partitioning within the Codexa system.

In the Codexa Service, incoming requests from users or outgoing notifications are handled through a Web or WAP server. The system uses XSL and XSLT to transform its XML document representation of data models to WML, HTML, or an XML stream for the system to process.

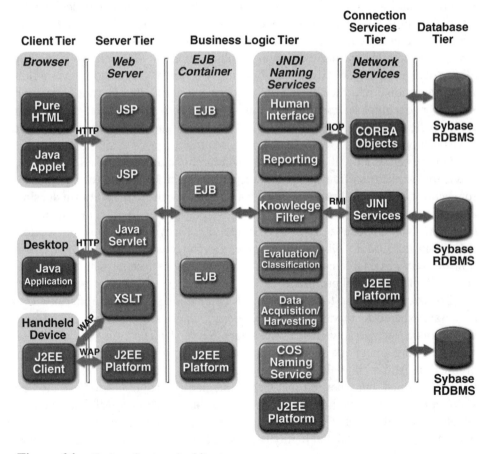

Figure 6.1 Codexa System Architecture

For the wireless channel, the international standard Wireless Application Protocol provides more-efficient Internet access than HTML because the communications stream is sent as encoded binary rather than bulky text. Wireless Markup Language (WML) provides simplified page descriptions and scripting for wireless applications, and lightweight Java Messaging Service (JMS) helps guarantee delivery of wireless communications. HTML on the Web side is ideal because it allows Codexa to provide information to client organizations without dealing with firewall issues. Codexa's JMS vendor, Softwired, has an implementation that uses HTTP for firewall tunneling, yet still supports guaranteed message delivery.

Requests from the Web or WAP server or outgoing messages to the client are handled through the servlet engine running on the GemStone/J application server. The servlet engine calls Enterprise JavaBeans (EJBs) running in Java virtual machines, which call other processes to assemble content from the GemStone/J persistent cache.

The beauty of this layered approach is that the presentation engine and the business engine don't need to know where the data is coming from or where it's going. Applications are channel-neutral because the WAP or Web server on the front end takes care of front-end communication issues and user interface issues. And because the layers isolate business information and rules from transport issues, Codexa can incorporate new front-end technologies simply by changing the front-end server.

6.4.1 GemStone/J Provides the Power

For more than 15 years, GemStone (Brokat's Java Server Unit) has helped companies build large-scale, distributed application architectures for the enterprise. As the industry moved to Java applications for e-business, the company applied its intellectual property and expertise to create practical solutions for the J2EE platform. This initiative provides a blueprint of proven, time-tested architectures and best practices for developing high-end Business-To-Business (B2B) sites and sophisticated distributed applications, such as the Codexa Service, based on J2EE technologies.

GemStone/J's chief contribution to Codexa is its Extreme Clustering architecture—multilevel resource clustering designed for high-volume, distributed environments and, able to support tens of thousands of concurrent users and many millions of transactions per day.

Extreme Clustering includes

- Multi-VM architecture. A distributed clustering architecture that transparently manages hundreds of virtual machines and other resources per server and across multiple servers

- Smart Load Balancing. Intelligent, multilevel load balancing that matches processing needs for specific operations to Java virtual machines configured to meet those needs

- Total Availability Technology. Multilevel failover to ensure continuous service and performance, plus tools and features that allow administrators to expand and adapt the e-commerce system without interrupting service

Extreme Clustering is supported and enhanced by GemStone/J's Persistent Cache Architecture (PCA), which enables users and processes to efficiently share access to business objects, and its Object Transaction Service, which provides flexible, multilevel transaction mechanisms to efficiently maintain transactional integrity across distributed business systems.

GemStone/J's Extreme Clustering architecture is designed with clustered resources at multiple levels to avoid resource bottlenecks. Figure 6.2 gives a detailed look at the server architecture behind the Codexa system.

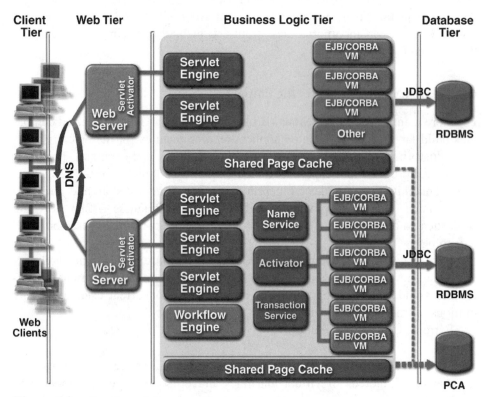

Figure 6.2   GemStone/J Extreme Clustering Architecture

- At the front end, requests from clients to Web servers are handled via routers and DNS scheduling. Codexa utilizes F5's HA+ for intelligent load balancing algorithms, such as lightest load or best response.

- GemStone/J uses HotSpot VMs, which provide a threefold to fivefold performance improvement over classic Java virtual machiness through improved thread handling and garbage collection.

- Each application server host supports multiple servlet engines, each in its own Java virtual machine. Servlet adapters in the Web servers independently balance requests across these servlet engines.

- Each GemStone/J application server manages pools of EJB/CORBA VMs across one or more hosts. The Global Name Service and the Object Transaction Monitor allow objects to be distributed and shared across multiple virtual machines and multiple hosts, while the Activator, using Smart Load Balancing, matches processing needs for specific operations to Java virtual machines configured to meet those needs.

- Pooled JDBC sessions optimize access to back-end relational databases.

- The GemStone/J Persistent Cache Architecture underlies and supports other resources. It provides fast, transactional access to objects through its distributed, shared-page cache; transparent object persistence to minimize object-to-relational translation for in-process data; and support for distributed, heterogeneous transaction control. It does not rely on Java serialization nor mapping to external databases.

6.4.2   J2EE Provides the Tools

To accommodate changing client needs, Codexa needs to be able to adapt or extend its applications continuously. To create a rapid application development (RAD) environment for prototyping and engineering iterations, all the technologies within the Codexa Service are based on Java technologies. Within its layered architecture, the Service relies on the J2EE platform and other technologies to provide security, scalability, reliable communication, and lifecycle management of business objects and processes. Figure 6.3 illustrates the technology stack.

In the top layer of the figure, Java Server Pages (JSPs) and Swing are used to build Web user interfaces (UIs), while InfoBus and JMS are used for system-to-system interface. (In this layer, the JMS is a producer for the InfoBus, with InfoBus as a static data bus for a presentation virtual machine.)

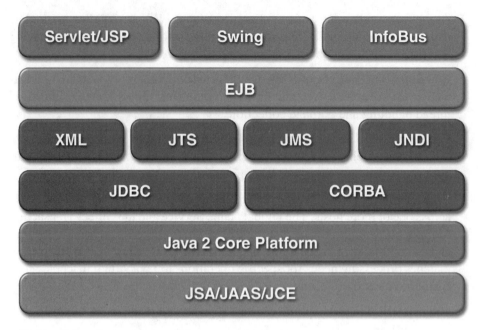

Figure 6.3 Codexa Layered Component Technology

Enterprise JavaBeans manage session state and "short-lived" behaviors, such as component-to-component data processing and client requests via servlets and JSPs.

The next layer provides lifecycle management for longer-lived objects in the system. XML Document Type Definitions (DTDs) represent the directory hierarchies and are used to depict domain objects and their relationships to other domain objects. EJBs can use these to create CORBA objects that are run on behalf of a namespace within the Java Naming and Directory Interface (JNDI), allowing for natural system and component partitioning, and register them with the JNDI. The JNDI is the main interface for locating objects in the directory structure and creating contexts for state and relationship management among logical components. Java Transaction Service (JTS) provides XA-compliant ACID transaction management, and Java Messaging Service handles message queuing for guaranteed data delivery.

The persistence layer is handled through GemStone/J's Persistent Cache Architecture. When a given object's useful life within the system has expired, JDBC is used to store it as historical information in the relational database.

Java Security Architecture (JSA), Java Authentication and Authorization Service (JAAS), and Java Cryptography Architecture (JCA) provide multilevel security for Codexa applications.

The whole system leverages the Java 2, Standard Edition architecture, using multiple VMs, distributed processing, and other features to create a scalable, highly available system.

6.5 Application Architecture: Billions and Billions of InfoBytes

Logically, Codexa's application is partitioned into a set of application services, including

- Data acquisition, the processes whereby the system gathers data of interest to Codexa clients from the Internet

- Data distribution, a messaging/event queuing service to provide the guaranteed data delivery that is critical to the Codexa system

- Data evaluation and classification, which evaluates and rates incoming data based on customer-specific criteria

- The KnowledgeMQ, a user-defined querying/reporting engine through which users interact with Codexa's application services

- Reporting, a user-defined data-formatting engine that enables users to specify logical information association and data delivery mechanisms (bulk file, cell phone, pager, Web page, and real-time alerts that leverage applets, Info-Bus, and JMS).

In the interests of flexibility, each of these components is designed to be independent of the platform, vendor-specific tools, security protocols, infrastructure, and even other Codexa components. This modular architecture is necessary because the Codexa system must enable client expertise to be applied at any level of the application, including client systems integration and asynchronous information delivery (see Figure 6.4).

6.5.1 Data Acquisition

Active data acquisition is one of the core technologies created by Codexa. The data acquisition module is responsible for acquiring data from a wide variety of Web data sources, including e-mail publications, news sites, message boards, closed-caption TV broadcasts, and corporate Web sites. Traditional sources include news, earnings, company information, SEC, and price feeds. After retrieving the data from these disparate sources, this module utilizes JINI technology to

Figure 6.4   Codexa Application-Services Architecture

distribute the processing necessary to strip the data of extraneous information and format it into a consistent, extensible, readable XML-based model. This complete process is referred to as "harvesting."

As of this publication, the data acquisition module brings in approximately 200,000 to 300,000 data items on a slow day and up to 500,000 items on a busy day. To handle peak loads, the system must be able to handle millions of items a day, some as small as e-mail messages, some as large as 300-page SEC filings.

Extracted data is stored in the Codexa system in the form of nested XML documents, accessed through the JNDI tree. As data is stored, the data model portion of the JNDI tree becomes, in essence, a map of relevant portions of the Internet, with XML documents representing data at a URL reachable through XML documents representing URLs, and so on. Notification of harvested data is published into the messaging system for evaluation and classification.

6.5.2   Data Distribution

The guaranteed distribution of data is central to the functionality of the Codexa Service. It is also essential for easing scalability issues, because it allows many operations to be separated into components, which can work in parallel but independent of one another. The Service requires a messaging/event queuing service that enables components distributed anywhere to communicate effectively with each other. A messaging service must be available to every server and every client in the system. Codexa wrapped and extended the functionality of Softwired's iBus//Message Server to satisfy this requirement.

Codexa has a few functional requirements beyond those of the average messaging service.

- A programmable interface for clients/user communication

- A network-centric client-side "lite" (small footprint) version for embedding in applications

- Functionality that supports the JavaBean property-change event notification model

- Support for a complete finite state machine model, including state management and transition management

The initial version of the Codexa KnowledgeMQ (the querying/reporting engine) implements JMS as a publish/subscribe message queuing system with which subscribers register interest in "topics," represented as locations in the JNDI hierarchy. This basic implementation includes support for distributed transaction-oriented messaging and is compliant with the Open Standards Group XA specification for distributed transaction processing (DTP). The transactional view of a message begins when the message producer creates the message and ends when all message consumers have received the given message.

For consistency, all messaging for KnowledgeMQ is structured as XML. All topics for publish/subscribe-based messaging use element and attribute node names in their hierarchical structure as topic names based on Codexa's implementation of the JNDI CompositeName specification.

KnowledgeMQ is a complete implementation of the JMS, supporting all the architecture defined in the JMS specification. The JMS architecture in its simplest form dictates the use of a `ConnectionFactory` that creates a specific type of `Connection` to a messaging server. The `Connection` is then used to access the `Session`. A `Session` is a factory for its `MessageConsumer` and `Message-Producer` references. A `MessageConsumer` is a subscriber to a `Session`. A `MessageProducer` is a publisher to a `Session`. With the addition of property-change monitoring, Codexa's KnowledgeMQ becomes a rules-based message distribution system, because property-change listeners have the ability to veto changes based on a set of rules and to force an understanding of state and transition. For example, the Codexa Service might have a base evaluation rule that multiple instances of certain keywords in a data item signal that a company is in legal trouble. If a client's rules are that some of those keywords aren't significant, the item might be judged unimportant, and propagation would be stopped before notification is sent to that client's users. This would imply patterns similar to deterministic finite automata (DFAs) in which the regular expression (RE) is substituted for rules and the KnowledgeMQ supports the propagation of state transition, including notions such as state concatenation, state alternation, and Kleen closure.

6.5.3   Data Evaluation and Classification

Data evaluation is one of the fundamental benefits the Codexa Service offers its clients. The Data Services include a set of evaluators—message consumer objects that add one or more evaluations to a harvested item. An evaluation is simply a determination that an item has a certain property (for example, that a message board posting contains a certain keyword). In addition, users can configure their own evaluators, so the types proliferate constantly.

The Data Services perform two basic types of evaluation and classification.

1. **Dynamic classification.** Classification is a subset of evaluation wherein an item is judged to be a member of a particular group (it is relevant to a specific organization, market sector, or an organization's business model).

2. **Dynamic constraints.** Constraints are data-validation modules. A constraint can veto the further propagation of a message based on its interpretation of the validity of the data. For example, if the system cannot classify a data item, a constraint removes all references to that item, and it is removed from the PCA.

6.5.4   KnowledgeMQ and Filters

The KnowledgeMQ, with its user-defined Knowledge Filters, is the front end of the Codexa Service, enabling users to interact with the application services in sophisticated ways. In the same vein as some commercial ad-hoc reporting tools, the KnowledgeMQ is a user-defined querying/reporting engine, except that it supports fuzzy logic-based queries, as well as standard reporting of data that is maintained by the system's real-time components. For example, a user can assign weight to data item attributes, then define a time scale for a weighted collection of events. When the aggregate weight of a collection of evaluations achieves the user's specified threshold within the time constraints, an alert is sent to the user's client process.

Knowledge filters are the user-defined "rules" that the KnowledgeMQ uses. The KnowledgeMQ uses the JavaBeans component architecture for rules definition. The rules are a standard XML document that follows the standard "bean customizer" pattern.

The core architectural paradigm for the KnowledgeMQ is as a real-time engine in which all communication takes place through a standard interface using a standard communications protocol. Through the realization of this design pattern, the Knowledge MQ becomes a scalable component that is accessed by server-side objects acting as proxies for organizations, organizational units, and users. Reports can then be delivered through the KnowledgeMQ.

The KnowledgeMQ offers a default set of reports, such as message volume ratios, earnings whispers, and market manipulation attempts. In addition, it can return alerts to a client, informing the client of events in which the client has registered interest, of new data available for reports the client has subscribed to, or of new information on a topic of interest to that client.

6.5.5   Reporting

Once data is fully classified, it is stored in the RDBMS, where it can be used for statistical analysis and reporting. Codexa clients access reporting EJBs through secured Java Servlets and Java ServerPages.

6.6   The Working Solution: Codexa in Action

Figure 6.5 is a visual representation of the flow of a data item through the Codexa system. The Harvester monitors Web and traditional data sources. When it finds an item of interest, the item is sent to an Extractor for conversion into a valid XML document. When the Extractor is finished, it stores the document in PCA and sends a JMS message to a Classifier, which decides which of the Wilshire 5000 companies are featured in the item. The Classifier stores its information, then passes the item on via JMS to appropriate Evaluators and Knowledge Filters, which operate in parallel to figure out what kind of information is in the item (for example, mergers and acquisitions, price manipulation, and so forth) and the relevance of the information. When the filtering is done, users are notified of items of interest via the KnowledgeMQ. Users can invoke reporting services to create real-time reports from items in the PCA or historical reports (trends and aggregates) of older items in the database management system.

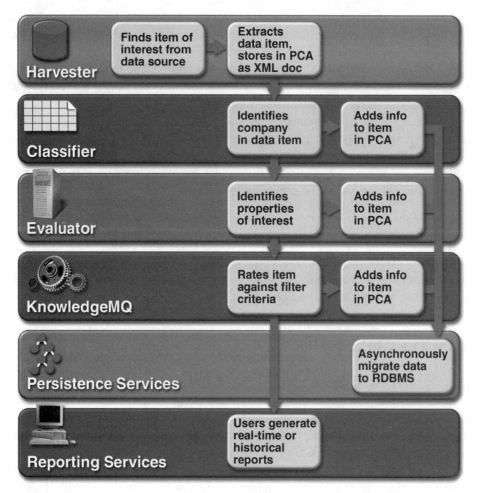

Figure 6.5   Data Flow Through the Codexa System

From the standpoint of the layered architecture, all user interactions with the system are much the same as shown in Figure 6.6, which shows a user request for a report from the Codexa Service. The request is handled by a servlet, which calls an appropriate EJB, which in turn goes to the JNDI to invoke a service in a CORBA process. The CORBA process returns the requested information to the user in XML form via the EJB and servlet.

Viewing Reports

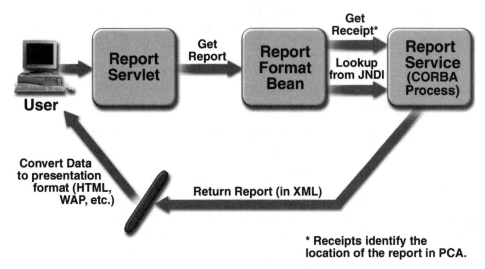

Figure 6.6   Servicing a User Request With the Codexa System

6.7   Achieving the Big Bang

So, how does the Codexa's Big Bang Service scale to meet requirements that would bring most networked systems applications to their knees? Let's look at some of the issues in more detail.

6.7.1   Channel Neutrality

The human interfaces to the Codexa Service can include a graphical user interface, a standard Web browser, e-mail information distribution (for example, newsletters), and consumer devices, such as palm-tops, personal communication service (PCS)-based cellular phones and alphanumeric pagers. Such a channel-neutral system requires the flexibility to access the same business applications using a variety of front-end technologies. J2EE technology is a natural fit for this kind of architecture, because it is inherently layered. Channel-specific processes are handled at the Web or WAP server level, while core business logic and processes are executed in the application server and shared among channels.

To separate application and presentation logic, all Codexa GUIs adhere to the model view controller (MVC) pattern for data access and manipulation. The model is the XML-based data model residing on the application server. Depending on the delivery channel, the view is either through the Java Foundation Classes (JFC, commonly referred to as Swing), HTML, Wireless Markup Language, or raw XML (for a system-to-system interface). The controller always resides on Codexa's servers as servlets, EJBs, or the KnowledgeMQ. When a user request comes in, the system uses XSLT to transform the XML document via Exstensible Style Language to the appropriate delivery format—HTML, WAP, or XML.

6.7.2 Scalability

The Codexa Service must scale to support tremendous volumes of data and peak loads, because system response is most critical to users at the same times the system is most heavily used. At times of financial crisis, both client usage and incoming data levels peak. The Codexa Service can meet these demands because its structure, with a highly distributed implementation of the J2EE architecture and GemStone/J's multi-virtual machine configuration, allows the system to scale within platforms and across many platforms transparently.

Figure 6.7 shows Codexa's deployment architecture. Each of the systems depicted in the deployment architecture is designed to scale, based on load. Web

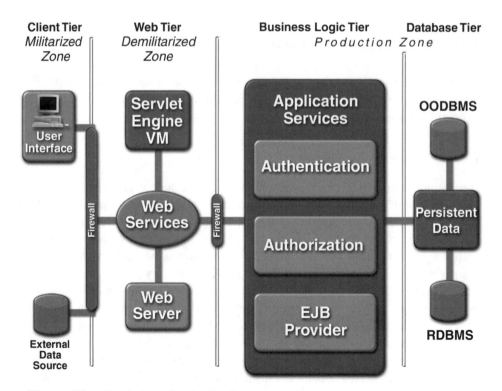

Figure 6.7   The Codexa Service Deployment Architecture

services scale in the traditional Web-site fashion, through intelligently applied algorithms for distribution of requests. One of the common pitfalls of any balanced access to Web servers is that during a long transaction-oriented session, DNS must return the client to the same Web server. To overcome this obstacle, Codexa's production application server uses GemStone/J's distributed session tracking feature. In GemStone/J, client session state is automatically stored in the persistent object cache, so client requests can be assigned to different Web servers and servlet engines. When the request comes in, the new servlet engine retrieves the session state from PCA using the client ID, and it services the request, enabling true round-robin access for DNS.

To achieve optimal per-process performance, Codexa takes advantage of GemStone/J's multi-virtual machine architecture. Processing and resource utilization varies greatly among virtual machines in any truly distributed system, and Codexa's needs are no different. Each component within the Codexa Service leverages a VM configuration specific to its needs. For example, a traditional "client" VM that a user would leverage is throughput-intensive, yet not CPU intensive. A system CORBA VM, such as the one used by the knowledge filter would require greater CPU capabilities per system.

The Codexa Service makes the most of its hardware by running multiple, specially tuned virtual machines in each application server to handle different kinds of processes. GemStone/J virtual machines have a number of configuration options: optimum/maximum number of clients, Java heap size, lifespan before they are recycled, code to initialize a given virtual machine's resources, and so forth. Therefore, the Codexa Service tunes one or more virtual machines to the needs of each process type and the GemStone/J Activator assigns each incoming request to an appropriate virtual machine based on its configuration and actual current workload. The throughput-intensive "client" virtual machine is configured for a large client load with a larger memory allocation, while the CPU-intensive system CORBA virtual machine used by the knowledge filter is configured for fewer client processes within a single virtual machine. The system can activate more virtual machines on demand to handle possible spikes in throughput. Codexa typically runs many dozen virtual machines at a time on each application server.

The other major issue with scalability is database access. Codexa's data stores are huge—the system stores several gigabytes of new data every day, and a terabyte of disk can be dedicated to persistent object storage alone. To speed access, domain data is divided among several GemStone/J databases, one each for Wilshire 5,000 company data, securities information, and earnings information. The Data Services' RDBMS is Sybase ASE 12.0, which has a number of mechanisms in place to support high availability and fault tolerance.

Finally, in order to achieve scalability in the Java platform, processes must be able to run in a federated fashion in multiple virtual machines. The management of the federation of processes is the responsibility of the application server.

Codexa leverages GemStone/J's PCA again to create a distributed object network that will enable not only federation of virtual machines but also horizontal scaling of the Application Services systems.

6.7.3 Security

Codexa requires air-tight security, because the search and reporting parameters its financial analyst clients set in the system are vital intellectual property that must not be visible to anyone else. Furthermore, Codexa has access to a number of on-line information providers for data used in its analyses. Some of this information can only be provided to clients in accordance with the clients' subscription agreements with the information provider. So, for example, Codexa may have clients who are authorized to see summary data, but others are permitted to view only some of the underlying details from various sources, which led to that aggregated data. Codexa keeps up-to-date security information about the clients who are authorized to see information from certain providers and enforces those agreements on the providers' behalf.

A combination of the Java Security Architecture (JSA), Java Cryptography Architecture (JCA), and Intel's Common Data Security Architecture (CDSA) enable Codexa to provide very high security for object access, within individual virtual machines and across its distributed system. The CDSA defines the core issues surrounding secure distributed systems: data and user authentication. The JSA addresses core issues surrounding security within a given virtual machine. The JCA addresses core issues surrounding public key infrastructure (PKI)-related technologies. The CDSA depicts a modular layered architecture (see Figure 6.8) that enables security infrastructure at any level.

This component-based security architecture enables the extensibility that is necessary as the system's security constraints evolve. Each of the base modules can exist on a per-machine basis, as well as in a federated model. The per-machine basis of the model can be enabled through off-the-shelf implementations of common security services. A federated common security services manager (CSSM) enables a programmatic interface that supports the JSA, JCA, and JAAS.

Security for the Codexa Service deployment architecture (Figure 6.7) is maintained through three "zones of trust." The first is the militarized zone of the Internet, which is protected through standard Internet security, such as SSL. The second is the demilitarized zone of Web services, which is protected by internal network partitioning and private address masking. The third is the production zone, where user authentication and authorization services control user access to methods and data.

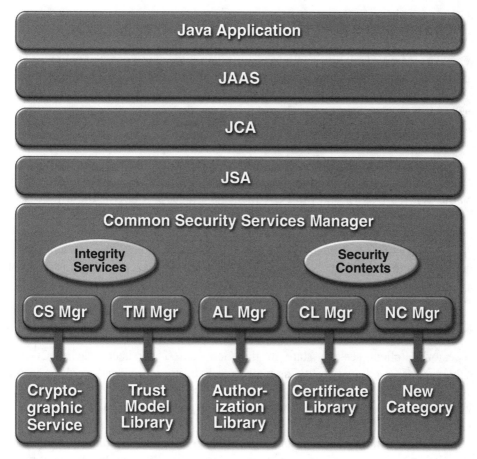

Figure 6.8   Codexa's Modular, Layered Security Architecture

6.7.4   Very High Availability

Financial institutions rely on the Codexa application to provide time-sensitive decision-support data whenever and wherever they demand it. The Codexa application, therefore, requires very high up-time. It must handle peak loads, and it must be able to incorporate improvements and upgrades, without taking the system offline. J2EE supports this because it is dynamic and layered, and Gemstone/J takes advantage of J2EE's architecture to provide precision failover of system resources and online deployment, upgrades, and maintenance.

6.7.5   Precision Failover

Often, availability problems occur at the lowest levels of a system's computing resources. Many availability solutions, however, must shut down the entire system to repair a minor problem. Codexa manages this issue by taking advantage of GemStone/J's Precision Failover technology, which monitors and handles recovery for critical software processes and reinitiates the process as necessary, without system down-time.

Perhaps most critical for Codexa is the GemStone/J "buddy system." The active Global Name Service (GNS), a JNDI service, monitors the other processes running in the system, including the Activator, the persistent cache's Repository Name Service (RNS), and the PCA manager process. If any of these processes become unresponsive, the GNS will stop and restart it. The active GNS in the primary server also tracks the GemStone/J processes in secondary machines. A "buddy" process monitors the active GNS. If the GNS fails, the buddy will shut it down and initiate a restart. Since many of these are separate processes, a failure of a component should not interrupt the active requests in the system.

6.7.6   Transparent Client Session State Persistence

By storing client session state in the GemStone/J persistent cache, Codexa achieves increased availability, as well as scalability. If a virtual machine in the system fails, the Activator automatically reroutes client requests to another pooled virtual machine or starts a new virtual machine, if necessary. If the replacement virtual machine is on the same machine, it may be able to continue processing objects already in the shared object cache. If a servlet engine virtual machine fails, the Web-server adapter can reroute requests to another servlet engine virtual machine, which then retrieves session state from persistent object cache using the client ID.

6.7.7   Lifecycle Management and Availability

To maintain full-time availability, the Codexa application must be functional even during system expansion, reconfiguration and tuning, and application deployments and updates. GemStone/J enables Codexa system administrators to dynamically maintain and upgrade the application, without taking the Web site, application, application server, or hardware server offline. The application can be dynamically configured for scalability by adding, removing, and reconfiguring new virtual machines or other software components or by reconfiguring for performance tuning.

Comprehensive APIs within GemStone/J also give the Codexa application dynamic control of all parts of a system. These tools include both command-line controls and a graphical UI, and configuration changes can be saved automatically without restarting the system.

New versions of the Codexa application can be deployed with the same name while clients are still executing the prior version of the application. New clients are automatically given the new version of the application. This is enabled through the use of CORBA and virtual machine management.

6.7.8   Extensibility

Extensibility is a key requirement and capability of the Codexa Service, as evidenced by this quote from an early engineering specification: "At first glance, Codexa's Data Services may appear quite complex, with the interdependencies among components not immediately clear. The apparent complexity only increases when one realizes that Codexa's set of core technologies must support not only Codexa's requirements, but those of its clients." Fortunately, the J2EE platform provides a set of standards that make extensibility both possible and practical.

The J2EE architecture includes JNDI, EJB, JSP, JMS, JTS, the Connector Architecture (which Codexa intends to embrace when it is finalized), CORBA, JDBC, XML, and Java Servlets technology. Through strict adherence to these standards and by exposing only the J2EE platform's standard APIs, Codexa has created a distributed information system infrastructure for which customers can write their own modules without having to learn proprietary APIs. And this applies to *all* third-party tools the system uses.

Going forward, Codexa will be able to apply vast amounts of working, production-tested components to the information synthesis needs of a broad array of financial and nonfinancial professionals. And as other divisions of Codexa appear to address new financial sectors, the systems that are developed will integrate seamlessly to share data with the currently running version of Codexa's Data Services. This paradigm affords huge savings in code reuse, and creates a significant win in the reusability and extensibility of the data.

6.8   Codexa Through Time

The Codexa Service has already had a "big bang" impact. Codexa's customers profit from improved, more-information-rich decision-making, while they enjoy significant productivity benefits in their information gathering and analysis activities. Codexa's client financial firms anticipate that the Codexa Service will continue to make their decision-making professionals even more effective over time, as they work with Codexa to tune and extend its Service to meet their needs.

Meanwhile, Codexa's developers strongly believe the J2EE architecture has already made them much more effective. Using the J2EE platform, Codexa's engineering staff has produced an extremely sophisticated networked information infrastructure in far less time than would have been required by previous generations of software technology. As an ASP, Codexa's imperative is to provide an enterprise class application to its customers on Internet time, and the J2EE platform's component-based layered architecture make this possible.

Forte/eTapestry

About the Authors

Scott Ganyo, co-founder and vice president of research and application architecture for eTapestry.com, built the eTapestry fundraising and communications software from scratch using the Java programming language. Ganyo is responsible for oversight of eTapestry.com's technological direction and application architecture, ensuring that eTapestry blends seamlessly with partner applications and creating a CRM (customer relationship management) package that can be accessed anywhere the Internet is available.

Tony Baer is a well-published IT analyst with more than 15 years experience in application development and enterprise systems. As president of Demand Strategies, Baer studies implementation issues in distributed data management, application development, data warehousing, and leading enterprise applications. He is also a columnist for *Application Development Trends*, frequent contributor to *Computerworld*, and chief analyst of *Computer Finance,* a journal covering IT economics.

Paul Butterworth is a distinguished engineer at Sun Microsystems, where he is the chief architect for the Forte tools division. He was a co-founder of Forte Software, serving as senior vice president of software development. He was also the principal architect of the company's pioneering distributed development platform. Butterworth is a recognized authority on object-oriented technology, multitier architectures, and distributed computing. He has served as chief technology officer and engineering vice president for a number of innovative companies during his 30-year career in the computing industry, including Forte, Servio Logic, and Ingres Corporation. He holds an MA in computer science.

CHAPTER 7

Java Technology Builds eTapestry.com ASP for Charities with Forte Tools

7.1   The Project

eTapestry.com was founded in August 1999 to deliver fundraising applications to the nonprofit sector using an Internet-based ASP (application service provider) model. The Indianapolis-based company chose Java technology because it provided an open, productive, and extensible application platform for developing an application to serve a rapidly evolving market segment.

The application uses a standard HTML front end, with Web pages generated by Java servlets and Java ServerPages (JSPs). The application, which first went live in spring 2000, makes extensive use of many J2EE architecture features, such as servlets and JSPs, the Java XML parser, and the Java Naming and Directory Interface (JNDI).

The application illustrates that J2EE technology is useful, even if the deployment scheme does not yet use a fully distributed environment. Significantly, the J2EE architecture provides eTapestry the capability to redeploy the application as appropriate once traffic levels warrant, *without* rewriting the application itself.

To build the application, eTapestry.com used the Forte for Java, Internet Edition as the integrated development environment (IDE), and is deploying the application using the Gemstone/J application server. The application itself is currently hosted by Genuity.

7.2   The Company

eTapestry's four cofounders had accumulated more than 30 years of experience developing solutions for the nonprofit sector. CEO Jay Love and COO Steve Rusche have each spent 15 years managing the operations of nonprofits, while CTO John Moore and Scott Ganyo, the vice president of research and application architecture, each have more than a dozen years with system design, database management, and programming. Prior to cofounding eTapestry, Moore and Ganyo had extensive object-oriented development experience working with C++ and SmallTalk. They began working with the Java language even before its 1995 public release.

The idea that eventually became eTapestry originated in the mid 1990s while the founders were principals of Master Software, a vendor that offered client/ server-based business applications for charitable organizations. "We realized that the Internet was the coming wave," says Rusche. "We had an R&D project on Web development underway at the time the company was sold to a competitor."

After their company was sold, the four worked for different companies in the Indianapolis area. "We still got together in our off-hours to thrash around our ideas," Rusche says, noting that thanks to their similar backgrounds in object-oriented design, Scott and John "were on the same page" when it came to developing the new architecture for the application.

Significantly, a major design goal was to offer the application as an application service provider (ASP), which at that time was an untested idea. "We knew the nonprofit world was populated with organizations that couldn't afford to buy or install their own software," notes Rusche, who adds that the design goals of simplicity and low cost became their "mantras." At their previous company, they had all learned that only a handful of nonprofit organizations had the resources to maintain IT staffs that could install and maintain the applications. According to eTapestry's Ganyo, in raw numbers, the nonprofit field is dominated by small organizations, most of which are run primarily by volunteers.

Nonetheless, because the ASP concept was so new, the cofounders hedged their bets. The new architecture would have to be modular and flexible enough to allow the application to be deployed either in conventional shrink-wrapped form or over the Internet as a service. It would be simpler to administer than conventional, Windows-based client/server applications because it would take advantage of the familiar, HTML Web-browser front end.

Today, eTapestry has become the first Web-based donor-management application for nonprofit organizations. It is also the first to offer this functionality through the ASP channel. After the end of its first year of operation, eTapestry.com has attracted a user base of 500 organizations; its ASP service handles an average of 50 concurrent sessions. And an independent customer poll, conducted by an outside market research organization, found eTapestry winning good or excellent ratings for its ease of use and prompt customer service.

7.3 Technology Adoption

Thanks to the design team's early experience with object-oriented development in C++ and Smalltalk and with object-oriented databases from Gemstone and ObjectStore, they were ready to embrace Java as the development platform for the new application. In addition, the founders were versed in client-server technologies, with backgrounds in Visual Basic, C and other third generation languages, and the Microsoft SQL Server and Oracle transactional databases.

When eTapestry was formed, the principals agreed to take advantage of Web architecture to produce an application that was more accessible, scalable, suitable for B2B integration, and standards-based. They also decided to use the object-oriented techniques that they refined from their previous experience. "The idea of modular code that can be encapsulated, managed, and reused carried a lot of weight with us," explains Scott Ganyo. He notes that this approach allowed them to focus on developing relatively simple modules of standard code, which could be assembled and reused when forming the final application. "This philosophy is very much in line with Sun's Java technology," says Ganyo.

7.4 Opportunity: The Business Problem

Today, there are more than one million nonprofit organizations in the U.S. Accounting for $650 billion in proceeds, the nonprofit sector ranks as the third largest industry in the U.S. Yet, like many sectors, in raw numbers the overwhelming majority of nonprofit groups are small to midsize organizations. In many cases, they rely in whole or in part on volunteer labor, and are therefore rarely capable of implementing or maintaining IT systems beyond a few stand-alone personal computers. The result is that most nonprofits are left to manage funds manually.

eTapestry entered the market to provide solutions to charitable groups that could not afford their own systems. Thanks to the reach of the Internet, eTapestry could build a standard application and offer it as a browser-based Web service that charitable organizations could rent for nominal cost. (They also offer an incubator program that provides free access to organizations that have only a single user and fewer than 1,000 donor accounts.)

Although charitable organizations are often considered unique, when it comes to transacting business, they share much with their for-profit counterparts. At the most basic level, both sectors need to track finances and manage customer relationships in order to operate.

In many cases, the differences boil down to terminology: For-profit businesses track orders and customers; nonprofits track donations and donors. Furthermore, repeat business is a key goal for both classes of organizations, because the cost of revenue acquisition is much lower compared with seeking out new customers or donors.

The realization that charitable organizations require sound business management solutions was the driving force behind eTapestry.com. Admittedly, the concept wasn't new. Fundraising management solutions have been in existence for many years. However, at costs ranging from tens to hundreds of thousands of dollars, few nonprofit organizations were large enough to afford them.

However, nonprofits, large or small, need business solutions that, in important ways, differed from the accounting and customer relationship management packages common to the corporate market. "The unique thing about nonprofit organizations is that they must manage soliciting the funds and recording gifts as they come in," says Rusche, who adds, "This can get very complex, because the donations have to be categorized according to the unique relationships of the fundraising process."

For instance, there are different types of gifts. Some gifts are considered "hard" donations; they correspond to the actual amount pledged by the contributor. However, in many cases, there are "soft" donations, as well, which consist of matching contributions many companies offer for their employees. The types of gifts vary. There are individual gifts that are contributed as part of a fundraising drive, and there are planned gifts that are dispersed by an institution or as part of the arrangements from the trust fund from someone's estate. In addition, memorial contributions may come with stipulations that relatives of the deceased be specially notified.

The following are some of eTapestry's major features.

- Donor Profiling. This feature accounts for various methods by which donors are to be contacted. For instance, they may have different mailing addresses or seasonal addresses. Donors are categorized by their roles, which in turn governs what pieces of mail should be sent. And they may have unique relationships to other donors, which must be acknowledged.

- List Management. Nonprofit organizations conduct numerous direct mass mailings. Like any direct marketer, nonprofits must carefully track these mailings to ensure that the recipients on a list receive the right mailings. This is especially critical for nonprofits, which cannot afford to oversaturate their members or donors with annoying duplicate mailings.

- Message Center. Because maintaining one-to-one relationships with donors is essential to maintaining donations, nonprofit organizations must conduct careful contact management. This is especially critical for the top 2 percent to 3 percent of donors who consistently make the largest contributions. They must track all communications with donors and groups of donors, and provide calendaring services that allow event notifications to be mailed. The eTapesty system allows donors to make appointments and schedule events that are posted on the organization's Web sites. It also conducts targeted and mass e-mail notifications based on donor profiles.

- Volunteer Profiles. Because nonprofits depend heavily on contributed labor, they must classify the skills and preferences of their volunteers when it comes to mundane operations. In addition, for tax and legal purposes, volunteer effort must often be recognized as "in kind" donations, with monetary value.

- Calendaring and Event Management/Notification. Special events play large roles in fundraising. Organizations require solutions that allow them to register donors or attendees, and in conjunction with the messaging functions, remind donors when events of interest are scheduled.

- Gift Processing and OnLine Donations. The order-entry function for nonprofit organizations has similarities to that of conventional businesses. However, differences include how "orders" are tracked, such as differentiating whether a contribution is "hard" or "soft," and whether other donors, organizations, friends, or relatives must be notified. Prior to the eTapestry application, no single solution combined online donations with the ability to record and track them.

- Audit Trails and Rollback Capabilities. Gifts contributed to charitable organizations are sometimes redirected; the system must be able to update, and in some cases, reverse previous transactions already recorded.

- Reporting. The application provides summary and drill-down reports covering campaign activity, such as how much money poured into a specific campaign, where it came from, and which activities were the most productive. Nonprofit organizations using the eTapestry application can also make ad hoc queries of their donor database and campaign activity.

- B2B Integration. With the use of HTML links and XML data integration, eTapestry users can take advantage of value-added services from a growing list of business partners. For instance, using an XML link, customers can use the PGCalc online application to calculate the tax implications of planned gifts.

The key to the power of the eTapestry application is its central repository for all transactional information, from contact information and donor activity to the services offered by eTapestry's partner sites. This provides a complete picture of donor activity—the lifeblood of charitable giving. Because the service is hosted on a secure server that supports 128-bit secure socket layer encryption, eTapestry customers are assured that all transactions are safe.

7.4.1   Challenges

The major obstacle was that Internet technology is a moving target. For instance, when the development team began work in late 1999, the J2EE standard had not yet been released. The result was that the development team created a number of services that subsequently became commercially available once the J2EE specification was made public. Some of the services custom developed included user authentication and the management of interactions among JSPs and servlets.

A prime risk in the effort was being caught with obsolete technology. eTapestry chose Java technology because it has become a major standard for e-commerce platforms and applications. Admittedly, because the J2EE platform was still emerging at the outset of the project, the team developed some home-grown application services that would have to be migrated once the technology matured matured. However, by adhering strictly to object-oriented application design practices, the code could be modularized and isolated from the rest of the application, allowing subsequent replacement with more-standard technology.

Like any application, the quality of development and deployment would play a do-or-die role. In this case, failure of the application would take the entire business down with it, since the company was founded around the new software.

Implementation concerns included scalability and flexibility. Because the company's long-range plans were based on concurrent usage levels at 10 to 20 times current volumes, the company could not afford to develop anything that would later require costly redesign or architectural migration. Besides the unwanted costs of new development, the company did not want to subject its customers to a shakeout process just as the business was taking off.

According to Ganyo, scalability requirements were one of the factors behind the Java decision. "If we went with a proprietary environment, we ran the risk of being locked into designs that might not handle the number of users we were targeting," says Ganyo.

In addition, eTapestry required a modular application architecture that would allow it to quickly add functionality in response to customer demand. For instance, the company recently added a calendaring function that allows donors to store appointments, and subsequently upgraded it with reminder-alert capabilities. Using a strict object oriented (OO) design enabled eTapestry to add functionality without disrupting the core application.

Finally, there was the challenge of supporting and introducing business-to-business integration to a market that was not computer literate. In some cases, eTapestry customers have stand-alone databases or spreadsheets that list donors, and calendaring systems that list events. In other cases, the source data was maintained manually. eTapestry had to develop a system that was open, yet simple enough to facilitate the entry or transfer of data from its would-be customers.

Furthermore, to make the service more compelling, eTapestry also had to design a system that would accommodate integration with business partners. That could include software or service providers who could add value to eTapestry's applications, service providers to its customer base, along with corporate donors, which might offer automated or institutional donations via existing HR or payroll systems.

7.5 The Solution

The challenges that eTapestry faced required that they make careful choices in terms of both the technologies they used and the vendors that they relied on to deliver the technology. Being at the leading edge of the technologies, it was important to select solutions and vendors that would meet the need both for the short term and the long term.

7.5.1 Technology Choices

Technology evolves rapidly and today's standards need to have both room to grow and wide spread support to ensure longterm viability. eTapestry focused on Java technology and XML standards as a way to achieve these goals.

7.5.2 Java Technology

eTapestry chose Java technology for its application platform for numerous reasons. The first was Java technology's object-oriented nature. Having decided to design the application using object-oriented principles, the development team (which, at the start, consisted of just two people) required an object-oriented language that was also highly productive. The team found the Java language to be a much simpler and more versatile alternative to C++ because of its lack of pointers, its use of garbage collection, platform-independence, and its ability to accept changes or fixes without having to recompile the application or take the server offline.

The decision for Java technology was reinforced by several key enhancements. For instance, Java JIT (just-in-time) compilers ensured that the application would perform efficiently. In addition, the emergence of the J2EE standard provided an upward migration path that would allow the application to be distributed as traffic levels warranted.

7.5.3 Extensible Markup Language (XML)

Extensible Markup Language data formats are used for several purposes. The obvious function is for B2B exchange of data from business partners. Much of the B2B integration work is still in progress. For instance, a bi-directional link with Acteva, which offers an event-management plug-in, is being developed. This would allow eTapestry customers to enter data on any scheduled event, such as a seminar, including information on membership dues and sponsorships, and options for donors who can't attend an event to contribute via a sponsorship or donation. Events open to the public could be listed with Acteva's own search engine. At this point, the mechanics for the XML data exchange have yet to be determined.

As part of its partnering strategy, eTapestry is working with several XML organizations to create standard APIs for specific business transactions. For instance, eTapestry has joined the Open Philanthropy Exchange (OPX) to develop standard electronic transactions from the newly emerging online charity portals (which manage donor funds) and the nonprofit organizations that are to receive donations. Typical transactions include automated processing of payroll deductions, volunteering opportunities, and providing electronic acknowledgements that the donations were accepted.

eTapestry is also working with SyncML, a broad-based technology group, to develop the standards for synchronizing data between personal digital assistants such as, Palm or PocketPC and calendaring and messaging applications (such as, Outlook). Such a standard would help donors download schedules of charitable events onto their own palmtops.

"XML standards are important to our customers and their donors because both sides want to ensure that their online transactions are handled accurately and seamlessly," says Rusche, who adds, "The standards allow us to concentrate on value-added functionality, rather than on writing and maintaining proprietary interfaces."

XML is also important to eTapestry's internal operations. The company uses XML to manage internal system configurations (for example, database properties and log settings). With the data stored in a neutral format like XML, it will be relatively easy to manipulate, using the XML editors contained in the Forte for Java development tool, along with the standard XML parsers specified as part of J2EE.

7.6 Vendor Selection

The major off-the-shelf components of the solution eTapestry acquired included an interactive development environment (IDE) and a combined application and database server. For the development environment, eTapestry chose Forte for Java, Community Edition, based on the flexibility and broad functionality options the open source-based tool provides. "Forte for Java gives us a double-barreled advantage. As open source, it is freely available, and it has the broadest selection of features and integration capabilities of any Java development environment that we evaluated," says Ganyo.

Among the features Ganyo found useful were its auto-completion capabilities with which the tool can complete partially written coding statements. "That provides a useful productivity tool," notes Ganyo. The Forte for Java product's capability to automatically generate Java property files was another productivity aid. Its XML, JSP, and servlet support, plus the comprehensive Javadoc-based help system, made the coding and debugging processes simpler and faster.

That the Forte for Java IDE was available as an open-source product was an important selection criterion. "Open source provides us the confidence that we won't end up with proprietary, dead-end technology," Ganyo says.

Open source significantly broadened eTapestry's options. With the source code freely available to the Internet developer community, eTapestry can benefit from third-party enhancements that are becoming available. For instance, the development team is considering using Ant, a Make environment for managing code dependencies, which is available through the Apache Foundation. They are also looking forward to small but valuable enhancements, such as the new "mouse wheel" support that open-source developers have made available to the Java community. "Little things like that add up and make a big difference," says Ganyo, who adds, "A bonus is that we won't have to depend on a single vendor to get all the improvements."

Furthermore, the modular architecture of the Forte for Java IDE provided eTapestry the flexibility to use only the functionality it requires. "You can trim down the memory requirements of Forte for Java if you use only the features you need, which really helps performance," notes Ganyo. For instance, while eTapestry currently uses most modules available as part of Forte for Java, the company has not installed modules covering JINI, FTP, or login. An added benefit of the product's modularity is the ease of upgrade, an important advantage now that version 2.0 is shipping. With this release, the core tool can remain in place with only the new or updated features needing to be installed as plug-ins.

When the Forte for Java Internet edition was released in beta, eTapestry quickly upgraded to the new tool to take advantage of several key features. "We were very interested in using the new JSP line-level debugging features that allow us to improve the way the system handles incoming HTTP requests," says Ganyo.

eTapestry chose the Gemstone/J application server as the deployment platform, in large part due to its embedded object-oriented database. The advantage of this approach is that the performance and complexity issues of object/relational mapping can be avoided. The embedded data cache stores data as Java objects. This approach simplifies matters for the development team, since they do not have to reconcile the object structures of the Java application with relational data structures. In addition, by using an object database, new functionality can be added more readily to the system.

7.7   Application Architecture

Because the application is still in its early phases, traffic can be accommodated on a single dual-Pentium-based, Windows NT server platform. However, modular design of the application will enable eTapestry to distribute functionality when patronage levels warrant. Although eTapestry does not yet use a fully distributed deployment, it uses key J2EE technologies.

7.7.1   Client Layer

Recognizing that many charitable organizations operate with older, donated machines, the front end was kept as simple—and thin—as possible. Accordingly, the user interface is entirely based on HTML and JavaScript, making the application extremely portable and resource-efficient. The application runs in any standard Web browser.

7.7.2   Web-Server Layer

eTapestry uses Microsoft Internet Information Server (IIS), which is bundled as part of Windows NT 4.0. The web server handles the incoming HTTP requests, which are handled through a standard Common Gateway Interface (CGI). SSL decryption is also handled at this tier to optimize internal communications between the Web server and application server.

7.7.3   Application-Server Layer

As mentioned earlier, all tiers of the application reside on a single server. For now, this means that application-server processes, such as load balancing and failover are not necessary.

The application layer contains numerous services, including the core application logic that provides the fundraising management functionality, plus supporting services, including directory and authentication, mail, SSL encryption/decryption, and XML processing. The processes are largely handled by servlets that are generated using the NewAtlanta ServletExec Servlet engine.

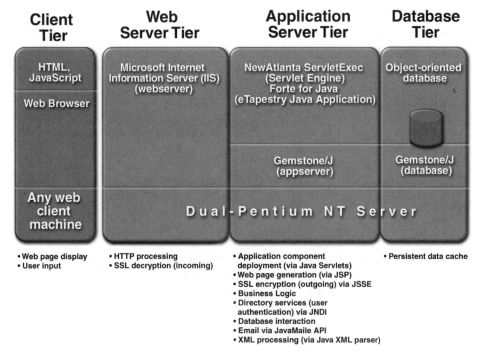

Figure 7.1   The eTapestry Application's Current Architecture

It also handles the all-important user authentication process. Users access the application through a standard login and password authentication procedure. This is preferable to alternatives, such as requiring users to obtain certificates from third parties, such as Verisign or Thawte. Although certificates in the long run might be more foolproof, requiring eTapestry users to install the necessary certificate management engines on their systems is not yet practical.

7.8   Solution Analysis

The application is currently quite simple. However, the development team designed the application using object-oriented approaches to provide an intuitive migration path once utilization grows. This approach will pay off as eTapestry begins to modify the deployment of the system as traffic to the suite grows.

7.8.1   Servlets and Java Server Pages

The goal of eTapestry's application designers was a highly dynamic, data-driven application that provides access to fully functional business applications through standard Web browsers. Almost every Web page sent back to the user is dynamic, containing customer-specific data.

The initial approach involved deploying Java applets, which provided limited application logic and graphics processing on the client. However, this architecture encountered performance problems for customers accessing through slower modem connections, using older desktop PCs or Macs—or both. (In some cases, the Java applets encountered problems passing through customer firewalls.)

Instead, the production version uses thinner, HTML clients, with all processing performed on the server. Java servlets are deployed at runtime. Based on user input, the servlets generate Java ServerPages, which in turn send HTML and JavaScript via HTTP back to the user.

7.8.2   Java Mail API

The eTapestry application bundles an IMAP (Internet Message Access Protocol) e-mail server to relieve customers of the need to implement their own e-mail servers. The Java Mail API was used to build eTapestry's e-mail modules, which handle custom and mass e-mailings to donors.

By relying on a standard API, eTapestry focuses on developing enhanced functionality, such as the ability to send mass-customized e-mails (mass e-mailings that are individually addressed to each donor) and the ability to store the contents of e-mails into each donor's journal. Without the JavaMail API, eTapestry would have to write individual low-level socket communications with SMTP, POP, and IMAP mail servers, a task that would have required extensive custom programming. "The JavaMail functionality allowed us to put together the whole e-mail package in just a few weeks, without forcing us to learn the innards of every kind of mail server," says Ganyo. Currently, eTapestry supports outgoing mail via SMTP and POP3, with incoming mail IMAP support scheduled for release in Q1 2001. "This will provide our clients full round-trip e-mail, allowing incoming mail to be automatically routed to the proper IMAP mail server," Ganyo continues.

7.8.3   Java Naming and Directory Interface (JNDI)

With the Gemstone/J application server, objects are retrieved using naming services via the JNDI API. In the future, eTapestry plans to use JNDI to add directory services to its basic e-mail functionality. With directory service integration, e-mail can be more tightly interwoven into other core eTapestry functions and modules. For instance, this would allow the e-mail system to integrate with the donor journaling feature (a form of contact management that tracks all interactions with the donor). With this integration, the donor journaling would have records of all e-mails associated with the contact. Other possibilities include the ability to conduct targeted mass mailings to different donor segments based on past activity (for example, send reminders to all donors who haven't made contributions in the past six months) or specific demographics (all donors in a certain census tract or membership level).

The use of standard interfaces, such as JNDI, eliminates the task of developing APIs from scratch. The benefits have allowed eTapestry to focus on developing functionality rather than inventing and maintaining custom interfaces.

7.8.4 Java Secure Sockets Extension (JSSE)

As a mission-critical transaction system for its customers, maintaining security is business-critical for eTapestry. The identities and activities of donors and all financial data are extremely sensitive.

Therefore, virtually all transactions are encrypted, using 128-bit secure socket layer (SSL) encryption. JSSE provides a standard API that allows Java applications to use SSL connections. JSSE provides eTapestry a far more economical alternative to buying proprietary, third-party algorithms for accessing SSL sessions.

7.8.5 Object-Oriented Database

As noted earlier, eTapestry relies on an object database as the sole data cache, an architecture that is fairly unusual. The rationale is that keeping the data represented as objects avoids the complexities of object/relational mapping, and it avoids the need for deciding which form of persistence to deploy—bean- or container-managed.

In taking this strategy, eTapestry weighed issues such as the availability of professionals skilled in object databases in a world dominated by SQL relational architectures, as well as data integration issues with customers and business partners who might otherwise use relational or flat-file data sources. eTapestry concluded that, as a small, Web-based application service provider, it did not require large teams of database administrators. Furthermore, when it came to data integration, because the data structures themselves were hidden from customers and business partners, there was little issue over whether eTapestry's data was object-oriented or relational.

The only issue here was that some customers, who already had rudimentary applications, might already have some data in relational form. Naturally, when migrating data between one database and another, conversions are always necessary. If the source data is relational, having an object database requires an extra conversion step. Considering the nature of eTapestry's customer base, these problems are fairly rare.

The issue, however, might become more relevant if eTapestry adds future integration with business partners whose systems are likely to be more sophisticated, and whose data is likely to be in relational form. As a bridge strategy, the Gemstone/J object cache does support SQL 92 query and indexing capabilities, which will allow business partners with relational systems to access data using familiar SQL calls.

Furthermore, because eTapestry's customer base is not computer-savvy, queries are made, not with SQL commands, but with a query and reporting facility that was custom built into the application itself.

Naturally, scalability is an issue, for application and database architectures alike. Given the market dominance of SQL databases, large transactional object databases are rare. However, at current levels of utilization, that is not an issue for eTapestry. Nonetheless, the development team is keeping its design options open, however, as utilization levels rise.

7.9   Future Directions

While the solution eTapestry developed meets its initial goals, there's always room for enhancement and evolution. Efforts are currently anticipated in several directions.

7.9.1   Distributed Deployment

Although the existing application sits on a single, dual-Pentium machine, it has been designed modularly to allow distributed deployment once patronage levels rise sufficiently. That will prove key as eTapestry takes the next step, possibly as early as the first half of 2001, to redeploy the Web server and SSL encrypting/decrypting functions on a separate server that would perform all the preprocessing. The reasoning is that SSL processing is extremely compute-intensive and therefore the most likely process to offload (from the main server) to improve performance.

As utilization grows, eTapestry expects it will have to redeploy application and database services. However, the company has not yet made any firm architectural plans, besides the assumption that the application will have to use the clustering, load balancing, and failover capabilities of the Gemstone/J application server.

eTapestry has not yet decided whether to use Enterprise JavaBeans in the future. However, if it does, it will actively consider use of modeling tools that can automate the generation of EJBs. The company is considering tools such as Together/J (from TogetherSoft) and Rational Rose.

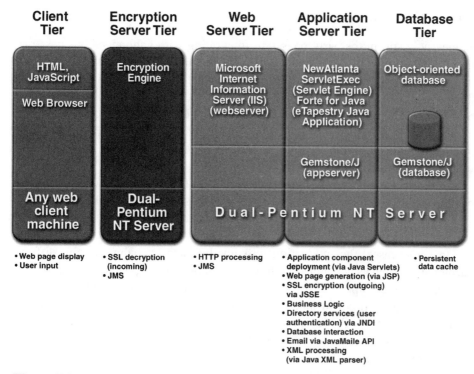

Client Tier	Encryption Server Tier	Web Server Tier	Application Server Tier	Database Tier
HTML, JavaScript Web Browser	Encryption Engine	Microsoft Internet Information Server (IIS) (webserver)	NewAtlanta ServletExec (Servlet Engine) Forte for Java (eTapestry Java Application)	Object-oriented database
			Gemstone/J (appserver)	Gemstone/J (database)
Any web client machine	Dual-Pentium NT Server	Dual-Pentium NT Server		
• Web page display • User input	• SSL decryption (incoming) • JMS	• HTTP processing • JMS	• Application component deployment (via Java Servlets) • Web page generation (via JSP) • SSL encryption (outgoing) via JSSE • Business Logic • Directory services (user authentication) via JNDI • Database interaction • Email via JavaMaile API • XML processing (via Java XML parser)	• Persistent data cache

Figure 7.2   The eTapestry Application's Proposed Future Architecture

7.9.2   Java Messaging Service API (JMS)

eTapestry is considering using the JMS API to provide tighter integration, both internally and with business partners. Currently, actions that trigger other systems, such as data insertions, must be handled by writing servlets that act inside the firewall.

Conversely, use of JMS would provide a standard means for adding messaging to Java applications. Examples might include transactions such as adding accounts, entering new gifts, and making pledge payments.

System-to-system updates or alerts could be sent individually or broadcast using publish-and-subscribe methods. The result would be a common approach to application integration, both internally and externally, using a standard rather than a custom API.

Furthermore, since JMS messages are stored and forwarded, this design feature will provide a higher-availability interface because it does not rely on the application server itself to be available. Consequently, if the application server is taken offline for maintenance, these messages can still be received and stored for processing later.

7.9.3   Partner Integration

eTapestry is still in the early phases of integrating with announced business partners. "Our strategy is to become a portal or conduit that gives nonprofit organizations access to all the tools they need to manage their operations, regardless of their size, background, or computing capabilities," says Rusche. This involves a best-of-breed strategy, in which eTapestry provides seamless access to complementary tools and services offered by its business partners. Examples include managing planned giving to donor tax planning, estate planning, and integration with print and mailing houses.

Access is now primarily through HTML/HTTP hot links. However, eTapestry has already begun building the first links with business partners, based on strategies such as providing XML-based transaction integration and Java-based plug-in applications that work atop the eTapestry engine.

In some cases, the integration will involve data exchange among different partner sites, such as is planned with Acteva. In other cases, partners are providing Java-based plug-in applications, which are bolted directly into the eTapestry application environment. For instance, eTapestry currently bundles a tax calculator for planned giving, from PGCalc, that uses a Java technology plug-in. The company is also working with eLetter to integrate the generation of printed mass mailings for charitable groups, through XML transactions that query eTapestry's donor database and produce mail/merges that are fed to the eLetter production system. In addition, eTapestry is partnering with financial institutions, such as credit card processors, to further automate online giving.

7.10   A Rich Tapestry

eTapestry is building a portal that is dedicated to the goal of making donor management accessible and affordable to any charitable organization with Internet access. "We're almost an integrator of services and a common pathway to get the functions they need. As an ASP, hopefully we can take the mystery out of it," says Rusche.

To accomplish that, eTapestry is relying on open, industry-standard Web technologies, including Java technology, HTML, and XML. "By using open, object-oriented technologies like the Java programming language, we can rapidly develop the functionality our customers need. With XML, our customers can be assured we can deliver a fully integrated best-of-breed service package," adds Ganyo.

The choice of a Java development environment was a key building block for eTapestry. "By using a modular, open-source tool like Forte for Java, we gained full support of open standards, such as Java technology and XML," says Ganyo. The modular design of the Forte for Java environment allows eTapestry to use only the features it needs and eases the installation of new upgrades. The product's foundation in open source means that eTapestry has access to enhancements, not just from the vendor, but the entire Java development community.

HP Bluestone/Altura

About the Authors

Richard Friedman is the chief technologist for the Bluestone Division of Hewlett-Packard Middleware. He has been with HP Bluestone for four years. Starting as a senior member of the Advanced Technology Group, he worked on all aspects of building enterprise applications for *Fortune* 100 companies using Java. He also developed and delivered Java training courses. Friedman served as a lead developer on Bluestone's management and deployment product, now called Bluestone Application Manager, focusing mainly on the packaging and deployment of applications to remote servers. Friedman also contributed to Bluestone's Enterprise JavaBeans 1.1 server, focusing on container-managed persistence.

Jordan Zimmerman is a senior software architect at Altura International. He is the lead developer of the Altura Merchant Operating System, Altura International's multi-merchant, multilingual, multicurrency, and multinational e-commerce engine. Zimmerman has worked as a computer programmer for more than 14 years on Macintosh, Windows, and UNIX systems.

CHAPTER 8

HP Bluestone's Total-e-Server at Altura International: Deploying J2EE for Performance and Scalability

8.1   The Company

Founded in 1997, and partially funded by Bill Gates, Yahoo!, and others, Altura International created the Web's first catalog-shopping portal, www.CatalogCity.com. Through a combination of product syndication agreements with major Internet portals (including Yahoo!, Lycos, NBCi, Excite, and others), custom shopping malls (such as www.gifts.com, www.ishopexcel.com, and www.goodcatalog.com), as well as its own destination Web sites (catalogcity.com, catalogcity.co.uk, catalogcity.de, catalogcity.fr, jp.catalogcity.com, and www.productcity.com), Altura International provides a one-stop business-to-consumer resource that provides consumers with easy access to more than 17,000 merchant catalogs and their products.

8.2   The Challenge

The development environment that Altura initially used to build and syndicate its customized online shopping malls proved difficult to scale when traffic to the sites suddenly began to increase. They also found flaws in the original development environment that caused unexpected crashes—yet a lack of sophisticated management and monitoring tools in that environment often left Altura IT personnel unaware that a server application had crashed.

Altura officials explored their options and finally concluded that there was no practical way to fix the problems their original environment presented. They could overcome the traffic management and server performance problems only by deploying a large number of servers to accommodate the increasing volume of traffic. However, managing a large number of servers without a centralized monitoring console created other problems, which Altura could only solve by writing its own specialized monitoring application and management tools. To get through the holiday shopping season of 1999, Altura did, in fact, run its site in this manner—with home-grown software monitoring more than 120 Web servers, each supporting no more than 15 to 20 users at a time.

However, even as they committed to getting through the shopping season by this route, Altura officials acknowledged this was a short-term solution and that the only viable long-term solution was to rearchitect their site. Without knowing exactly what shape that solution would take, they knew what it should include: a scalable, highly available, standards-based application-server architecture that would be Java language–based, J2EE specification compliant, and hardware agnostic.

8.3   The Solution

After considering several application-server implementations, Altura chose to rearchitect its site around HP Bluestone Total-e-Server, the company's J2EE-technology based application-server foundation. Altura developers rewrote the multivendor, multilanguage, multicurrency shopping cart and other core business technologies in the Java programming language and built a new production architecture around Total-e-Server.

8.3.1   Benefits of the HP Bluestone Implementation of J2EE

HP Bluestone Total-e-Server builds on the J2EE specification to deliver linear scalability, customer-facing fault tolerance, high-transaction reliability, and greatly increased performance to Altura and its sites. Because of Total-e-Server's implementation of the J2EE platform, individual physical servers can handle hundreds of user sessions—a dramatic improvement over the 15 to 20 sessions the old architecture allowed. This increase in performance—on the same Windows NT server-based systems Altura had always used—enables the company to reduce its Web-server farm from more than 120 servers to fewer than 30. In addition,

Total-e-Server provides Altura with a single management console from which Altura's IT personnel can manage all their servers from one location. Again, that represents a significant improvement over the use of 120 separate consoles and custom-built software to track the health of each application.

8.4 Altura Merchant Operating System

Catalog merchants have, over long years of trial and error, developed a very successful business strategy. They rent mailing lists, ship catalogs, take orders, get revenues, and then mail out more catalogs. It is a simple but elegant model that has proven itself over and over again.

But it is, as officials at Altura International realized in the mid 1990s, a strategy that entirely ignored the emerging world of the Web. Even in its infancy, the Web was turning the tables around and creating an environment in which customers did not need to wait to receive a catalog to place an order. Indeed, the Web was clearly evolving into an environment in which a consumer could actively seek out, compare, and purchase products quickly—from the comfort of an armchair, the same location from which the customer might purchase an item from a catalog.

Altura officials could see that the Web presented some compelling opportunities for catalogers—and that catalogers themselves had not quite figured out how to make the most of those opportunities. Some catalogers had already developed Web sites to extend the reach of their paper publications, but no one had taken what, to Altura officials, was the real giant step—the creation of a Web site that would be for catalog shoppers what Amazon.com was for book shoppers, a single location on the Web where a shopper could access, browse, and order from thousands of catalogs.

For shoppers, such a site would offer unprecedented convenience, enabling them to find virtually anything that could be purchased via catalog. For individual catalogers, such a site would drive more business toward their individual offerings—particularly if the site were designed with cross-catalog search engines, organized by product lines and/or affinity groupings. A shopper searching for office furniture, for instance, might see catalogs they did not even know existed—and those catalogers might then have their wares presented to customers they never knew about.

So Altura officials took that giant step and began the development of CatalogCity.com, a single site that aggregated the best of the world's direct-mail catalogs. They even cataloged the catalogs themselves, organizing more than 17,000 publications into hierarchical categories—autos, books, beauty, clothes, electronics, and so on—with each high-level category branching into subcategories for further differentiation. By navigating the hierarchies, visitors could quickly access the catalogs of interest to them.

For catalogers, even those with existing Web sites, Altura's approach offered a significant value proposition. By affiliating with Altura, a catalog merchant could have its publication, and a link to its existing Web site (if one existed), included on CatalogCity.com. The more catalogers Altura officials could recruit, the better it would be for all catalogers, because the CatalogCity site would then gain the mass it needed to become known as the de facto standard for catalog shopping on the Web. In Altura's vision, consumers could shop across hundreds of catalogs with one sign-in, one set of privacy preferences, one password, one date reminder, one gift registry, and one easy-to-use navigational process.

Moreover, Altura was talking to catalogers about providing support for online purchasing through a sophisticated multivendor shopping cart—and for catalogers in particular, that discussion was very exciting. Even by 1997, it was clear that businesses accustomed to working face-to-face with customers had significant culture shock when working with customers on the Web, but catalogers were already accustomed to doing business with customers in other than a face-to-face mode. In fact, Altura's math made the Web appear to be even more efficient and more cost-effective than the traditional call-center approach to taking customer orders. A visitor to an Altura site would not even have to call the merchant to order from the catalog. With a few mouse clicks, an order would be in the fulfill-ment system as effectively as it would have been if an operator in a call center had taken the call. Yet no operator would take the call. No one on either side of the transaction would even pick up the telephone. Such orders would effectively be executed in a lights-out mode.

8.4.1   Constructing the Altura Merchant Operating System

Altura engineers began to construct the company's flagship site, CatalogCity.com, in October 1997, long before the J2EE specification was finalized. They selected a proprietary deployment environment that ran on top of Microsoft Windows NT 4.0, with Microsoft Internet Information Server providing Web-server support and Microsoft SQL Server providing database support.

Using these proprietary tools, Altura's developers began to build the core technology that would inform the company's sites—the ideas for which were quickly multiplying. This core technology soon became known as the Altura Mer-chant Operating System (AMOS). AMOS enables a wide range of unique fea-tures, prominent among which is a very sophisticated multivendor shopping cart, one that can hold virtually any item from any catalog on the site and one that can be pushed, as it were, from catalog to catalog, before the visitor pushes it to the checkout stand.

"We looked at hundreds of catalogs," explains Vince Hunt, executive vice president of engineering at Altura, "and asked the question: '*Which products could potentially be in our database?*' And the number of products—and the number of permutations—is huge. In our database, we have apparel products that have characteristics such as color and size. We also offer electronic items, and there you might have color or voltage as the important characteristics. We even offer products such as saws, where you can select the number of teeth on the saw. We took every product characteristic and shipping permutation into account and created a shopping cart that is completely flexible. It was designed to support *any* type of merchant and any type of product there is."

Figure 8.1 shows the resulting Web site, CatalogCity.com, offering a variety of customer conveniences. With the AMOS shopping cart, a shopper can add any number of items from any number of merchants. The shopping cart also allows shoppers to change the quantity of items they have added and also to save items for later. The Save For Later feature allows shoppers to remember products, without having to shop again for items they may want to buy later. A shopper's AMOS

Figure 8.1 The CatalogCity.com Home Page from Altura International

shopping cart is persistent, too. The shopper can add a product on a Monday, log off, and come back two weeks later to find the shopping cart still intact.

Other AMOS features were just as compelling for catalogers.

- E-gifts provides a way for gift recipients to select the gift they want. Gift-givers can select categories of products and enable the recipients to choose from those categories.

- E-cards enable shoppers to send a customized electronic card to anyone with an e-mail address.

- Date reminders enable shoppers to build up a personalized calendar of reminders in advance of gift-giving events.

- Gift registry enables shoppers to identify items they would like to receive for wedding, anniversary, graduation, or other presents. They name their registry and then send e-mails inviting friends and family to shop in their registry.

- Multicurrency and multilanguage support enables AMOS to support merchants and buyers worldwide.

- Powerful search capabilities enable a visitor to search for products across virtually all the pages in a site. Shoppers can find merchants by name or description (that is, search by catalog), find products by name or description, and even search for items (by name or by SKU number) within a given catalog. Within the search results, shoppers can refine their search by selecting a price range or jumping directly into a category of products in which they may be interested. Also, to help refine a search even more, shoppers find related search words. These words are derived from tracking similar searches across the AMOS network.

- Personal shopping accounts provide facilities through which a shopper can enter shipping information and billing information once, store it securely, yet make it available to any merchant from whom the shopper is purchasing merchandise, through the use of a single password.

This combination of a well-organized collection of catalogs, a multivendor, multicurrency, multilanguage shopping cart, and the other rich features of AMOS opened up yet a new business opportunity for Altura: syndication. In addition to developing its own sites (in the United States, as well as regionalized sites in Europe and Asia), Altura began working closely with Web portals, such as Yahoo!, Excite, and Lycos, to deliver catalog-shopping sites specially packaged to cater to the shopping needs of those portals' members. The multivendor shopping cart fit neatly into portal owners' desires to deliver ease of use to their members,

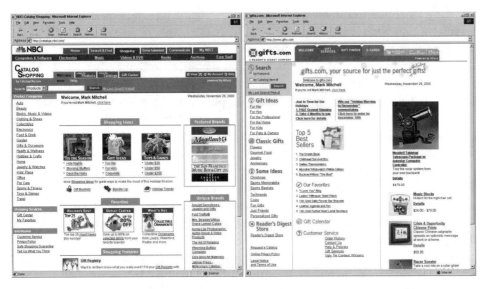

Figure 8.2 Sample Home Pages from Other AMOS-Powered Altura International Sites

since the preponderance of shopping carts available at the time were geared to support a single vendor at a time. Altura's ability to order from multiple vendors with a single shopping cart was a clear advantage. Indeed, the AMOS shopping cart not only enables shoppers to add items from multiple catalogs on the CatalogCity.com site, but it also enables shoppers to add items from *any* Altura mall, even multiple Altura malls. The same cart stays with the shopper across all Altura-powered malls until checkout, so a shopper can add items from gifts.com, quixtar, ishopexcel, CatalogCity.com, and other malls (see Figure 8.2) and go through checkout with all these items from any of the AMOS-powered malls.

Yet these same advantages precipitated the complication that would eventually lead Altura officials to migrate many aspects of the site off their original architecture and on to an architecture that conforms to the J2EE specification.

8.4.2 Growing but not Scaling

From the beginning, traffic to Altura's site grew rapidly, thanks in large part to the strategic relationships it was forging with leading Internet portals. However, as traffic increased, IT managers at Altura began to notice some performance problems they were unable to overcome.

"There appeared to be flaws in the way our original deployment environment managed and completed threads," says Hunt. "We could watch a thread going in, and then we'd notice that it took a long time to come out—but we had no way of knowing what was going on while that thread was inside the box. We simply had no insight into what was going on."

Yet a far greater problem lay just around the corner. When quixtar.com opened its newly syndicated catalog shops to portal members in September 1999, Altura officials discovered they could not scale the site efficiently to meet demand. The original environment simply would not support more than 15 to 20 visitors on a given Web server. In order to accommodate the influx of traffic that these two newly affiliated portals unleashed, Altura had to expand its Web server farm from some 30 systems to more than 120.

Unfortunately for Altura, this vast expansion created more problems than it solved. The solution they were using offered no centralized services for managing multiple Web servers. Instead of one console that could manage the 120 servers, Altura had 120 consoles. Moreover, the original solution provided no failover, intersession, or intermachine communication mechanisms. If the Web application crashed, the user could not failover to another server, thus causing lost sales and lost customers. To compensate for this problem, Altura developers had to write more code to provide failover and user-data-caching mechanisms.

Beyond the challenges of avoiding potential data loss and managing multiple servers centrally, the expansion of Altura's original architecture created two other problems that Altura officials knew would have serious short- and long-term consequences. The first problem was that the crashes they experienced usually occurred in the Web-application layer, not at the Web-server layer, and the Web application itself provided no inherent mechanisms for reporting that an instance of the application had crashed. So 20 visitors might be stranded on a server, but Altura IT personnel had no notification that there was a problem. Indeed, because Internet Information Server was still running, the Web server and everything above it *seemed* to be functioning properly.

That fact gave rise to the second problem. Because Internet Information Server was still running but there appeared to be no IP traffic to or from that Web server, Cisco LocalDirector, which Altura had configured to provide load-balancing services across its 120 Web servers, perceived that *that* Web server could accept and handle more traffic. LocalDirector would consequently route *new* visitors right to the Web server on which the Web application was *not* running. Those visitors, of course, would get nothing but a blank screen. Compounding this problem was a sticky-bit feature Altura administrators needed to invoke in LocalDirector that automatically routed return visitors to the server on which they had held their last interactive session. Those visitors who were on the Web server when the Web application crashed often attempted to restart their session by leaving the site and quickly return—but as a consequence of this sticky bit, they would *land right back* on the original server with the dead application. Unless Altura IT personnel had discovered and restarted the dead application before they returned, the user would get nothing but a blank screen again. For those users, the entire site appeared to have died, even though it may have been only one Web server's application that was down.

"For an e-commerce site, this is a real problem," notes Hunt. "People who land on dead servers get instantly frustrated and don't come back."

Altura developers were eventually able to code (in C++) some monitoring tools that kept them apprised of the state of the application running on these 120 Web servers, which increased the speed with which IT officials could respond when the application had a problem. Yet even as they succeeded in putting a band-aid on those problems, Altura managers could see that their original architecture would be unable to provide a viable long-term solution. Without greater efficiencies in scalability and manageability, the original Web-application architecture would simply never provide a sufficient return on investment.

"The cost of adding a server to support 15 to 20 users was between $6,000 and $10,000," says Hunt. "There was simply no way to justify that based on return-on-investment, considering we also had to write the management software, pay the monthly colocation and software maintenance fees, and pay a support staff to run it all.

"We knew we had to get through the 1999 holiday shopping season, though, and this approach would get us through. But we also knew we had to rearchitect our site. There was nowhere else to go, given the proven limitations of the proprietary solution we'd been using."

8.4.3   Sourcing a Viable Solution

"Our original environment had not been a true application-development environment," says Hunt, "but a scripted environment. Our Web application, including the multivendor shopping cart, relied on more than a million lines of script, and we really wanted to move all that into a true application-development environment. But what to use? And how were we going to get this script into the real world? We started to write a compiler to move all the script into C++, but the more we looked at where we expected to go and at the languages people were learning, the more C++ did not seem like a great option. We had some Java programming experience, but we also knew that as we grew we'd be recruiting a lot of new people—and increasing numbers of them would be coming out of UC Santa Cruz and UC Berkeley, where they learn the Java programming language as part of a computer science degree. We also wanted the flexibility to run our application on whatever platform would best suit our business needs. All this pointed us to Java technology. We were specifically interested in using Java Servlets, which were the new industry standard."

Yet Java technology was only a part of the solution Altura officials knew they wanted. Given the problems in the existing environment with server-farm management, failover, fault tolerance, scalability, and performance, they decided to rearchitect around a J2EE platform-based application server. In January 2000, Altura officials set out to find a technology partner that could meet their needs. After considering and testing several vendor's solutions—including solutions from IBM, BEA, and SilverStream—Hunt and his IT team chose to rearchitect Altura's proprietary Web application around HP Bluestone Total-e-Server, an application-server infrastructure built entirely on J2EE technology.

"When we decided to go with Java technology, we got better development tools, better debuggers, and a better overall application platform for our site," says Hunt. "Then we looked at what we would need to support that application optimally. J2EE technology was a prerequisite. We knew we wanted to do servlets, and we thought we wanted to do JSP. We also knew that Enterprise JavaBeans (EJBs) were something we'd like to explore in the future. So conforming to the J2EE specification was a hard and fast requirement. On top of that, we needed server-farm management, high reliability, support for load balancing, and of course, high performance.

"In the performance tests, we set up a system to mimic between 20 and 300 users hitting a Web server to see how our application-server candidates would scale," Hunt continues. "Our old architecture supported around 20 concurrent users on a Web server, which is pretty poor. We had several hundred users on Total-e-Server without a significant performance impact—and these were the same Intel-based boxes we had been using all along. We even unplugged one of the HP Bluestone servers—and lost nothing. The user sessions continued, and the whole thing continued to work. And HP Bluestone Application Manager offered something else of critical importance—centralized server management. With HP Bluestone Application Manager we no longer had to manage each of our servers individually. We could manage them all from a central point.

"HP Bluestone also works with any JDBC compliant database. Our old application made calls to Microsoft SQL Server using ODBC, but SQL Server is also JDBC-compliant, so going with HP Bluestone meant that we did not have to change our database at all.

"Finally, the fact that HP Bluestone Application Server is based 100 percent on Java technology ensured that we would have full platform independence. We could run our systems on Sun Solaris, HP-UX AIX, Windows NT, even Linux— whatever we feel is best for our business. With our old solution, we had no choice but to deploy to Windows NT Server—with support for some UNIX platforms promised in the future. HP Bluestone and the Java technology give us options we did not have before."

8.5 HP Bluestone Total-e-Server and the J2EE Specification

HP Bluestone Total-e-Server provides a proven, flexible, secure, highly scalable, and fault-tolerant infrastructure for all types of e-services—including application development, deployment, integration, and management. Total-e-Server provides a certified J2EE 1.2 platform implementation. It includes all the required APIs, including the EJB 1.1 specification—plus Message Driven Beans from EJB 2.0. Robust implementations of JSP 1.1 and Servlet 2.2 are included, as well. It also provides implementations of JTA and JTS, guaranteeing that transactions adhere to two-phase commit.

Building on the J2EE platform design in this way, Total-e-Server allows developers to create new applications using a variety of loosely coupled, portable modular components. As a result, Altura's developers can extend and add new functionality to its new Java technology–based application framework—the Altura Merchant Operating System (AMOS)—quickly, easily, and at a lower cost than they could using their script-based proprietary solution.

Total-e-Server consists of several integrated components.

- **HP Bluestone Universal Business Server** is the application server at the heart of HP Bluestone Total-e-Server. The Universal Business Server is the implementation and glue for the services that allow containers like J2EE to be implemented upon a common set of enterprise services. The Universal Business Server architecture is also responsible for providing the scalability, fault-tolerant, and overall enterprise-class features to all containers built on top of it.

- **HP Bluestone XML Server** provides the ability to exchange XML documents dynamically—externally, with customers and suppliers, as well as internally, among different back-office data systems.

- **HP Bluestone Universal Listener Framework** constantly monitors server ports to identify the presence and protocol of an incoming message. This allows the Universal Business Server to process a wide range of incoming data requests correctly. The Universal Listener Framework supports an extensive list of protocols—including HTTP, JMS, XML, FTP, SMTP, and WAP—and interacts with a wide variety of client devices. The Universal Listener Framework allows servlets and message-driven beans to process e-mail messages just as flexibly as HTTP requests and JMS messages.

- **HP Bluestone Application Manager** is an advanced, agent-based management component that provides real-time performance and status information on the entire Web infrastructure. It monitors all user interactions and ensures the quality, performance, and integrity of all work performed over the Web.

- **HP Bluestone Security Console** provides user, group, and role-based access control to every system level. A user can establish security levels for applications, pages within applications, user interaction points on pages, or each application-accessed data resource. With Total-e-Server, a business can take advantage of the latest encryption and security certification technologies on the market.

8.5.1   Total-e-Server's Universal Business Server and the J2EE Specification

Total-e-Server's Universal Business Server is based entirely on Sun Microsystems' J2EE specification. It is a J2EE certified application server that implements the complete set of J2EE API's. This includes Java ServerPages, Java Servlets, and Enterprise JavaBeans. For support of ACID transactions, Total-e-Server ships with a Java Transaction Service.

HP Bluestone's support for EJBs ensures that developers can focus on developing the business logic for an application. They don't have to worry about developing the infrastructure for enterprise-class distributed components. HP Bluestone Total-e-Server helps with the development, deployment, and interfacing of these EJB components. HP Bluestone's implementation of EJBs includes an out-of-the-box implementation of Container Managed Persistence that allows for related entities and cross-table joins. Total-e-Server also ships with a production-quality implementation of Message Driven Beans, as defined in the EJB 2.0 specification. This gives the developer the ability to add asynchronous beans to his or her architecture.

Total-e-Server also supports Sun Microsystems' Servlet 2.2 specification. Servlets provide developers with a simple API that extends the functionality of a Web server and allows developers to process requests. Servlets can make use of JavaBeans and Enterprise JavaBeans to build the logic to handle a request, and they enable developers to create Web-based applications quickly, with loosely coupled reusable components.

Total-e-Server also provides full support for the JSP 1.1 specification. With JSP technology, developers can easily and quickly create dynamic Web pages that leverage existing business systems. Using JSPs facilitates the separation of the Web-page design from the business logic itself, enabling designers to change page layout, without changing the underlying dynamic content. By separating the content generation from the user interfaces, JSPs greatly reduce Web-based application development and maintenance times.

In addition to EJBs, servlets, and JSPs, Total-e-Server also provides support for Tag Libraries (TagLibs) as described in the JSP 1.1 specification. Tag Libraries further simplify the application-development process by providing a pre-defined set of instructions to conduct an application routine (such as accessing a database). TagLibs are entered within JSPs as a single line of code (tag), which greatly reduces the amount of programming needed to create new applications. Programmers can easily select one or more of these tags from a library of previously defined TagLibs. TagLibs can also be reused on multiple applications quickly and easily.

HP Bluestone Total-e-Server includes a bundled TagLib package with predefined TagLibs, such as SQL, formatting, JMS, and EJB, and plans are in place to add many more predefined TagLibs in future editions. Developers using Total-e-Server can easily create their own TagLibs for commonly used routines, or they can draw from the wide selection of publicly available TagLibs.

8.5.2 Developing Applications for HP Bluestone Total-e-Server

HP Bluestone has reduced the learning curve for new Total-e-Server environment users by incorporating the latest open Java technology standards and by avoiding proprietary development tools. At Altura, many developers are using Metrowerks CodeWarrior for Java, but developers there are free to use whatever HTML/JSP or Java development tools they like. Total-e-Server allows developers to utilize any IDE, GUI creation tool, and UML tool. The platform does not tie developers to any single vendor's development software. This is true for the "comprehensive" tool suites, as well. With Total-e-Server, developers can pick and choose the IDE from one vendor and the GUI tool from another.

As part of Total-e-Server, HP Bluestone offers HP Bluestone J2EE Developer, which provides a point-and-click interface for developers deploying JavaBeans and EJBs. J2EE Developer includes a container-managed persistence tool that maps an entity EJB's fields to databases via XML and provides support for fine-grained objects. J2EE Developer also contains tools for generating home and remote interfaces, as well as deployment descriptors.

8.5.3 Deploying Total-e-Server

HP Bluestone Total-e-Server provides a wealth of application services—from dynamic load balancing to application isolation and comprehensive state management—and these are key to meeting Altura's needs. They provide rapid responses to user interactions while guaranteeing interaction integrity, regardless of whether those interactions involve simple database queries or complex electronic commerce transactions. HP Bluestone Total-e-Server places no restrictions on the number of CPUs or the mixture of platform configurations in a given deployment environment. It can run on a single CPU or across a network of computers (see Figure 8.3). This flexibility effectively ensures unlimited linear scalability for enterprise-wide production applications.

Figure 8.3   Deploying HP Bluestone Total-e-Server on Multiple Machines

And because Total-e-Server is written entirely in the Java programming language, it runs on any platform that supports a Java virtual machine (JVM), including Microsoft, Sun, IBM, HP, and others. A production environment can contain from zero to *n* instances of the application server. Each application-server instance can support any number of applications, in any combination. An application can also deploy on many applications-server instances. The flexibility to place these applications and application servers at different points in the deployment architecture in a controlled manner optimizes bandwidth, performance, and CPU resources.

Deploying applications to a production site is simplified with HP Bluestone Application Manager, which provides tools to pack and deploy applications. An application is packaged with all its components, Web pages, images, servlets, JSPs, TagLibs, EJBs, and any dependent classes. Then, using HP Bluestone Application Manager deployment capabilities, it is a drag-and-drop maneuver to deliver those packages to 1 or 100 machines. The package and deployment capabilities of HP Bluestone Application Manager enable developers to build and deploy newer versions of applications to a host machine quickly. HP Bluestone Application Manager also makes it easy to manage and configure those applications, providing access to all the applications, even in a distributed system, through a single console window.

HP Bluestone Application Manager also provides Altura International with HP Bluestone Hot Versioning deployment system (see Figure 8.4), which guarantees true 24x7x365, nonstop operations. With Hot Versioning, a Web application stays online and user sessions remain uninterrupted even while an organization's IT personnel upgrade or perform maintenance on the application. The Hot Versioning deployment system delivers the ability to change the version of a running application dynamically—and the version change can be forward or backward. HP Bluestone Total-e-Server even allows application-version selection to occur on a group basis or at the individual instance selection.

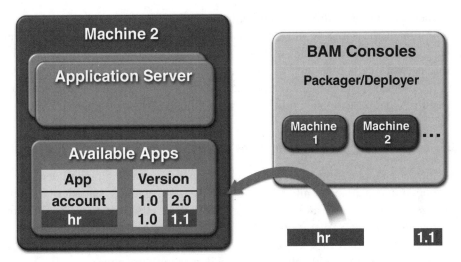

Figure 8.4   HP Bluestone Application Manager (BAM) Provides Powerful
                   Capabilities for Rapid Deployment and Hot Versioning.

8.5.4   HP Bluestone EJB Server

Built on the latest EJB 1.1 specification, Total-e-Server's EJB server provides
enterprise services for EJBs such as container and bean-managed persistence,
threading, transactions, security, database connectivity and more. The high performance of the EJB server is achieved through optimizations such as object pooling,
database-connection pooling, lifecycle management, and optimizations in the process invocation of beans. Total-e-Server ensures the scalability of the EJB server
through the use of load-balancing features. In addition, in order to protect business
technology investments, HP Bluestone EJB server is implemented in plug-and-
play components. The security, Java Naming and Directory Interface (JNDI), and
Java Transaction Server (JTS) components are all replaceable. This interface-
based approach enables users to build their own implementations, plug in third-
party implementations, or leverage their current infrastructure for those services.

The EJB implementation within Total-e-Server also includes an implementation of Message Driven Beans. Message Driven Beans are an EJB type specified
in version 2.0 of the EJB specification. They are asynchronous beans that provide
a standard mechanism for writing and deploying components to process messages.
These messages could be delivered through JMS or any other messaging implementation. HP Bluestone has delivered an implementation of EJB 2.0 that has
been tested with many industry-respected JMS implementations. The combination
of Total-e-Server with Message Driven Beans and the Universal Listener Framework allows e-mail messages, FTP messages (and any other Universal Listener
Framework listener type) to be processed via Message Driven Beans.

When operating within the application server, JSP and servlet engines can also be run in the same application server instance as the EJB Server. This in-process deployment technique, which is unique to HP Bluestone, eliminates the remote network calls that degrade Web and EJB application performance. Moreover, the process ensures that JSPs and servlets enjoy the fault tolerance, scalability, security, and performance provided by the Universal Business Server.

8.5.5   Monitoring J2EE Applications

HP Bluestone Application Manager provides more than packaging and deploying of applications, it also monitors application servers, gathers statistics, triggers alerts, generates reports, and much more. Together, HP Bluestone Application Manager and Total-e-Server monitor and provide statistics on more than 25 activities, and more activities can be monitored, depending on customers' needs. Should one of Altura's application servers fail, or should response time fall below a defined threshold, HP Bluestone Application Manager can generate an alert and force an e-mail or page to be sent to the administrator. HP Bluestone Application Manager was a huge win for Altura International, which no longer needs to rely on hand-developed screens or scripts for managing its applications. With HP Bluestone Application Manager, Altura no longer wonders whether servers are running or requests are being handled within proper request time limits.

HP Bluestone Application Manager allows statistics and alerts to be switched on and off from a management console. With the flip of a switch, for instance, administrators can monitor an application server's memory use. They can view reports on the information gathered from the servers within a domain, too. HP Bluestone Application Manager uses an agent-based technology to reduce the overhead associated with monitoring server activities.

8.5.6   Load Balancing

HP Bluestone Total-e-Server provides Altura with dynamic load-balancing support through HP Bluestone Load Balance Broker and through assistance from HP Bluestone Application Manager.

The Load Balance Broker runs as a Web-server plug-in, and Total-e-Server provides versions compatible with Netscape, Microsoft, and Apache Web servers. A generic Load Balance Broker that will run on any Web server is included, as is a servlet version of the Load Balance Broker for Web servers supporting Java technology. It automatically determines when to start additional instances of application servers and where to route incoming requests. The Load Balance Broker keeps track of the load (how many active users/requests) and status (running, not running, not responding) on each application server. It starts application-server instances as appropriate for load conditions and performs auto-application restart if a failure is detected. By continuously monitoring and managing tasks assigned to all applications, Universal Business Server meets peak loads, without affecting the performance of the entire system.

8.5.7 Fault Tolerance

Because application crashes were a serious problem in Altura International's early Web-application architecture, it was critically important that its new application architecture be impervious to failure. HP Bluestone Total-e-Server delivers precisely the fault tolerance Altura needs. With no single point of failure and support for robust persistent state management, Total-e-Server is designed to support customers who need to be running on a 24x7 basis. Total-e-Server even provides fault tolerance for JSP and servlet requests, as well as EJB requests.

With Total-e-Server, individual application servers—even whole machines—can go down without customers noticing. Applications can be configured to use the Universal Business Server's Persistent State Server, a server configured so that all state information is written to a JDBC database. If the CPU hosting the application server goes offline, no state information is lost. If a visitor to an Altura site, for example, begins the checkout process and then the CPU hosting the application fails, a new CPU comes online, the application server is automatically reinitiated, and all user state information is regenerated from the JDBC database. The shopper never sees a problem.

HP Bluestone Load-Balance Broker also helps ensure this customer-facing fault tolerance by constantly directing and redirecting requests to running application servers. The load-balance broker also can request that new instances of the application server be created. Thus, even with a small number of machines, a production site can offer fault tolerance and scalability. A site that needs to grow has to do very little to increase the number of machines available to the load-balance broker.

8.6 Configuring the Altura Merchant Operating System Framework

Today, when a visitor comes to CatalogCity.com or another of Altura's sites, the content and applications presented on the Web page are delivered through the use of HP Bluestone Total-e-Server. Java Servlets running on Total-e-Server manage the interactions between the Web interface and Altura's Microsoft SQL Server database farm.

"We're using plain Java technology with servlets," explains Jordan Zimmerman, Altura's senior software architect. "We are not currently using EJBs or JSPs for the main application, though we do use JavaMail and JDBC. We were originally going to recode all our original scripts in C++, but thankfully we discovered Java Servlets, which offered a much better platform for what we were doing. There's a rich set of APIs for building Web pages, and many of the mundane tasks associated with handling HTTP requests don't have to be coded from scratch. This saved us six months to a year, at least."

A team of two Altura engineers started the process of rewriting the entire application framework—including the multivendor shopping cart, personal accounts, checkout routines, and utilities—in the Java language in December 1999. Within four months, 85 percent of Altura's site had been rewritten and was running on HP Bluestone.

8.6.1   A Structure of Servlets

Altura's AMOS framework actually relies upon a small number of servlets—not even a one-to-one ratio of servlet to Web page. Partially based on model-view-controller and partially based on Model II, the AMOS framework is something of a coding-model smorgasbord. A controller servlet called cc serves up all the site's pages based on URL parameters. In fact, the same servers, the same database, and the same code delivers 20 to 30 different Web experiences, and all these experiences arise from the same implementation of the cc object.

"A Web request comes into the cc servlet and creates an internal class called cc_request," Zimmerman explains, "which manages all the logic of the application—from analyzing URL parameters to performing database queries and building pages around the resulting information. cc_request is essentially the broker for all the classes subsequently developed to support the application."

There are, in fact, three objects that form what Zimmerman calls the "trinity" at the core of the AMOS framework.

"Even more fundamental than cc_request," says Zimmerman, "is an object called cc_site, which Altura International uses to build Web sites. Each of the Altura-powered sites, whether CatalogCity.com, gifts.com, or any other, is a singleton in memory that extends the cc_site object, and each of these instances contains the non-request-related data that comprise a site—its name, various options as to what kind of site to display, cache paths, and the images that make up the site.

"cc_request is the second object in the trinity. A cc_request object is created for every request to the site. It contains request-specific data that isn't particular to any site—browser information, URL parameters, and so forth. It looks at cookies and loads in the correct shopper objects, and it looks at the parameters

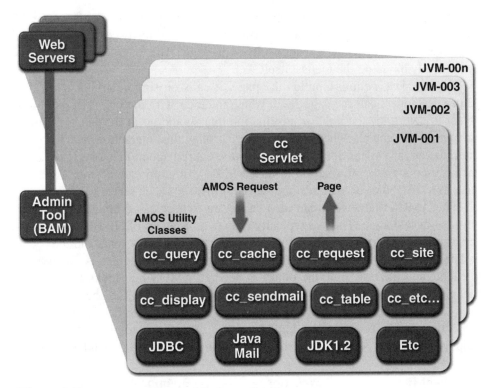

Figure 8.5   Altura's High-Level Software Architecture

coming in with the request and determines which kind of request it is. In all of our URLs, you'll see a parameter called `main`. That's what we call the 'context' and that's how we know what page to deliver. We have many contexts—`main=ccn`, `main=product_categories`, `main=gift_center`, and many others. The `main=ccn` context has subcontexts—`ccn_last_request`, `ccn_checkout`, `ccn_account`, and others."

Typical URLs appear as follows:

```
http://amos.catalogcity.com/cc.class/cc?main=ccn%5Fprivacy&ccsyn=1
http://amos.catalogcity.com/cc.class/
cc?main=departments&trk=HomePageSale&pcd=561885&ccsyn=173
```

"`cc_request` keys off the `main` parameter to create the third object in the trinity called `cc_site_request`," Zimmerman goes on to explain. "For each unique site and each unique context, `cc_request` creates a unique `cc_site_request` class to handle that request. It is objects that extend `cc_site_request`—in fact, that deliver the content displayed to the user in response to a request. So if the site they're looking for is shopping.NBCi.com, an

NBCi.com version of `cc_site_request` gets the shopping.NBCi.com page. If the request is for www.catalogcity.com, a catalogcity.com version of `cc_site_request` gets the catalogcity.com page. The pages are all created dynamically based on the request itself."

As `cc_site_request` builds the page, it calls on some common code that Altura developers call the page shell, which interacts with the `cc_site_request` object to determine the kind of information that should go in the header, the left navigation bar, and elsewhere on the page. Through this interaction with the page shell, the `cc_site_request` object builds the entire page in memory. If the page has no user-specific information in it, it will be written to disk as an HTML file (also as a GZIP file) on Altura's high-speed, full-page cache server.

The AMOS framework can also cache any object using both memory and physical disk storage. The site typically runs two instances of HP Bluestone Universal Business Server on each of its 16 application-server systems and the cache is shared among all of them. When an object is loaded in memory, it is also written to cache, and the next time the object is needed, AMOS first looks for it in the cache. If found, the cached object is used instead of creating the page, running a query, or performing whatever action precipitated the need for the cached object.

Altura developers have also built a set of utility classes to provide additional support at different points in the process. `cc_query`, for instance, bundles the myr-

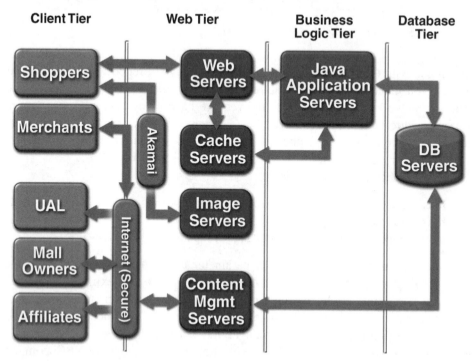

Figure 8.6 Data flow within the AMOS Architecture

iad APIs and classes of JDBC into one class. It handles everything the AMOS framework needs in the area of querying the database—from formulating the query to managing the transaction. Another class—`cc_loaded_query`—holds an entire results set of a query in memory, where it can be readily reused or cached.

Other objects include abstractions for each shopper, called `cc_shopper`, `cc_shopper_address_book`, `cc_shopping_cart`, and so on. All these are stored in the Java session and accessed as necessary during a shopper's visit to the site.

8.6.2   The Role of XML and JSPs

In addition to the Java servlets and Java classes that comprise the Web application and the multivendor shopping, cart, Altura is using XML and JSPs. At any moment, Altura enables visitors to purchase merchandise from more than 600 merchants, and those merchants provide their content to the site via XML. Altura's custom-built, Java-based content-management system moves XML docs into the SQL Server database.

Altura has built numerous intranet and extranet tools using JSPs.

- **Merchandising Management Tool.** Internal Altura employees and employees who work for syndicated mall owners (such as Readers Digest, owners of gifts.com, and NBCi, owners of shopping.NBCi.com) use JSP-based tools to manage the merchandising content and layout of their sites. They have control of which products display on the home page, in advertorial sections, and in departments. They can even define new departments and populate them.

- **Content Management Tool.** Merchants, mall owners, and employees can upload, change and remove products or product attributes. Merchants can change a product price, product description, categorization, or inventory detail through the use of this browser-based tool.

- **Promotional Tool.** This tool allows Altura's marketing group and Altura's mall owners to create custom coupon codes that can be used as incentives for shoppers. Promotional coupons might offer free shipping, a percentage off an order, or a free product with each purchase—and these coupons can all be created using this tool.

Altura's IT managers envision creating more tools with JSPs, and note that many of their pure HTML and C developers are initially more comfortable developing JSPs than they are in taking the leap directly into programming in the Java language. They can use JSPs and all the existing class libraries that have been developed in Altura to create powerful tools very quickly, without having to move immediately into the Java language itself.

8.7   Benefits of the J2EE Platform and HP Bluestone to Altura

The J2EE platform and HP Bluestone have both delivered significant and tangible benefits to Altura. There are increases in efficiency at every level. Developers are more productive; 16 application servers and 8 Web servers now accomplish what previously required 120+ Web servers to do (on essentially the same hardware, running the same operating system); administrators can now use a single management console to oversee the entire Web application infrastructure. And for visitors to the site? They enjoy the experience of high performance and high reliability— which can help foster a high return rate for Altura and its merchants.

"Going from our original environment to Java technology and J2EE was like being in hell and going to heaven," says Zimmerman. "What we used before was not a programming language; it was a scripting language, and its capabilities were limited. In the beginning of our move to HP Bluestone, we had to build up a lot of Java classes before we could be productive. So initially we were more productive in our old environment than we were in the Java environment. However, after nearly a year of development in the Java environment, we have such a large library of Java classes that we're much more productive now than we ever were in our original environment. It's an object oriented library, it's an extensible library, it's reusable. I can debug in a source-level debugger using a variety of tools, I can use a variety of profilers. It's the difference between batch programming on punch cards and a modern programming environment."

The day-to-day management and maintenance of the Altura site is greatly simplified, too, says Hunt. "With HP Bluestone, we can support a lot more users, more sessions, and more connections per server. We can pull a server out, without pulling down the whole site. We can also maintain our code more efficiently. If we wanted to add a feature in the old architecture, we would have to bring down the site, deploy the new feature to the servers, test it, and then bring the site back up. With HP Bluestone, we do all that on the fly. When a new feature is ready, we can make it available across all shopping malls within minutes, without taking anything offline."

If a machine fails, the failover mechanisms in HP Bluestone ensure that no user sessions are lost. Altura site managers now have a site-wide management console—which someone other than their own developers maintains. Altura no longer has to devote its own development resources to the creation of a centralized management system—instead, it can deploy those resources on projects that add real value to visitors coming to the site.

Finally, the benefits of Java technology, HP Bluestone, and J2EE extend far beyond just being able to develop a tool quickly and manage a site more efficiently. The reusability and extensibility of the J2EE objects and the ability to deploy entire sites dynamically make it easy for Altura to syndicate their content to other shopping malls quickly—even to develop whole new sites for new customers in a very short period of time.

"If someone comes to us and says, 'We want a new mall, and we need it up and running in two weeks,' we can do it. Even if it's late November and they want a mall with 100,000 products online in time for holiday shoppers, with their look and corporate character, their color schemes, and integrated with their back-end infrastructure. We can do all that because of Java technology and the J2EE platform—and we can do it for anybody, anywhere, in any language, and in any currency."

IBM

About the Authors

Jeff Reser is product manager for the IBM WebSphere Application Server, and was one of the original WebSphere architects. Reser works in IBM's technical e-business and network computing architecture group in Research Triangle Park, North Carolina. He joined IBM in 1981 with a BS in astronomy and computer science, from Penn State University. Reser has worked in various development, research, strategy, and technical marketing organizations within IBM, with an emphasis on Web-enabling technologies and network computing software.

Jose Antonio Sesin is senior technology editor for Brodeur Worldwide, where he helps clients communicate key messages through written materials, and provides intellectual-property consulting services to technology clients. Sesin's area of expertise covers software, hardware, middleware, e-business, and telecommunications. Before joining Brodeur Worldwide, Sesin delivered technical expertise and know-how to VaultBase Information Systems, a pre-IPO database security company. Sesin graduated summa cum laude from the University of Massachusetts, Amherst with a BA degree, and received a JD degree from Northeastern University School of Law.

David Kulakowski is the application development/technology manager of Honeywell International, in South Bend, Indiana. He and his team are responsible for supporting the ALS (aircraft landing systems) and ESA (engine support and accessories) businesses of Honeywell International, which has revenues of more than $600 million annually. Dave's team developed the Nonconformance Corrective Action System (NCAS) using VisualAge for Java and WebSphere Application Server in a three-tier architecture. His experience covers many subjects including CICS, DB2, IMS, OO, EDI, and others. While attending Purdue University, Kulakowski was the computer-center manager with a staff of 15 people.

Randall J. Mowen is CEO and principal consultant for Surefire Solutions Inc. whose customers include a wide range of private companies, colleges and universities, and start-ups. He holds a Master's degree in information technologies from Nova Southeastern University. As project manager for The Bekins Company's first e-business initiative, Shipment Tracking, Randall delivered a product later *A.D. Trends 2000* e-business Application of the Year.

CHAPTER 9

Honeywell and Bekins Succeed with IBM

THIS chapter analyzes how IBM clients have successfully used tools that leverage J2EE technology to enter the e-business marketplace. The chapter is divided into three parts. The first section describes IBM's role in developing the J2EE platform, and the next two sections detail how Honeywell and Bekins successfully used J2EE technology to solve computing needs.

9.1 IBM and the Evolution of e-Business

Computers and the Internet have transformed our lives by changing the way we get information, the way we shop, and the way we do business. Computers have been making our lives easier since the 1950s, and the Internet has opened up an unimaginable wealth of information that did not exist just a few years ago.

A pioneer in the computing industry, IBM realized early on that this mix of computing power and wide-reaching access of the Internet could propel businesses into another level—and e-business was born.

In theory, e-business is a simple concept—connect an organization's critical business systems directly to its customers, employees, suppliers, and distributors across the Web. By linking these key aspects, organizations realize a synergy that would not exist without the connection.

In order to make e-business a reality, there has to be a common element, such as the Java language, that can communicate with any client device and run on any platform. What makes the Java platform such a key ingredient of e-business is that it enables rapid application development and just-in-time deployment due to its simplified constructs and write-once, run-anywhere properties.

9.1.1   IBM Application Framework for e-Business

IBM's blueprint for e-business technology, the Application Framework for e-Business, defines the tools for designing, building, and maintaining e-business applications.

The IBM Application Framework for e-Business is designed to enable businesses of all sizes to build and deploy Web-based applications quickly and easily. To accomplish this, the Framework is based on open standards, such as Java technology, that are widely adopted by the computer industry.

The Application Framework for e-Business architecture incorporates clients, Web application servers, and connectors to external services. It is fundamentally based on Java technology, J2EE standards, and the Enterprise JavaBeans (EJB) component technologies. Together, those technologies deliver the benefits of "write once, run anywhere," which serve to lower development expenses while delivering higher-quality business applications.

Several key technologies enable the Framework.

- The Java platform

- An application-programming model based on servlets, Java ServerPages (JSP), JavaBeans, and Enterprise JavaBeans

- A network infrastructure based on industry standards

9.1.2   The Java Platform

More than just a programming language, the Java platform provides the base upon which the next generation of business applications can be built and deployed. The Java platform provides the JavaBean component model to enable construction of class libraries that are easily manipulated by programming tools from multiple vendors.

The Java 2 Platform, Enterprise Edition extends the JavaBean component model to encompass Enterprise JavaBeans, which are server-side extensions that enable components to adapt to the database and transactional services needed in many business applications. With EJBs, component developers do not need to know ahead of time which database, for example, will be used when the application is finally deployed.

Enterprise JavaBean components execute on a server within the context provided by a container. This container provides management and control functions to the component, such as access to the operating system processes and threads. Containers can be provided by Web application servers, database management systems, or transaction monitors. The container provides isolation of the components from the unique characteristics of the underlying services.

9.1.3   IBM and the J2EE Standard

IBM is deeply committed to industry standards that best support the multi-platform, multivendor, and dynamic environment that the Internet has enabled. The J2EE standards are designed to allow businesses to easily connect data and applications residing on disparate platforms. IBM believes that e-business is all about cooperating on standards and competing on implementation.

With the largest Java technology team in the industry, IBM contributed to the definition of more than 80 percent of the Application Programming Interface (API) specifications in Sun's J2EE platform, including Enterprise JavaBeans, Java ServerPages, Java Servlet, Java Interface Definition Language (IDL), JDBC database connectivity API, Java Message Service (JMS), Java Naming and Directory Interface (JNDI) Java Transaction API (JTA), Java Transaction Services (JTS), and RMI-IIOP. IBM is fully behind the Java technology and will continue its involvement in the evolution of this great technology.

9.1.4   Key Java Technologies

Tools for building and running robust applications based on Java technology are an essential part of the framework. VisualAge for Java is a Java application-development environment for building Java applications, applets, servlets, Java-Bean, and Enterprise JavaBean components.

WebSphere Application Server, the platform that powers the runtime environment for the application's business logic, is IBM's application server of choice. It is implemented using various Internet and Java technologies, including the HTTP server and the Enterprise Java services that enable rapid development and deployment of applications in a distributed network environment.

Applications run as a combination of Java servlets, Java ServerPages, and Enterprise JavaBeans in the Web application server and its Java virtual machine. These server-side components communicate with their clients and other application components via HTTP or IIOP, and make use of the directory and security services provided by the network infrastructure. They can also leverage database, transaction, and groupware facilities.

9.1.5   Application Programming Model

The application programming model supported by the Framework provides a rich set of component interaction capabilities based on industry standards. For example, components can communicate with each other using the Web-based HTTP protocol or the CORBA-based RMI-IIOP. The content can be HTML, Dynamic HTML, or XML. Other protocols and interfaces specific to particular applications, such as database access, are also accommodated.

Based on Enterprise JavaBeans components, the application programming model provides dynamic binding of new business logic to the underlying data storage and transaction services, as well as to clients, existing data and applications, the network infrastructure, and the server platform. The benefits of this dynamic adaptability are realized in greater flexibility for deploying, managing, and reusing business logic.

Java ServerPages enable applications, as seen by the user, to be assembled and delivered on the fly to the user, meaning that both the content and the form of the content can be tailored to the user and the device.

For clients, this means the application's business logic can be independent of the characteristics of the client device. The Framework supports clients that range from pervasive devices, such as PDAs, smartcards, and digital wireless telephones, to network computers and PCs. Server-side proxies and transcoding are examples of how servers can be leveraged to provide universal client access and extend client functions for devices with limited functionality. When the client is disconnected from the network, data synchronization services can be supported to provide asynchronous access to data and applications.

9.1.6   Network Infrastructure

The Framework's architecture includes a set of secure network infrastructure services that provide consistent, coherent, scaleable facilities for e-business applications. These services are based on established and emerging industry standards, including TCP/IP. Industry standard APIs and protocols are used for networking, security, access to directory services, and network file and print services.

With its support for distributed applications and the J2EE standard, IBM is able to help customers like Honeywell and Bekins find best-fit solutions for the challenges they face in the networked economy.

9.2   Honeywell

We've all heard the saying, "This isn't rocket science." Well, in Honeywell's case, it is. From spacecraft components to landing systems to nylon ropes for hot air balloons, Honeywell's products and technology touches everything that flies. Honeywell builds fuel control systems, wheels, and brakes in Indiana, cabin pressure systems California, engines in Arizona, and navigational equipment on the

East Coast. While creating those high-precision components, the company faced a difficult obstacle: how to implement new technology while ensuring zero errors.

9.2.1 Computing Environment

Honeywell has been using computers since at least the early 1970s. "If you look at somebody that's been building applications for 30+ years, you're going to find a collage of zillions of programs with logic scattered all about, data scattered in many files, and the same bits of data repeated many times. It got to the point where if you had to make a change to business rules, you had a pretty massive analysis and test effort," says Dave Kulakowski, development and technology manager, Honeywell.

About six to seven years ago, a group of two or three engineers tried to come up with a better way to build applications. At that time, Honeywell started exploring object technologies. The idea was to pull the logic out of those "zillions" of programs and build business components for those items. The main goal was to create a computing environment in which they could create an object and reuse it over and over again.

The team first started building objects with IBM SmallTalk. They later switched to the Java language because it was easier for application developers to learn, there was an abundance of schools teaching the language, and industry was embracing the technology.

Why Java Technologies?

"We chose Java technologies because, first they use an object-based approach that could fulfill our vision of reusable business components. Second, there is an abundance of resources in hardware, software, and people educated in the technology. Third, we really liked the idea of the JVM in which you could run an application anywhere, without having to deploy application software on the client machine. Those were the reasons we were moving to the Java language three or four years ago," says Kulakowski.

"We've actually backed off a bit on one of the above reasons, which is to place applets out on the desktops. Now we've moved to a servlet middle-tier arrangement with Java technology and very thin implementations of the Java platform on the desktops," says Kulakowski.

9.2.2 Computing Infrastructure

Worldwide, Honeywell has two data centers, one in France and the other in Tempe, Arizona. In the U.S., most sites use the mainframe data center in Tempe.

There is a collage of OS/390 boxes running approximately $24 billion worth of the company. "We have OS/390 mainframes, AS400 systems, UNIX servers, Windows NT servers, and all kinds of desktop hardware. We have a vast array of operating systems, database technologies, computer languages, and supporting system software. We've got a little bit of everything. That can happen when a large company like Honeywell has been doing computing since the late sixties or early seventies," says Kulakowski.

9.2.3   Company Vision

The key to writing a successful application is being able to keep up with the business. Businesses are so dynamic today, requiring modifications and enhancements to their computer-based business systems. e-Business has added to this load, and requires modifications and enhancements at an even quicker pace. "With our old development model we couldn't keep up with the pace," Kulakowski notes. "We were looking for something that could meet the business demand. We believe the component/object development model could."

Honeywell envisioned building an application infrastructure that not only met their current business needs, but could be easily modified and adapted to meet future requirements (see Figure 9.1).

"The whole idea is that if components are built that represent things within a business, one would be able to plug-and-play those components into any kind of application built in the future. You may have to change the user interface, maybe

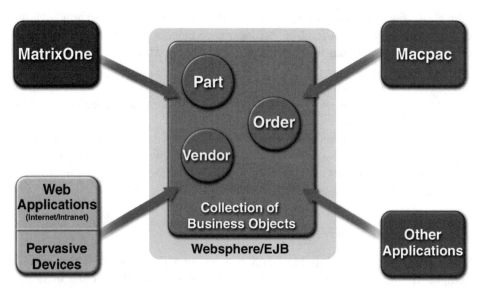

Figure 9.1   Honeywell's Enterprise Business Components and Their Use

look at the business processes, and then wire those things together into the application," notes Kulakowski.

9.2.4   J2EE Technology Projects at Honeywell

In beginning to work with J2EE technologies, Honeywell identified three projects that would benefit: the Non-Conformance Corrective Action System (NCAS), the Shop Floor Application, and the Matrix to MACPAC interface.

NCAS

Honeywell embarked on its mission to build a component-based infrastructure by building the Non-Conformance Corrective Action System (NCAS), a three-tier Internet application used to track defects and corrective actions on the shop floor of its manufacturing plant in Rocky Mount, North Carolina.

To build NCAS, the core Honeywell development team of about six people leveraged technologies that included VisualAge for Java, MQSeries, DB2, MVS, and Windows. The three-tier architecture features a user-friendly interface made up of reusable objects created with VisualAge for Java, running on thin-client workstations via the Internet. The business-logic tier was also built using VisualAge for Java running on a Windows NT server. The third tier, the enterprise tier, is composed of legacy wrapper programs that enable developers to leverage business rules within legacy core-business applications. To tie in the whole system, MQSeries acts as the link between business layer and the enterprise server.

The team's goal for NCAS was to develop a better user interface. Previously, users had to go through several screens and reenter the same data in different places to do their jobs. The team cut the process down to two or three screens, called editors. When users fire up one of the editors, they can run up as many as 20 CICS transactions.

"The problem we ran into with the NCAS system is that the users expected the response times to remain the same as the old system," says Kulakowski. "How do you take 27 CICS transactions that are running and make them run in 3 to 5 seconds?"

Honeywell reduced response times dramatically by having MQSeries run the processes in parallel. The team broke down the 27 transactions into groups of three or four, based on how they work, and launched them at the same time. It appears on the mainframe as if five to six users are running three or four transactions at the same time. The team built its application and satisfied its response time requirement, using only a few screens (Figure 9.2).

"With the parallel processing capability we gain through MQSeries, we've improved response times sevenfold. We can now create all kinds of applications that weren't possible in the past due to unwieldy response times," notes David Kulakowski.

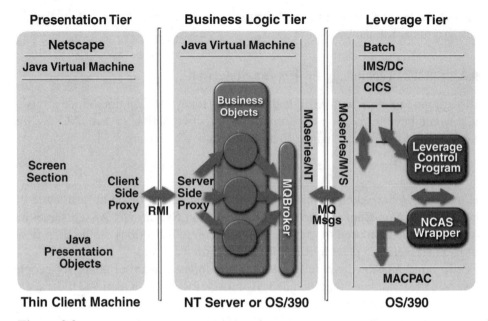

Figure 9.2 Honeywell's NCAS Multitier Architecture

"I would say that we didn't get very many business components out of NCAS. What we got most out of NCAS was a basis for building multi-tier applications and knowledge of middleware and Java technology," Kulakowski continues.

Shop-Floor Application

Honeywell's second project, the shop-floor application, is designed to streamline the processes of making engineering changes available on the shop floor. The effort was the development team's answer to a slow design process. In the past, it took a few hours to compile new specifications on paper and make them available for production. With the new Web-based application, the process happens near real time, electronically.

Based on the NCAS architecture, the shop-floor application was built with VisualAge for Java and designed to run on WebSphere Application Server. The solution uses servlets running on the application server to put shop paper on the factory floor. "That project gave us a good sense of what WebSphere was all about," says Kulakowski.

"By using a Web-based application model, we have reduced our software deployment costs by 98 percent," Kulakowski continues. "We can distribute software and updates centrally, from a developer workstation, rather than distribute software to each desktop as we had to do in the past. This approach gives us the added advantage of improved version control, as well. We know everyone is using the same release."

Matrix to MACPAC

Taking VisualAge for Java's J2EE technology capabilities to the next level, the development team used EJBs to build an interface to join two of their core business applications: Matrix, an off-the-shelf commercial application that engineers use to design and build new products, and MACPAC, Honeywell Aircraft Landing System's MRP system (see Figure 9.3).

The team's first application leveraging EJB technology, the interface is designed to allow engineering data to flow more quickly to manufacturing. The EJB technology is based on the Java programming language, so components can be deployed on any platform and operating system that supports the Enterprise JavaBean standard, and on any operating system.

Enterprise JavaBean servers reduce the complexity of developing middleware by providing automatic support for middleware services, such as transactions, security, database connectivity, and more.

"We achieved significant productivity gains by using the built-in functionality provided in the EJBs," says Kulakowski. "Our goal is to be able to turn around working code in a couple of weeks, not months. Once we amass 20 or 30 core

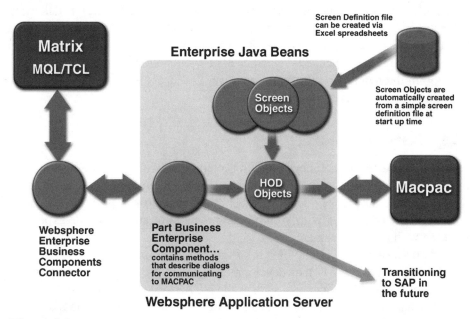

Figure 9.3 Honeywell's Architechture for Connecting Matrix and MACPAC Applications

business objects, we expect to see an explosion of new applications coming quickly into production. The sparks are already starting to fly."

The team used Enterprise JavaBean security capabilities, as well as some of the locking logic features available with EJBs. "We are depending on the security components that come with WebSphere and Enterprise JavaBeans. Authentication and authorization of who can use what with the business object can all be defined within WebSphere," Kulakowski notes. "The security is a great piece because it is something we really don't want to build into the application code. We did that in the past and learned our lesson—security administration can be a real nightmare when security code is embedded in the application software," he says.

In the past, Honeywell would use old procedural concepts when working on this type of project. The result would be an interface built for these two applications alone. With EJBs, the team is now building objects and applications that can be reused over and over. "We're using proven technologies, like VisualAge for Java and WebSphere, that all work smoothly together. As a result, our development processes are faster and more flexible," says Kulakowski.

With these Java projects, Honeywell is doing much more than simply building a new application. "We're building a collection of core-business objects that can be deployed rapidly to build new applications. This speed to market is particularly important for our evolution into e-business. It will ultimately redefine the entire role of our development team. We see ourselves becoming far more proactive in showing how technology can transform our business," continues Kulakowski. "Our direction is to take EJBs running under WebSphere Application Server and build new links to our business data. We want to be able to download information easily to wherever it's needed—whether it's a workstation on the shop floor or a palmtop in the hand of a sales representative. Our users will have information at their fingertips, wherever they go," he says.

9.2.5   Lessons Learned

The NCAS project was Honeywell's first attempt at writing an application using the Java platform. The team states that it may have been too big a project for its first such undertaking. The team members tackled a project with no experience with MQSeries on NT or with Web-based applications, and with little experience working with the Java language.

"If you look at this technology, it's frightening and probably scares off many people. The good news is that development time improves dramatically. If you look at our first few applications, such as the NCAS system, the development time was not that good. As we began to build other systems, our development time improved dramatically. What took 10 months could be done in three months. In some cases, we provided solutions in weeks instead of months. A lot has to do with the fact that we were reusing parts of components from prior development efforts, and our people became more knowledgeable about the component approach and technologies," says Kulakowski.

"You see the difference when you build something quickly and you see the enthusiasm grow. Then you know you're on the right track and you're almost to the point of achieving what you set out to do," he says.

"If people want to build Java applications or business components, they don't just buy a tool and go do it. You can't do that and expect everything to work. You have to take steps and a natural evolution within the IT department to understand how to use those technologies. If you decide to use contractors or outsource the effort, you still need to be involved in the architecture so that it fits within your business," Kulakowski continues. "You won't build the most grandiose thing with the product in the first six months or year. You have to create a plan, figure out what your vision is, and then tackle it in workable pieces."

The development team's biggest obstacle was probably the fact that this was its first time through. The project took about 10 months from beginning to end. "Some of that effort was thrown away or lost when we went down the wrong paths with the technology," says Kulakowski.

Honeywell turned to IBM because "IBM is always there and will probably always be there. With core technologies, this is the type of vendor you want. This is important because it takes significant effort to establish the technology within the organization. I want a vendor and a product that is going to be around," he concludes.

9.2.6 Results

Honeywell's vision both before and after embracing Java technology remains the same: to build plug-and-play components so that applications can be built quickly and cheaply. The company has met this goal and the business is there to confirm it.

The development team has been receiving positive feedback from customers and employees alike since embarking on their Java technology–based projects. "Feedback had been pretty negative before we built our Java applications. People weren't happy with us because we couldn't deliver applications fast enough," said Kulakowski.

Winning the 1999 *Intelligent Enterprise Magazine* RealWare Award for "Best Enterprise Application Integration Implementation" and runner-up of the 1999 AD Trends Magazine Innovator Award for "Best Object-Oriented/Component-Based Development," confirms that Honeywell is on the right track.

9.3 Bekins

A traditional moving and storage company since its founding in 1891, Bekins has been the typical brick-and-mortar company for generations. Highly innovative during its first years of operation, Bekins switched from horse-drawn carriages to motor trucks in 1903. Later, Bekins became the first company to build reinforced steel and concrete warehouses in Los Angeles. But its latest technological jump presented Bekins with its greatest challenge yet—adopting the Internet.

Bekins' vision was to provide agents and customers with Web-based access in order to place orders, view inventory, and track orders. Never having undertaken such a large development project, Bekins turned to a trusted name in the industry—IBM.

9.3.1 Who is HomeDirectUSA?

Technology demands for home moving are fairly low. Basically, we're talking about moving someone's household possessions from one place to another.

The HomeDirectUSA business, on the other hand, is a dedicated branch of Bekins that provides organizations with inventory and moving services. The company's markets are logistics and technology. In other words, HomeDirectUSA delivers products from the manufacturer all the way to the consumer. Generally, it involves large items that companies like UPS and FedEx do not handle. HomeDirectUSA handles inside deliveries and installations of complex equipment, and two-van deliveries of heavier, larger items, such as big-screen televisions.

Customers are perceived to be anyone who needs to move or manage inventory. Traditionally, the company's bread and butter has been catalog sellers and retailers. In the past couple of years, dot-com retailers have evolved as a growth area. HomeDirectUSA specializes in general retail products up to bigger business-support products, such as paper copiers, coolers, refrigerators, vending machines, and appliances.

Companies hire HomeDirectUSA to store their inventory in warehouses and then to deliver the products to consumers when the products are purchased.

9.3.2 Company Vision

With more than three dozen warehouses, 50 agents, and a host of e-tailers demanding Web-based shipment tracking, HomeDirectUSA embarked on an ambitious project to bring them all together.

The first priority was to build a Web-based application that would allow the company's agents and customers to track shipments online, anytime, anywhere.

Such capabilities could gain new Web-based retailers and greater customer satisfaction.

The second part of its technology makeover involved upgrading its order-management and inventory-tracking systems and linking them all together.

9.3.3 Initial Obstacles

With an ambitious plan in the works, HomeDirectUSA faced one small obstacle: No one in the IT shop was experienced with the Java programming language or in supporting the WebSphere Application Server. And the team had never delivered an application to the Web before.

"It was a really big challenge because there were a lot of unknowns. How many users do we need to support? How do we spec the hardware? What are the expectations in terms of performance? How do we handle customer service and technical issues that might arise. From a support perspective, we had to ask ourselves, 'What are we getting into?'" says Randy Mowen, director of data management and e-business architecture at Bekins.

From an architectural point of view, there was a learning process. The programmers had to learn the Java language and VisualAge programming. "We also had to change our programming paradigm and change our management process because now programmers working on the client and middle tier had to work with mainframe programmers," says Mowen. "They had to interface with DBAs and understand the connectivity all the way through our architecture, and understand how to manage it."

"Everybody had to understand what the impact of this application would be on their piece of the puzzle. We had some rough numbers of what we could expect, but the big picture really was unknown," Mowen says.

9.3.4 Why Java Technologies

HomeDirectUSA chose the Java platform because it wanted a server-side application or programming language. "The decision came down to whether we wanted to write it in the Java language, Perl, or CGI scripting," says Mowen. "We took a look at the servlet technology and really liked its efficiencies. We liked connection pooling, multithreading, and some advantages servlets had over straight CGI programming. Now there is fast CGI and some other things, but when we were looking, those technologies weren't proven. We liked the fact that server-side processing was available, and we liked how the Java environment supported applications," he notes.

Another factor was the Java platform's ability to provide visibility or the option to create different types of EJBs, both stateless and stateful. Using VisualAge for Java, the company could easily control Enterprise JavaBeans in terms of connectivity and attributes. "Those properties can be defined within VisualAge for Java. We chose to work with VisualAge and WebSphere, so there is a seamless process for deploying objects once they are created," says Mowen.

J2EE Technology

The development team designed and built the applications to be open and to take advantage of the J2EE technology. "In our development efforts, we are far ahead. We are using the J2EE standards to make sure all the pieces can talk to each other now and remain compatible for the future. We can see the potential. Once we start scaling this environment with different objects on different boxes, it makes sense to keep compliance so that we know we can support those objects. Having a standard makes it much easier to communicate among our array of computing environments," Mowen continues. "We don't know if we'll be acquiring another company, being acquired, working with other customers, or becoming a trading hub. But if we know we are compliant, we'll be in good shape whatever happens," he notes.

EJB Components

The development team's first application, shipment tracking, was servlet-based. Team members did not jump right into EJBs, and initially they also looked at the CORBA standard.

They looked at defining high-level objects in order to simplify some of the programming tasks. EJB simplified the programming tasks by allowing them to define EJBs to contain specific information so that programmers below their level would not have to worry about connectivity issues or about the architecture. Using EJBs, business-level programmers need only know which object they need to talk to in order, to get the information they want.

A big factor in the decision to use EJBs was the team's desire to save programming time and effort by building reusable objects. "When you have only one project, you don't expect to reuse a lot. When we leveraged and built the Order-Management and Inventory-Management systems, we started reusing objects and began to get a web-like effect in which different objects rely on other objects. We are now starting to realize the economy of scale of reusability. It is a curve. In the beginning, you build the objects for the first time, knowing that you will reuse them. It is not until you have multiple applications that you can take advantage of it," says Mowen.

Right now, about a third of the objects are reused. The team designed about two-thirds of the objects to be reusable. About one-third of the servlets and EJBs are support-type code that is not reusable by nature.

9.3.5 Architecture

Developing the architecture behind HomeDirectUSA required thinking on several levels, including accomodating legacy code, identifying useful interfaces between applications, and selecting projects well-suited to the EJB component model.

Back-End Applications

HomeDirectUSA relies on legacy code that is about 10 to 15 years old to support its business, which has changed dramatically in the past 10 years. The code is still fundamentally solid and sound and can scale to support large numbers of users. "It's very stable, so there's no good reason to get rid of it," said Mowen.

IMS transactions, the underlying foundation for all the applications, run in the OTMA (Online Transaction Manager) region of the IMS system. IMS transactions are available and can run in parallel with their Web-based systems. HomeDirect-USA did not want to turn off the older system and go live with a new one right away. The company wanted to roll out the new application while mitigating its risk through its ability to revert back to the old system. Going forward, the team anticipates adding quite a bit of new functionality for the Web-based application.

Currently, HomeDirectUSA simply leverages IMS transactions and/or DB2 subroutines and stored procedures. "It's more efficient for us to do that, since they are all mainframe applications. We felt it was more stable than managing everything in WebSphere, with EJBs that had stateful sessions," says Randy Mowen. Basically, everything that is delivered to the EJB is stateless. In other words, the data is useful as a snapshot. If you need to update the information, you need to rerun the transaction to get the new data. "To us, that was the most stable option and as efficient in terms of performance, which is another thing we wanted to ensure," he notes.

Applications that Interface

All new applications will be driven by DB2 database. However, the company still relies on data stores and transactions that store IMS data. Moving forward, the team anticipates more inventory-centric needs, more-detailed or granular-level visibility into inventory turnaround, and aggressive types of inventory management functions. "As we build these applications, there will be more interfacing to a more robust, centrally managed inventory system. That's going to involve program changes that that will probably make extensive use of stored procedures. Much of this effort will focus on calling the stored procedures from EJBs and servlets to present information on the Web," says Mowen.

Thinking Behind the Application

There were certain types of information for which the team felt the EJB concept was especially suited. For example, customer profile and customer inventory information sit well in an EJB format. Defining that kind of data as EJBs made more sense than doing it at the servlet level because with EJBs, you can make more-complex relationships easier to understand.

"Everyone can understand the concept of customer inventory. We have defined it to have certain attributes, such as a make and model number. If the items have a serial number, there is a description, location, and other attributes associated with it. We can use those objects, or EJBs, and know that is where we will retrieve the information, and that it will be a repository for that type of information consistently. Other applications that rely on customer inventory know they have to talk to that bean to get that type of information," notes Mowen.

9.3.6 Projects

HomeDirectUSA completed three applications to streamline its business and take it into the twenty-first century. Its Shipping and Tracking application (STS) is a Web-based application that allows agents and customers to track shipments. Customers can place orders across the Web with the Order-Management application, and the Inventory-Management solution allows customers to view warehouse inventory and place orders directly.

A servlet-based application, STS allows customers to perform shipment tracking. The two latest projects address more-fundamental business applications. The Order Management application is the company's central application that allows customers to place orders. It is an efficient way for customers to tell HomeDirectUSA how to move their inventory or freight through the system, and is the focal point and centerpiece of all the applications.

From there, the development team built the Inventory-Management application, which allows customers to place orders with full visibility of all inventory in the HomeDirectUSA system.

9.3.7 Shipment Tracking

The Shipment-Tracking application provides more visibility of shipments that have already been ordered and displays the status of the orders. Now the application is expanded to allow customers looking for specific pieces of furniture to search the company's inventory and to attach available pieces of inventory to an order (see Figure 9.4).

The STS application was completely new to HomeDirectUSA. The Order-Management and Inventory-Management projects were basically rewrites of Cobalt applications into the Java language using EJBs. These two projects involved more legacy conversion than writing a new application.

STS is designed to be a robust, flexible, and easily maintained system, based on multitier architecture. Each architectural layer has clearly defined responsibilities, with minimal dependencies between layers. The team took the time to look at the overall architecture in order to create a more robust solution. By taking this approach, it created a nice end-to-end solution that is neatly integrated with back-end legacy systems (see Figure 9.5).

Each component is implemented with minimum development dependencies. As a result, modifications or improvements at the component level can be made easily, without affecting the rest of the system. The cost of each change is proportional to the size of the change, not to the size of the system.

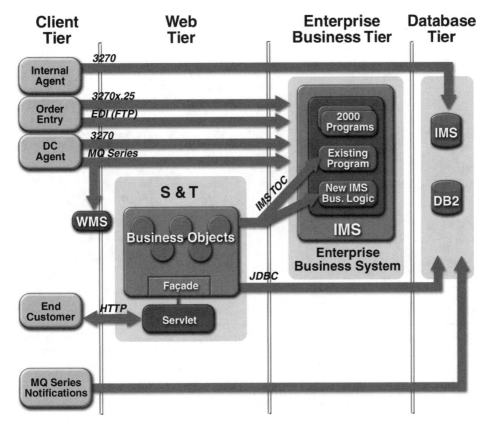

Figure 9.4   Bekins' GNS Shipping and Tracking Application Architecture

The presentation tier is built independently of the database and contains no complex business logic. Developers without business programming knowledge can create completely new views or modify existing views independent of the business-object layer. With the help of VisualAge for Java's drag-and-drop view construction, even nonprogrammers can build new views. Using VisualAge for Java, the team can change the user interface quickly. There is no need to change, redeploy, or retest server components when view changes are made. In fact, the team estimates a 25 to 50 percent reduction in the time it takes to create new views.

A mapping layer between legacy data types of column names enables the existing mainframe tables to change, without affecting every e-business user. Only the mapping layer need be updated.

The result is that business programmers are shielded from database knowledge. Currently, HomeDirectUSA has WebSphere Application Server accessing a DB2 database, both residing on Windows NT Server. In the future, the team plans to optimize persistence behavior and possibly migrate distributed databases over to the IBM S/390 MVS mainframe. And it will all be transparent to the business programmer.

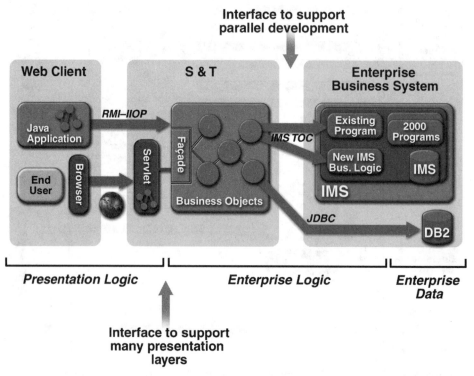

Figure 9.5   Bekins' GNS Shipping and Tracking End-to-End Configuration

Through STS, customers can access accurate, timely information about shipments using any standard Web browser. Every time an item moves within a warehouse, onto a truck, or is delivered, its item-level bar code is scanned and the information is available immediately via the Internet.

STS revolutionized the way HomeDirectUSA defines customer service by launching the company into e-business with a high-performance, scalable, multi-tier infrastructure. The company is now positioned to provide additional functionality quickly to its Web-based application.

Order Management

It came down to two options when considering which route to take with the Order-Management architecture. Either design a simple servlet-driven application like STS, or use more robust EJBs. The team chose EJBs, which make up the core of the base logic. Some servlets also support the application.

"We knew we wanted to use VisualAge, WebSphere, and Java architecture because of the success we had and also because of the scalability factors. Our hardware architecture was built to spec to support it, and we already had the skill sets from the administrative and coding sides. We didn't look at any other languages or at any other base-level tools. We use mostly WebSphere Studio," says Mowen.

The company wanted to have an application that would allow accessibility to the system from anywhere. The Order-Management application is designed to allow anyone, anywhere, with Internet access, to enter an order or place an order into the system. That was the main motivating factor.

Methodology for Order Management. The methodology for this project was a little different than it would be for a new application because it was a legacy application being rewritten in the Java language. The business logic had already been designed, and the team just had to "Webify" Cobalt transactions running as IMS transactions or Cobalt subroutines. The team had faith in the Cobalt business logic and believed it was rock solid.

The Order-Management project was a matter of pairing a Java language programmer with a Cobalt programmer to establish which program should be leveraged, or called, by the EJB to enable the business logic. In essence, it was a matter of mapping out which EJB would call which Cobalt program. Once the developers knew the layout, they cut and pasted the specific Cobalt code into the VisualAge for Java code generator to create the appropriate Java code for talking to the application.

This was the first time the team used the generator, which creates Java language code and classes that developers can look at. "Some parts are encrypted, but the majority of code is visible, including the parameters and the I/O. We could look at it and make sure it was correct. As we worked through the task, the tool worked the way we thought it would, and made the appropriate calls to the appropriate subroutines or transactions," explains Mowen. "I don't know how we could have done this project without the reverse generator in VisualAge for Java. We wouldn't have known or had the expertise to even approach it. We could not have made calls to the existing program and would have had to rewrite it entirely in the Java language. It would have easily taken five times longer to code the enterprise beans and required the cost of an additional programmer, doubling expenses for the project," he continues.

The Old System. The order process in place before the team started the project was a series of 3270 screens based on IMS transactions. The screens varied, depending on the type of order entered and on criteria entered to define how to process the order. The system was not intuitive. It was designed for someone who knew the business, understood the Bekins order process, and knew the codes and acronyms necessary to place an order.

HomeDirectUSA wanted to simplify the process so that someone with no knowledge of Bekins' order policies could place an order correctly. The new application was designed to make things easier and more intuitive. The application went further and validated up-front that information was in the acceptable range of entry, whether or not it was correct.

Keep It Simple. "The first order of business was to keep it simple. We supported everything on a Windows NT platform and replicated the data that used to be supported for the shipment-tracking application. From that point, we wrote SQL statements against it to provide shipment visibility. We kept most of the moving pieces simple and concentrated on writing and supporting the code," says Mowen.

Once the team had the application working, they moved into their true workhorse environment—the mainframe. Since the team was already replicating shipment-tracking data from the mainframe systems, they decided to move all the STS data residing on a DB2 database running on Windows NT platform back to the OS/390. "We made a conscious effort to build all the connectivity features and functions onto the mainframe to allow Java applications to speak to the mainframe. We looked at the IMS toc connector from IBM to allow us to connect to IMS transactions. And installed DB2 Connect so that we could easily make calls to DB2 OS/390 data from Java applications," explains Mowen. "Now that we have all the architecture set up, and WebSphere configured and connected to the system, it is very easy to plug in new applications and go after that data because the architecture doesn't really change."

Inventory Management

The discussions on the inventory visibility project began in February 2000, as it was driven by the Order-Management project. The Inventory-Management application was a natural extension of Order-Management capabilities.

A screen on the Order-Management application acts as a door into the Inventory-Management system. A screen in the Order-Management application asks for line items or inventory. Clicking on a button takes you to an inventory screen that asks for an SKU or model number, to view the entire inventory in a specific region, warehouse, or nationwide. Clicking on an item populates the order. HomeDirectUSA actually provides inventory information back to the customer.

The Order-Management solution is an IMS-based system that is completely transaction-based. Inventory is managed in a DB2 database running on the S/390 platform. The inventory-management application is all stored-procedure driven. All the logic is written in DB2 Cobalt stored procedures and the EJB simply calls stored procedures.

The stored procedures retrieve a certain number of rows of data based on the parameters entered into the query. For example, you may have make, model, and agent location; or make, model, and region; or all makes and models across the inventory in the Bekins system nationwide. The application displays as inventory by region and by location. It also provides serial number and date, so orders can be removed in a Last-In, First-Out (LIFO) or First-In, First-Out (FIFO) inventory-management structure. However, customers choose to complete an order Bekins gives them the information. Then it's as easy as clicking items to fill in the order form.

"We have real-time inventory positions managed by EXE Technology's Exceed Management System which are run by each of our warehouses. The application runs locally at each agent facility, so they can keep up to date on our inventory positions. These, in turn, feed the central DB2 database," Mowen goes on to say. "We use MQSeries as the interface between all those warehouse management databases and DB2 databases. It's the message interface we use to replicate the data up to that DB2 repository." The Inventory-Management application complements the other two applications by providing more depth and greater inventory visibility to clients.

9.3.8   Development Team

The development team included a lead developer, a system architect, an object modeler, and a database administrator for the Shipment-Tracking project. "An outside resource helped us with the initial architecture and got us started with the Java language code. Basically, it was a five-person team," says Mowen.

For the Order-Management application, the team started with three internal Java programmers and two outside resources who strictly wrote Java language code. Randy Mowen designed the architecture. The systems programmer on the OS/390 side helped set up the IMS table-of-contents connectivity, the IMS sessions, and the DB2 Connect environment. Two junior programmers worked on inventory movability.

9.3.9 Computing Environment

The workhorse is Big Iron, an OS/390 system supported by the IBM Center in Dallas (see Figure 9.6). Bekins connects to Big Iron through TCP and SNA. The SNA connectivity supports all the 3270 users. TCP/IP supports all the Web activity and DB2 Connect. Internally, Bekins has a regular Ethernet network setup. The WebSphere environment has two Compaq servers running Windows NT supporting it. Two HTTP servers support the HTML code, which acts as a portal to the Web. A DB2 Connect machine allows Java applications and users to connect to DB2 data. It is also a gateway for an IMS table-of-contents connection so that Java applications can talk to IMS transactions.

Bekins has SQL Server warehouse-management databases that connect via MQSeries send-and-receive channels to the central DB2 database running on OS/

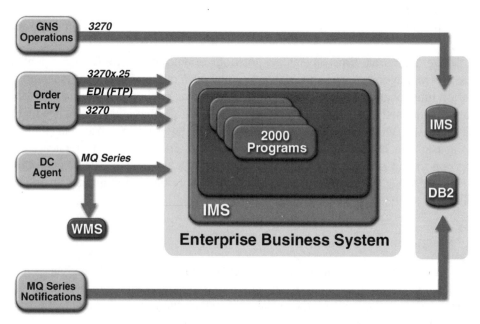

Figure 9.6 Bekin's GNS Mainframe Architecture

390. Agents connect through frame relays and TCP/IP into the company's virtual private network.

9.3.10 Lessons Learned

"From an efficiency point of view, we became more conscious of documenting, following procedures, and understanding where our code lives. Under the old paradigm, if you wanted a change you had to do one of two things. You could either complete an impact analysis and make changes to the existing code if possible. Alternatively, you made a carbon copy, copied that code, and did it again. Often, you missed a business rule or something else that was key, resulting in problems. With more than 2,000 Cobalt programs on the mainframe, there is redundant code and the potential for missing a business rule. Because we have copied, copied, and copied again to support a new function, reusability guarantees that you use the same rule every time. That is huge for us," notes Mowen.

On the development side, the team learned to leverage the power of the Enterprise Edition of VisualAge for Java. Even without prior training or experience with the toolset, developers were able to produce a complex, dynamic application in just three months. The application has a rich feature set. The centralized repository, for example, was a big benefit for the team, allowing developers to share written code and save valuable time. With VisualAge for Java's servlet-builder tool, the team was able to generate servlets quickly, without having to hand-write code to generate HTML pages.

HomeDirectUSA realized order-of-magnitude productivity gains, and coding is at least 75 percent faster compared with alternate tools and methods.

9.3.11 Maintenance and Performance

The new applications have been extremely stable, and the team has not had any problems. They have one WebSphere administrator and one network administrator. Most important, the new applications have not increased demand for more administration.

The team members reached their goal of sub-second performance for STS. The other two applications have seen similar performance to the old 3270 application, which was the goal. "In certain cases, there is a lot more information than we anticipated but we still remain within the performance range that we strive for," says Mowen.

9.3.12 Outcome

This redirection of its order processing system is a major step in the right direction for HomeDirectUSA, both from a customer-service perspective and from a technological perspective. The company is putting up barriers, and the competition is starting to lose ground.

"In our environment, we know who the major players and the major customers are," says Mowen. "Retaining our own customers and even attracting some that are with our competitors are both important. Self-service applications, in our experience, increase customer response times and increase satisfaction tremendously. So the more we can offer self-service applications on the Web, the higher our retention rate. And we feel that we'll be able to obtain a market share."

Building applications based on J2EE technology was a big step for Home-DirectUSA. "Some virtual type of logistics companies have the technology, but they don't have the infrastructure and are not brick-and-mortar companies at all. The key is that a traditional company that actually delivers the services is bolting on this technology. We really have an end-to-end solution from logistics to delivery," Mowen continues.

The Shipment-Tracking application has resulted in total financial benefits of more than $10 million (U.S.) in increased revenue projected annually, and Bekins won a number of important new accounts due to its ability to deliver online STS functionality. Information is provided electronically over the Web, reducing operating expenses $250,000 annually.

Improved customer service and satisfaction resulted from faster access to information. In the past, it could take hours for customers to get answers, via telephone or fax, to their questions on shipping status. With STS, both the direct customers and their end consumers can access shipping reports instantly across the Web. They have full supply-chain visibility and can track an order to the exact moment of delivery. Consequently, retailers can bill the consumer faster, improving their cash flow position. At the same time, STS frees HomeDirect customer-service representatives to focus on handling exceptions. All this results in high overall customer satisfaction.

An important benefit in planning for future growth of the e-business service channel, the Java technology-based system encompasses multiple operating systems. It currently uses both IBM S/390 MVS and Windows NT.

9.3.13   Future Direction

In the future, the development team sees information flowing much more dynamically and more seamlessly through their applications. They foresee that the need for more front-end applications will probably diminish, with enterprise application integration, data transformation, and response to other people's demand for open systems increasing.

The Shipment-Tracking application was customer-driven. A large dot-com customer demanded that its customers have order-tracking visibility. "From there, we expanded to include assessing customer complaints, customer requests, and internal demands for increased turnover of revenue. It gave every aspect of our business a benefit. Now we will probably focus more on different target groups. We'll extend this to whichever markets and niches offer benefit. These two applications were fundamental," explains Mowen.

iPlanet

About the Author

Torbjörn Dahlén is a senior Java architect at Sun Java Center of Sun Microsystems Professional Services division, where he specializes in legacy system integration and J2EE-based financial applications. Before joining Sun in 1997, he worked with distributed systems and CORBA at Ericsson, in Sweden. Dahlén earned an MS degree in Computer Science at Uppsala University in 1993. Since then, he has participated in numerous development projects, building distributed, object-oriented applications in C++ and Java. Dahlén also writes articles for the "Architect's Corner" column in *Java Report.*

CHAPTER 10

International Data Post Brings Snail Mail to the Internet Age with iPlanet

INTERNATIONAL DATA POST (IDP), a Copenhagen, Denmark-based postal technology solutions company, is taking the communications realm of postal operations to the Internet age, using Java 2 Platform, Enterprise Edition (J2EE) technology. The company, owned by seven global postal operators, is a pioneer of "hybrid mail," which streamlines a letter's delivery cycle by enabling electronic delivery from the sender to the post office. There—rather than at the sender's site—the document is printed, stamped, and physically delivered to the recipient. By using IDP's solution, postal organizations can grow beyond providing only communications logistics services, and add e-messaging to their repertoire. And organizations from a multitude of other industries can license the solution to capture new revenue opportunities.

IDP's hybrid mail management system, ePOST, was first developed in the late 1980s on a mixed infrastructure, of IBM mainframe computers and legacy middleware. Since then, the system has enjoyed incredible acceptance from both postal operators and corporations. In 1998 alone, IDP customers produced more than two billion hybrid mail letters.

A little over a year ago, IDP decided to extend ePOST by incorporating a front-end, Web-based access channel for the solution. Its engineers, however, lacked expertise in developing Internet-based applications. IDP consulted a half-dozen leading IT vendors to determine the type of technology and solution that would garner the most success. After talking with Sun Microsystems, the company was convinced that the total package from Sun—including J2EE technology, for its growing reputation as a highly flexible Internet application development platform—offered the most attractive option. IDP called on Sun Professional Services to architect and design the application, called WEB ePOST. WEB ePOST was developed with J2EE-compliant iPlanet Application Server and iPlanet Web Server running various Java and J2EE technology components, including Enterprise JavaBeans (EJB), Java ServerPages (JSP), Java Servlets, and Java applets.

Now, IDP customers can mail letters using a standard Web browser, saving significantly on printing, administration, and postage costs. And traditional postal operators, whose market has been under pressure from new technologies and new competitors, finally have a Web-based offering that ties into their core business and helps them exploit new markets to grow their revenues and build their businesses. Currently, several postal operators—who reach more than one billion addresses and represent more than 75 percent of the worldwide postal mail volume—have licensed WEB ePOST. As for IDP, J2EE technology has given the company a rapid application development environment that can easily be leveraged for future projects.

10.1   Company Profile

Imagine sending colorful brochures to thousands of physical mailboxes—all with a click of the mouse. No more envelope stuffing, stamp licking, or traveling to the nearest post office. Thanks to cutting-edge technology from IDP, that day has arrived. Using IDP's hybrid-mail solution, which brings together electronic and physical delivery of mail, businesses are sending letters, paper invoices, and other printed materials directly from their PCs. "We call this the next-generation mail system," says Jacob Johnsen, vice president of research and development at IDP. "We're bringing the postal service to the Internet while saving corporations substantial dollars in the process, and enhancing the service standards and accessibility of the postal network."

IDP worked with Sun Professional Services to be at the forefront of this revolution, offering complex messaging software and related services that make Internet mailing a very practical reality. More than a dozen companies have prelicensed IDP's state-of-the-art WEB ePOST, the Internet channel for its hybrid-mail system. As IDP continues to extend the market introduction of WEB ePOST, the company anticipates attracting even more licensees.

Unlike the many Web-born companies that have met their financial demise over the past year, IDP is an established IT company with a solid foundation. It garnered tremendous support from industry stalwarts. Shareholders include seven of the world's top public postal operators (the equivalent of the U.S. Postal Service) in Australia, Denmark, Finland, France, Germany, Norway, and Sweden. As noted earlier, these postal operators reach more than a billion addresses and represent more than 75 percent of the worldwide postal mail volume. IDP has 50 employees, half of whom are technical support, customer service, and testing staff. The other half of the workforce includes staff from product management, consulting, sales, and administration.

It is no wonder hybrid mail systems are attractive to postal operators. Hybrid mail presents a way by which an old industry can profit in the new economy. And the timing could not be better: With a growing range of electronic communications in our connected society—e-mail, electronic attachments, faxes, and cellular phones, to name a few—postal operators are facing significant competition in an ever-expanding market. Reliable TCP/IP connections and emerging technology such as digital signatures enable companies to send and receive corporate invoices and purchase orders—once the bastion of the physical letter—in the domain of the Internet. And as for letters that still find their way into a mail carrier's sack, the contrast with e-mail messages that arrive in minutes—even seconds—after the writer hits the "send" button is enough to make any postal operator want to go electronic. According to IDP, more than 70 percent of postal letters are originally created on computers and then printed out, placed in an envelope, stamped, and dropped off in a bin—an operation that can be inefficient, especially where mass mailings are concerned.

For postal operators, hybrid-mail systems are fast becoming the high-tech tools of choice for breaking into new market opportunities. "Hybrid mail secures the position of postal operators as trusted parties in the electronic communications age, creating a digital channel for efficient message delivery," explains Flemming Skov Hansen, senior project manager at IDP. "For customers, our solution is attractive because it provides them with the ability to conduct high-volume mailings at lower prices and with shorter delivery times. What was once a cumbersome mailing project, particularly in terms of the logistics and resources needed, now becomes a streamlined communication process." Indeed, IDP studies show that corporations using WEB ePOST cut mailing costs nearly in half, replacing time- and cost-intensive manual labor with lightning-fast, Internet-based automation.

IDP licenses its software to corporations, telecommunication carriers, Internet portal operators, ASPs, and of course, postal administrations. More than just a technology solution provider, IDP also offers an array of professional services, ranging from strategy consulting and marketing to technology implementation and operation. "We are a center of expertise for e-messaging solutions, technology, and markets," Johnsen says.

10.1.1 Hybrid Mail: The Technology Evolution

Hybrid-mail systems emerged, with little fanfare, on the high-tech scene in the 1980s, The slow start had much to do with the fact that postal operators traditionally thought of themselves as logistics carriers, rather than as having a role in electronic communications. Still, a handful of European countries saw the seeds of something spectacular; in 1992, Nordic Data Post, which included postal operators in Denmark, Finland, Norway, and Sweden, began developing its own hybrid mail offering. Intrigued by the solution's potential, postal operators in France, Germany, and Australia jumped on board over the next couple of years, and Nordic Data Post became International Data Post.

Shortly after, postal operators in 18 countries, including Italy, the United States, Singapore and Portugal, started licensing ePOST. These international companies realized they could suddenly and cheaply conduct mass mailings in countries where postal operators embraced ePOST. In other words, companies could send documents electronically to a country—possibly overseas—and have the documents printed there, rather than pay hefty charges for shipping bulky paper.

An early hybrid-mail application, ePOST/VM, was built on the IBM VM mainframe platform and ran on IBM S/370- and IBM S/390-compatible hardware (this version is being phased out). IDP then decided to build an access solution for PCs, called PC ePOST. It is a Microsoft Windows-based application that acts as a virtual printer—that is, PC ePOST users can submit print jobs directly into a hybrid mail system, sending electronic versions of their mailings through cyberspace and eventually to a printing company. (The carrier in this system is standard SMTP e-mail transport system.)

The next system, ePOST/Open 1—and later ePOST/Open 2, released in late 1998—is a UNIX-based system that supports printer servers such as IBM Info-Print Manager, IBM PSF/6000, and Oce Prisma APA. It utilizes middleware from Oracle, as well as IBM MQSeries. Its major routing system runs on IBM AIX and HP-UX, though it is currently being ported to Sun's Solaris Operating Environment for greater stability.

The eventual rise of the Internet and the ubiquity of Web browsers triggered a momentous milestone in the evolution of IDP's hybrid-mail system application. In its quest to become the worldwide leader in postal e-messaging, IDP knew it needed to provide a Web channel to ePOST. This newest iteration of its solution eventually became known as WEB ePOST.

To develop WEB ePOST, IDP recognized it required powerful Internet-based software built on standard components and protocols that would enable customers to prepare sizable electronic documents for safe and reliable transport over the Internet. The software would need to work with just about any production tool or word processor and connect to both enterprise-scale server infrastructures and legacy mainframe environments. Moreover, IDP officials saw this as a big opportunity to brand the company and its postal operators as Web-savvy organizations. It was at this moment in its evolution that IDP remembered the promise of Java technology.

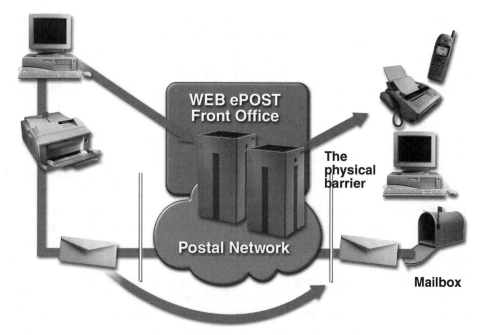

Figure 10.1 Postal Customers Save Substantially by Sending Hybrid Mail Through WEB ePOST

10.1.2 Why J2EE Technology?

The decision to extend ePOST using Java technology and a multitiered architecture was based on the need for flexibility and scalability, as well as on the ability to speed up future application development. WEB ePOST also needed to be easy to integrate into customer IT infrastructures and work seamlessly with nearly every production tool used for creating documents and graphics.

Since a company might possibly send thousands of mission-critical documents daily, IDP needed a multitiered architecture so that it could add servers quickly, to handle sudden and massive transaction spikes. Early on, IDP also envisioned organizations other than postal operators licensing WEB ePOST, so it wanted to be sure its solution could be customized for a variety of industries so that it could capitalize on new business opportunities. A restaurant chain could, for example, customize WEB ePOST to enable users to send postcards, birthday cards, or registered mail. Using the various components of the J2EE platform, IDP could save some time and effort because of the reusable business-logic code inherent in J2EE technology.

For WEB ePOST to be a practical, attractive solution, it had to require little or no end-user training. The fewer barriers to adoption, the more likely corporations long familiar with traditional mailing methods would switch over to hybrid-mail systems—without concern about overcoming challenges that any new technology can bring. This meant WEB ePOST had to connect seamlessly with popular Web browsers, such as Microsoft Internet Explorer and Netscape. It also needed to work with packaged address books, such as Microsoft Outlook, with a MAPI interface or in conjunction with an LDAP or ODBC-based database.

After speaking to several vendors, IDP found the flexible development environment for building its multi-tier enterprise application—the J2EE platform. By basing enterprise applications on standardized, modular components, and managing many details of application behavior, without complex programming, J2EE technology simplifies their development. "Java technology offers the most flexible solution for this kind of development, because it can operate on any platform whatsoever," notes Hansen. "In addition, from a marketing perspective, the Java brand has a lot of power with our customer base. Java technology was a natural choice."

But even with the promise of application development ease, IDP engineers knew little about Java technology and the J2EE architecture—only that the technology was fast becoming the de facto standard for developing flexible applications, and for extending existing applications to the Web. The engineers desperately needed experienced professionals to work with them. "We were very new to the world of Internet development," says Johnsen. "We had developed on big UNIX servers, built production-class software that ran 24x7, and even made some PC developments. But these were largely unconnected to architecting, building, and deploying a J2EE platform. We needed someone to guide us through the design and implementation phases."

Consequently, IDP turned to the services firm that logically had the most Java technology expertise, Sun Professional Services. "Our main reason for choosing Sun Professional Services was that its proof-of-concept seemed to be a solid solution that met our criteria for reliably bringing our hybrid-mail system to the Web," says Johnsen. "Another key reason was the reputation of Sun Professional Services in architecting sophisticated platform infrastructures based on Java technology." He adds, "And the brand name of Sun was also an obvious factor."

Of course, providing a Web front-end access point for an application such as ePOST using Java technology—or any other technology, for that matter—isn't as simple as it sounds. To begin, powerful functionality needed to be built into the front end so that users could send Hybrid Markup Language (HML) documents to IDP's hybrid message management system, where addresses could be inserted and the completed file routed to a post operator's paper-based distribution system. In addition, there was a need for a complex server-side portion of the Web application to handle business logic and transaction processing.

10.2   Problem/Opportunity Profile: The Applet Dilemma

The biggest challenge in developing WEB ePOST was building the client-side Java applet—the lynchpin for the entire system, which performs complex tasks, as well as interfaces with different Web browsers. The problem was that this applet kept growing because IDP wanted it to be packed with functionality and graphics. As the development of the application progressed and more and more functionality was embedded in this applet, it reached a little more than a megabyte. At the same time, the company did not want the Java applet's size to become a barrier to adoption.

The Java applet provides the graphical user interface (GUI) and a rich array of functionality for the WEB ePOST user to send postscript files and select postal delivery options, as well as letter and envelope formats. Users can select a set of standard enclosures—residing at the core printing system—to be added with each letter. For example, a pitch letter offering a credit card with low interest rates might be paired with a flier describing a free gift for those who sign on. The applet also has a built-in calculator that enables users to calculate the cost of sending the letters, depending on their formats and delivery options. In addition, the Java applet is responsible for generating the HML file wrapped around the postscript file. (HML takes into account delivery attributes, such as addresses, document layout, and enclosures.)

The applet integrates seamlessly with a variety of address databases: Microsoft Outlook, through MAPI; Lotus Notes, through LDAP; and Microsoft Access, through ODBC. This enables users to select any number of recipients and enter data fields into the letter. Users could also preview a bit map of the letter, including recipient addresses, reserved fields, and other information, via the applet. The remaining functionality for WEB ePOST, such as document management and security, resides within the solution's server, iPlanet Application Server.

Sun and IDP decided to identify an alternative that would help ameliorate the challenges associated with using a large Java applet. Instead of having users download the applet over the Web every time they wanted to use WEB ePOST, they would have to download it only once and store it on their hard drives. Simply put, a megabyte would take too long to download over and over again from a narrow bandwidth, such as dial-up lines. By downloading the applet once and storing it locally, a user would have ready access to the application whenever needed.

Still, the size of the applet somewhat limited WEB ePOST in terms of the platforms it supported. The applet can run from two major browsers—Microsoft Internet Explorer and Netscape Communicator—and on Windows 95, 98, and NT. It should also work on any operating system (such as Macintosh and UNIX) that supports these browsers. "Our customers' IT environments vary incredibly, but the one thing they have in common is a browser," says Michael Olsen, a software engineer at IDP. "That's why developing WEB ePOST was vital to the future success of our company."

10.2.1 Collaboration with Sun Professional Services

The Sun Professional Services Java Center, in Stockholm, Sweden, was initially engaged to provide an architectural assessment for WEB ePOST. The proof of concept and other accompanying documents used IDP's service-level requirements as the basis to architect a multitier platform infrastructure with layers that contain the various J2EE components. And after developing an implementation plan, Sun Professional Services worked with IDP to build and deploy WEB ePOST. Although Sun Professional Services was an important component in architecting and building WEB ePOST, Hansen notes, its biggest contribution was in knowledge transfer: "From a technical standpoint, we found Sun Professional Services to be very skilled and extremely professional in its understanding of Java technology and moreover in mentoring our Java engineers."

Part of the services-driven methodology used by Sun Professional Services is based on the rational unified process (RUP) methodology for software development, which was leveraged in the development of Web ePOST. Developed by Rational Software Corporation, RUP is a case-driven software development process. In essence, it provides a roadmap that helps to ensure that the development of certain applications coincides with end-user requirements, not to mention coalesces with other applications in development. With RUP, you can focus on eliminating risks early by implementing and testing the most critical use cases first—typically, during the inception phase—and then building out the bulk of applications during the elaboration and construction phases. Since each RUP iteration results in an executable part of an application, performance testing can start as soon as the first iteration. Johnsen notes, "The consultants from Sun Professional Services trained our engineers in the RUP methodology, which helped us stay on track to deliver the product in a timely manner. And now that our IT staff has both a practical and theoretical understanding of the RUP methodology, we will likely be able to speed development cycles of projects in the future."

Along the way, IDP and Sun overcame the challenges that can come with any first-time collaboration and built a strong working relationship that promises to continue delivering benefits well into the future. Other technology providers played smaller roles in the development and enhancement of WEB ePOST. For instance, Cap Gemini Ernst & Young subcontracted with Sun to design the graphical user interface. EOS, a Danish IT start-up, developed JAD'K, a Java/RMI server for credit card authorizations, which IDP used in the solution's testing phases.

After working with consultants from Sun Professional Services for more than a year, IDP engineers say they now have a strong understanding of Java technology—and this has opened the doors to other revenue streams—namely, joint professional services. In addition to being a product company, IDP offers consulting, systems integration, and even custom-development of WEB ePOST's Java applet. "There is an opportunity for us to offer consulting services to our installed base," says Paul Donohoe, director of product management and professional services at IDP. "And Sun Professional Services may be able to play a role in this future, as well."

10.3 Solution Analysis: The Lifecycle of a Hybrid Letter

The way in which hybrid mail is created by the end user is quite simple: A company or organization visits a participating postal operator's site and registers its name, address, credit card information or other payment method, and then downloads the Java applet to run WEB ePOST. This large applet carries a variety of functionalities, including calculating mailing costs and previewing copies of the letter before shipping.

After creating a document, the user starts the applet from a Web browser with a built-in Java virtual machine (VM) and enters various criteria, such as recipients, paper choice, speed of delivery and envelope format, which are then sent to iPlanet Web Server. It routes the file to the business-logic tier, where a Java servlet running on iPlanet Application Server prepares the document for delivery, inserts the appropriate addresses, and sends a copy back to the user for review. This process is repeated until the user is satisfied and a final version of the letter is ready internally; it is then sent over the Web to the postal operator's system for processing and delivery.

The Java servlet has four primary functions: managing communication between the user and the application server; communicating with the UNIX-based application server that renders JPEG images from HML documents with embedded Postscript files and passes these back to the applet for preview; storing Postscript documents on the file system; and calling up stateless session EJB components, which keep track of users actions with WEB ePOST in real time. IDP also worked with Sun Professional Services to map several Data Access Objects (DAO), which are responsible for inserting data into the Oracle8*i* database, handling searches of items end users save and managing the JDBC connection to the database tier.

The EJB components verify users and credit cards, maintain their security, authorize special functions, and register completed transactions. As soon as a transaction is validated, WEB ePOST notifies the end user using the Java applet, which also provides document previewing. In addition, IDP offers an administration system that can be hosted at a customer's location. The system essentially transfers HTML forms via JSPs from the postal operator's system to a company's site, enabling new users to create profiles, existing users to change names and addresses, and hybrid mail jobs to be tracked—all accomplished while staying within their companies' firewalls.

WEB ePost users fall into three primary categories. There are those who create and send letters (the end users). There are administrators, who run the WEB ePOST server in their environment (IDP's licensees). And there are help-desk personnel who monitor usage. All of them use JSP pages that generate HTML forms, which keep track of information and enable users to conduct their respective administrative tasks.

Since postal mail has a history of security and reliability—"through rain, sleet, or snow"—IDP wanted to bring these high standards to its Web-enabled system. WEB ePOST uses secure sockets layer (SSL) encryption, which encrypts the transmission of the document from the client to the application server. All the data retrieved from the client, such as credit card numbers and passwords, is encrypted with up to 128-bit algorithmic technology, so it can traverse the Internet securely.

In summary, a transaction that goes through the WEB ePOST infrastructure tiers follows these steps:

Step 1: A new user registers at the WEB ePOST site and downloads a self-installing .exe file. This file contains the Java applet and a printer driver, which is installed on the hard disk and can be launched from a browser, or directly from the printer driver.

Step 2: The Java applet connects to the site where a Java servlet, working in conjunction with an EJB, authenticates the user.

Step 3: Users write a letter or attach a Postscript file, then select recipients from Outlook, ODBC or LDAP, or write them manually. Users then select a registered payment option, letter option and delivery option.

Step 4: The Java applet creates a preview of the letter and sends it back to the user for approval. Prior to being sent, the electronic letter is wrapped in HML. The letter is then routed to the appropriate stateless sessions EJB.

Step 5: The user selects appropriate delivery options, service types, payment options and confirms the transaction via the Java applet.

Step 6: An EJB receives the letter, authorizes the transaction through credit card payment servers and places the electronic letter into the WEB ePOST server for delivery.

10.3.1 Future of Hybrid Mail

IDP and Sun have only scratched the surface of this nascent market—a world of opportunity awaits. According to the "Hybrid Mail in the Third Millennium" report,[1] the potential of hybrid mail messaging (in computer mail processing mar-

---

[1]   Source: Mackintel Ltd., 1999 published report.

kets) will increase more than 460 percent between 1998 and 2005. And thanks to an aggressive first-mover advantage, IDP stands to become the de facto standard hybrid message management system provider. Moreover, it is not just the technology that gives the company its edge; rather, it is also the fact that IDP was heavily involved in the development of HML (Hybrid Mail Language), which was approved by the European Committee for Standardization (CEN) in January 2001. IDP serves as a technical advisor to the committee.

HML is a superset of Extensible Markup Language (XML), the standard protocol for describing Web documents. J2EE technology defines a set of descriptors in XML, making it easy to implement customizable components and to develop custom tools. HML allows applications to exchange mail or messages according to a standard, the "electronic envelope." In this way, any document format can be exchanged between systems.

Prior to being sent, an electronic letter is wrapped in an HML formatted file so that it can be sent over the Internet and read by the receiving Web server. However, not all XML—or in this case, HML—documents are created equal. XML uses HTML-style tags not only to format documents but to identify the kinds of information in documents so that it can be reformatted for use in other documents, as well as used in information processing. For example, lawyers have a very different way of describing a particular event than, say, a marketing professional. HML is already being adopted by major postal operators as the industry's standard document type definition (DTD).

"IDP has been a major driver in defining hybrid-mail language," says Olsen. "We have helped introduce HML as the interface language between Java technology–based transactions, developed by Sun Professional Services, and the back-office system that we developed." Messages are collected in WEB ePOST and transferred from the customer to the application server using HML. These messages are then routed by an appropriate EJB component through the JDBC layer to the back-end systems. Explains Johnsen, "HML gives us the flexibility to draw from, create, and exchange documents in multiple formats. That means our customers can count on WEB ePOST to support most business or personal communications."

10.4 A Multitiered Architecture

IDP hosts the servers and handles the transactions that flow through Web ePOST. The platform infrastructure reflects a multitier architecture: Web server, application server, database server, and directory server. There are industrial-strength printing servers connected to the infrastructure, as well. Corporations also have the option of hosting the application in their own IT infrastructures. Physically, all these servers can run anywhere—even inside a corporation's firewalls.

To Web-enable IDP's ePOST application, IDP and Sun Professional Services utilized three different EJBs—administration-service bean, customer-service bean, and hybrid-mail service bean. Each of these EJBs is a stateless session bean running on iPlanet Application Server, which is based on the EJB specifications. The use of stateless session beans provides IDP with high scalability, since a user's request can be executed in any application server process in such a replicated system. Two subsequent requests from the same user can be executed in two different processes on two different hosts. So if the WEB ePOST licensee has integrated the solution into a clustered environment, the application server always directs requests to the least-loaded host. "With stateless session beans," notes Hansen, "our customers can accommodate as many hosts as they need, without affecting user response time." The initial production hardware comprises any number of Sun Enterprise 450 servers running Solaris 7 (the number of servers is dictated by the WEB ePOST licensee).

The use of iPlanet Application Server and iPlanet Web Server was recommended by Sun Professional Services—a recommendation IDP didn't take lightly. iPlanet Application Server is a J2EE technology–compatible e-commerce platform that extends the reliability and portability of the J2EE environment through its failover capability, container-managed persistence, and transaction monitoring. iPlanet Web Server features a high-performance Java application platform that supports Java Servlet extensions, JSPs, and in-process, plugable Java virtual machines. "We're pleased with this recommendation because together, these iPlanet solutions provide a reliable backbone to support our J2EE technology–based solution. As we grow our customer base, and in turn the transaction volume, we're confident we have a platform that will keep pace with us," notes Johnsen.

Each EJB handles requests from one of the various types of clients: hybrid-mail administration, customer administration and postal office administration. The EJBs authorize the request from the client, based on the user ID and password obtained during log in. They then read and write to the database. The hybrid-mail EJB also communicates with the credit card verification and payment server provided by the WEB ePOST licensee.

The GUIs for the customer administration, postal office administration, operator and help desk are provided through HTML pages generated by JSPs. Of course, these pages reside on the application server, along with servlets and EJBs. JSP pages consist mainly of forms and tables filled with data from the database. Each of WEB ePOST's 111 JSP pages provides unique functionality.

- The postal administrator can view and modify customer data, as well as register new customers.

- The operator can view logs and update application-server configurations, and the help desk can view customer data. The operator and help desk are not included in the Java applet; they are functions accessible through HTML pages for use by the postal organization or other IDP customer.

- The customer administrator can view and modify select data concerning the company, and can also add new users from the same company.

In terms of tiers, Web ePOST's underpinnings were distributed along the following lines as shown in Figure 10.2:

- Client tier: Java applet and Web browser running from a PC. The Java applet presents the graphical user interface, integrates with address databases, calculates shipping costs, and lets users send HML files with embedded postscript.

- Web tier: A client PC running Netscape, Microsoft Internet Explorer, or another Web browser downloads the Java applet. iPlanet Web server also resides on this tier. Firewalls and SSL encryption provide security.

- Business-logic tier: Java Servlets and JSPs running on iPlanet Application Server powered by two Sun Enterprise 450 servers. Java Servlets perform previews, store HML documents on the file system, and locate stateless session EJBs using Java Native Directory Interface (JNDI). JSPs consist mainly of generated HTML forms and tables with data read from the database using DAO, enabling postal operators to update application-server configurations.

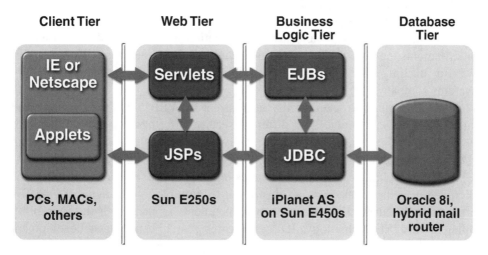

Figure 10.2 IDP Application Architecture

EJBs, JDBC, and a Postscript parser/JPEG renderer, to parse Postscript files and render them as JPEG images, run on Sun Enterprise 450 servers. EJBs authorize requests from the client, read/write to the database via DAO, and communicate with the credit card verification and payment server. JDBC 2.0–compliant Oracle OCI drivers are used to retrieve information stored in Oracle8*i* for the requesting EJB component.

- Database tier: When iPlanet Application Server receives an HML letter, a process is initiated that takes the HML document and places it in a directory on Oracle's server, a Sun Enterprise 450. EJBs put a record in a certain table, called hybrid-mail transact, and also trigger payment functions. A UNIX-based process then goes into the transact table to check for new print jobs, as well as for timestamps. If jobs exist, the process sends a call out that triggers the printing process. Also residing on the database tier is JAD'K, the credit card authorization application that IDP used when testing WEB ePOST.

10.5   A Bounty of Benefits

After a little more than a year of development and testing, IDP's Web-enabled hybrid mail system is up and running, and will eventually handle multiple channel delivery protocols, such as SMS, WAP, HTML, XML, and PDF. Several postal operators have already licensed WEB ePOST. "The driving principle behind all our development efforts is interoperability," explains Johnsen. "And it has paid off."

J2EE technology gives IDP flexibility and ease of use. The company expects that licensees will market the solution for direct marketing, business-to-business communications, and other needs. And IDP envisions selling its solution to other ASPs for even greater penetration into corporations, while growing sales revenues outside its core base of postal operators.

"Since WEB ePOST is an Internet application, it can be used in a variety of environments, not just within the postal industry," Donohoe says. "We are on our way to fulfilling our vision of really being an end-to-end electronic messaging systems company."

IDP also wants to leverage the Java applet in WEB ePOST by reusing and customizing an appearance for different service offerings on the Internet. For example, an oil company could conceivably place privately labeled kiosks using IDP's Java applet in its gas stations to offer simple messaging. Vacationing travelers, while pumping gas, could send a quick letter, postcard, or if a digital camera is mounted near the kiosk, even a self-portrait to multiple family members—delivered either electronically or as a paper document. In fact, with the reusability inherent in J2EE technology, IDP anticipates that it can reduce development

Value Chain Benefit ➞	IDP	IDP's Customers	End User
Faster Application Development	●		
Revenue Opportunities	●	●	
Improved Productivity	●	●	●
Cost Reduction	●	●	●
Strengthened Relationships		●	●

Figure 10.3 The WEB ePOST Value Chain, from Postal Providers to End Users

cycles for future J2EE technology-based applications significantly—so it can get a head start in meeting the needs of a wide range of industries.

At any rate, a postal operator can play the role of message manager, taking these documents and other communications and delivering them using IDP's back-end infrastructure. In turn, this will further solidify the place and importance of postal operators in today's new economy. "An oil company may want this kiosk to be branded with its own brand, which we can easily do with Java technology," explains Donohoe. "But in the back end, there is a postal connection."

Kiosks are not the only interface; IDP engineers are looking at wireless implementations, too. Many J2EE technology–based application servers also support wireless communication forms. All of which has IDP excited. "We could use a lot of our existing components for that application," says Olsen. "Because of this, coupled with the knowledge transfer we received from Sun Professional Services, future development could proceed more quickly."

The hope is that an international business traveler sitting in an airport will be able to make a wireless connection to the Internet and send a hybrid letter to anyone in the world using his or her laptop computer or personal digital assistant. "Our vision includes both wired and wireless connectivity, bringing greater efficiency to the way people do business," explains Donohoe. "And the flexibility of J2EE technology is key to evolving WEB ePOST to meet ever-changing needs of consumers and businesses."

For more information about iPlanet, visit http://www.iplanet.com. For the IDP Web site, visit http://www.idp.dk.

Oracle/CERN

About the Contributors

Derek Mathieson is project leader and principal software engineer, at CERN. Mathieson has a BSc (Honours) in electronics and computer science.

Jurgen De Jonghe is a software architect at CERN, and holds a MSc degree in computer science/applied mathematics.

Anand Ramakrishnan is the principal product manager for the Oracle9*i* Application Server, at Oracle Corporation. He holds an MS degree in management science and engineering.

Ellen Barnes is the senior technical editor, server technologies, at Oracle Corporation. She holds a degree in psychology.

Kuassi Mensah is the group product manager for Server Technologies Java Products at Oracle Corporation. His academic background includes post-graduate computer science studies at the Programming Institute, Paris-VI University

Mike De Groot is the software development director of business components for Java at Oracle Corporation. DeGroot holds a BS in information and computer science from the University of California, Irvine.

Moe Fardoost is the group manager of Oracle9*i* Application Server marketing at Oracle Corporation. Fardoost holds a BS in electrical and electronic engineering.

Roel Stalman is the Director of Product Management, Oracle Corporation, and holds an MS in Computer Science

Sudhakar Ramakrishnan is the principal marketing manager of Oracle9*i* Application Server, for Oracle Corporation. Ramakrishnan holds an MS in computer science.

CHAPTER 11

CERN Simplifies Document Handling Using the Oracle Application Server

CONSEIL Européen pour la Recherche Nucléaire, more commonly known as CERN is the world's leading particle physics research laboratory. Some 6,500 scientists, half the particle physicists in the world, use the facilities at CERN. The business of CERN is pure science, exploring the most fundamental questions of nature. The tools of the laboratory, particle accelerators and detectors, are among the largest and most complex scientific instruments in the world. CERN is currently working on the construction of a new 27-kilometer accelerator, the Large Hadron Collider (LHC), due for completion in 2005.

When CERN was established in the 1950s, it set the standard for European Collaboration in science—with the LHC, it is set to become the first truly global laboratory. However, as with many businesses in the current economic climate, CERN is expected to continue to grow, even though staff levels are planned to shrink in the coming years—in essence, achieving higher productivity with fewer resources. One way of accomplishing this is to use fast, efficient, and streamlined organization-wide electronic workflow.

11.1 EDH Application

Among computer scientists, CERN is more often remembered as the birthplace of the World Wide Web (Tim Berners-Lee and Robert Cailliau) than an organization that has been awarded several Nobel Prizes in physics. In this context, it is important to remember that the World Wide Web was developed to meet the needs of CERN physicists, collaborating and exchanging information in a global physics community. Similarly, an organization-wide e-business system at CERN must be available and must meet the requirements of the physicists and engineers working or collaborating with CERN, whether they are on the CERN site in Geneva or working from their home institutes in California, Moscow, or Delhi. Currently, CERN collaborates with more than 500 such institutes around the world.

CERN's internal e-business application is known as EDH (electronic document handling). EDH currently has more than 5,000 active users, with more than 1,000 users a day. An electronic document is processed every 20 seconds. The system is multilingual, uses a Java servlet architecture for its Web tier, and runs Oracle Workflow as the routing engine. Oracle Workflow enables information to be routed according to a set of business rules.

CERN uses EDH to

- Purchase any of 16,000 standardized items from the CERN *Stores Catalog*

- Create purchase requisitions that are processed and transmitted to any of CERN's 20,000 suppliers or any new supplier in the world

- Create requests to import or export goods

- Create requests to attend a course from CERN's on-site training catalogue

- Create requests to attend external training, conferences, or other events

- Create requests for vacation time

- Create requests for overtime compensation

- Create requests for additional human resources for a project or activity

These tasks, using EDH, generate about 100,000 electronic forms a year. Paper forms are no longer used for any of these tasks. Other smaller, low-volume procedures are also under consideration for integration into EDH.

EDH understands the structure, roles, and responsibilities of the organization and can employ this knowledge to accelerate procedures even further. For example, EDH never sends a document to someone who is absent. If a document is not signed within a given timeframe, it is automatically routed to a deputy or someone else with equivalent responsibilities in that domain. Oracle Workflow also offers tools to show and edit the workflow graphically, thereby fostering streamlining and standardization of procedures across the organization. In addition, Oracle Workflow supports both synchronous and asynchronous processes, and enables post-notification by allowing functions to be executed. The net result is that the average processing time of an e-document takes less than a few hours, compared with days, if not weeks, for the previous paper process.

11.1.1 Why Move to J2EE Technologies?

Using servlets with JDBC, access to a database can easily serve dynamic content. But this approach lacks scalability if the Web applications become more complex or the client base grows. A key performance measure for the Web is the speed with which content is served to users. Caching is one of the key strategies to improve performance. Oracle addresses this problem with its Web cache to improve the application server performance, and a database cache to improve the performance in the database tier. In addition, the Internet calls for rapidly changing user interfaces, making it important to clearly separate the business logic tier from the presentation tier.

More particularly, our goal is to decrease the complexity of application development by using the system-level services of the Enterprise JavaBeans container, including security, resource pooling, persistence, concurrency, and transactional integrity. By acquiring off-the-shelf components, the sheer amount of code developed in-house is reduced, at the same time increasing internal reusability within the confines of a standardized component model. Use of frameworks enables developers to productively build application components out of smart, reusable parts. Oracle offers a comprehensive component framework and tool set for writing server-side business applications. Called Oracle Business Components for Java, the framework significantly simplifies the construction of Java- and XML-based application components.

The J2EE platform thus emerges as an industry standard, and many vendors provide solutions in the area of UML tools, integrated development environments (IDEs), EJB application servers, monitoring tools, and so on. By using the best products that come out of this competitive environment, and by adhering to standard, well-documented J2EE technologies, the goal of CERN is to reduce the learning curve for its new team members, allowing them to quickly integrate into their projects. Because CERN is partly a training facility, it has a particularly large turnover of temporary student programmers who work on an application for only a short time.

11.1.2 Why Use EJB?

Although the EDH application has existed since 1990, a complete rewrite using Java technology was begun in 1998, with the relatively new EJB specification in mind. At the time, few commercial application servers implemented the EJB specification, and those that did were thought to be insufficiently scaleable for the relatively large user population at CERN. To ensure forward compatibility, CERN implemented a component architecture closely following the EJB specification, with the intention of migrating to fully compatible EJB components once commercial implementations of the technology matured. The EDH development team believes this maturation is now taking place.

11.1.3   Why Choose Oracle J2EE Products?

Given the existing business relationship between CERN and Oracle, it seemed logical to start the J2EE journey at Oracle. Although the multivendor support is a major argument in favor of J2EE, Oracle's offering is a compelling choice, because Oracle offers products for all J2EE tiers.

Oracle9*i* offers a unified Java-XML-SQL environment for both the Oracle9*i* database and Oracle9*i* Application Server (Oracle9*i*AS). From native data storage (such as XML documents) to standards-based data access (such as JDBC) to common APIs for complex application processing (such as messaging, queuing, transactions, multimedia and file management, online analytical processing, and data warehousing), the three languages can be used in combination to write applications. This approach ensures that applications rich in these languages will never suffer from interlanguage incompatibilities, and it allows Oracle to ensure optimal performance and scalability.

Furthermore, Oracle is uniquely positioned to distribute the logical tiers of a distributed application over different physical tiers, depending on the operational requirements. Oracle9*i*AS and Oracle9*i* database have a complete implementation of the J2EE enterprise APIs, including servlet, EJB, JSP, XML, JMS, and JNDI. Oracle9*i*AS builds on Apache's extensible architecture by adding modules to extend the core functionality. Oracle9*i*AS Web Cache provides cacheability rules for both static and dynamic content created by J2EE components. Oracle9*i*AS intelligently distributes loads across multiple servers and provides no single point of failure using its sophisticated listener-dispatcher architecture, Web cache load balancing, and architecture of Oracle HTTP Server. In particular, all logical tiers can be collapsed into the Oracle9*i* database featuring EJB 1.1 support and an integrated servlet engine. Because the EJBs reside inside the database in this scenario, access to the database can be highly optimized. In multitier configurations, EJBs run in Oracle9*i*AS. Servlets running in the Oracle Enterprise Java Engine have direct in-memory access to EJBs and benefit from a shorter-path JDBC driver. Another boost in performance can be expected from the ability to compile the final production code into native code that gets linked dynamically with the database.

11.2 The EDH Component Model

As mentioned previously, the existing EDH architecture is based on the EJB specification, but it does not use any commercial EJB container. Figure 11.1 summa-
rizes the main components of the existing EDH architecture.

11.2.1 EDH Document Servlet

Each electronic document in EDH has its own specific Document servlet. The role
of the document servlet is that of a dispatcher. It uses a cookie stored on the user's
browser to identify the user's `ServletExecutor` instance and then forwards the
call directly to it.

11.2.2 EDH ServletExecutor

The `ServletExecutor` is the component that holds the conversational state information about the current interaction. An instance of a `ServletExecutor` exists
for each open document on the user's screen. Its role is to hold references to the

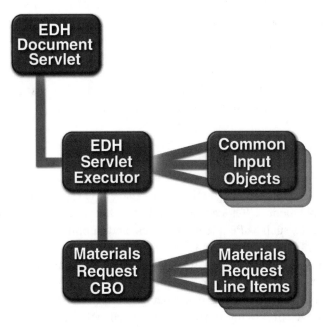

Figure 11.1 CERN's Electronic Document Handling
Application Architecture

common business object (CBO) representing the document being edited and its user interface components, and to coordinate their activity. Oracle EJE addresses the scalability of such stateful components with a virtual machine architecture that reduces the response time by making sure each session perceives its own *virtual* Java virtual machine, Java global variables, threads, and garbage collector. The underlying runtime supplies the needed scalability. This enables the virtual machine to efficiently perform memory management, provide a low session footprint, and perform advanced garbage collection.

11.2.3 Common Business Objects

Within the EDH application, the equivalent of an Entity Bean is the Common Business Object (CBO). This object effectively provides an object representation of one of the application's business objects—for example, a purchase order, a person, or a currency. CBOs provide `getX` and `setX` methods for their properties, implement access control, have the ability to be persisted to the EDH database, and implement any necessary business logic (such as calculation of totals) and business rules (such as requiring mandatory fields, permitting only allowed types of cost center, and so on).

In accordance with the EJB specification, the application gets its CBOs from a Home interface through its `findByX` and/or `create()` methods. An EJB client first obtains a reference to the home interface with the Java Naming and Directory Interface (JNDI) mechanism. Oracle EJE behaves like a namespace server by implementing a JNDI interface resulting in location transparency. This is particularly useful when changes to the server environment must be made without seriously disrupting the client. In addition, the namespace has fast access to indexed entries in the cache, resulting in performance improvement.

11.2.4 Common Input Objects

The Common Input Objects (CIOs) are a set of classes responsible for building the user interface for our Web applications. Each CIO represents a single data type within the document. CIOs can be Numbers, Dates, and Text, as well as more-complex objects, such as People, Currencies, and Suppliers.

Within an EDH document, a CIO instance is created for each field. When the HTML form is submitted, the CIO is responsible for parsing the data from the user and performing some basic validation, such as maximum string length for Text input objects, or verifying if the person exists for Person input objects. One of the advantages in moving to frameworks such as Oracle Business Components for Java is that it provides mechanisms for defining, implementing, and executing validation logic in the business logic tier. The validation framework provides a consistent programming model that hides internal implementation details.

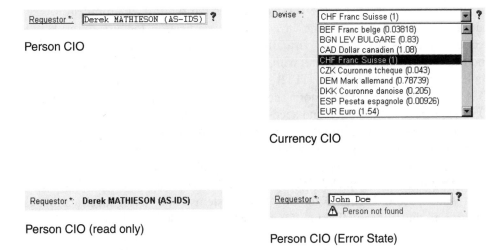

Figure 11.2 Generating a User Interface Employing Common Input Objects

When a response is sent back to the user, the CIO is capable of creating an HTML representation of its value that can be substituted into an HTML template.

Figure 11.2 illustrates two CIOs in operation. As you can see, the CIO can represent itself in a manner that is appropriate to the data type and can also take into account the user's preferred language (the currency CIO is rendered in French). Oracle supports one of the richest sets of multilanguage character support in the market, incorporating many open and vendor-specific character sets within the database. Among the standards supported by Oracle is UTF8, or Unicode 2.1. Thus database utilities and error messages, sort order, date, time, monetary, numeric, and calendar conventions automatically adapt to the native language and locale.

11.2.5 Runtime Scenario

Two classes, a `DocumentServlet` and a `ServletExecutor`, provide the user interface to the common business objects.

A single instance of the `DocumentServlet` exists for each type of document and is shared by all users. Its job is to find the appropriate `ServletExecutor` for the user and forward the requests to it.

A `ServletExecutor` instance is created for each open document window during the session. The job of the `ServletExecutor` is to interpret the information in the user's request and make the appropriate calls to the CBO. Once the `ServletExecutor` has processed the entire request, it then creates the response HTML by substituting placeholders in an HTML template with the values from the now updated CBO.

The Oracle Servlet Engine (OSE) provides the runtime environment to execute servlets. OSE supports the Java servlet specification for processing HTTP requests. OSE is designed for virtually unlimited linear scalability and supports thousands of concurrent users, with an extremely low session footprint. The mod_ose plugs into the Oracle HTTP server architecture and routes requests to the OSE. The OSE offers in-memory access to EJBs, enabling better performance. OSE supports authentication and access control, as required by the servlet specification. Servlets running in OSE efficiently use the Oracle9i application Server data cache, running in the same process space as the data cache SQL engine.

The OracleJSP implementation is highly portable across server platforms and servlet environments. OracleJSP can run in any servlet environment that complies with version 2.0 or higher of the Sun Microsystems Java servlet specification. In addition to the JSP specification, OracleJSP supports SQLJ programming in JSP scriptlets, and JML tags to support XSL transformations within a JSP page. OracleJSP has been ported on all Oracle servers and tools: Oracle9i, Oracle9iAS, and Oracle JDeveloper.

Figure 11.3 illustrates the sequence of events and how each object interacts when a user submits a form.

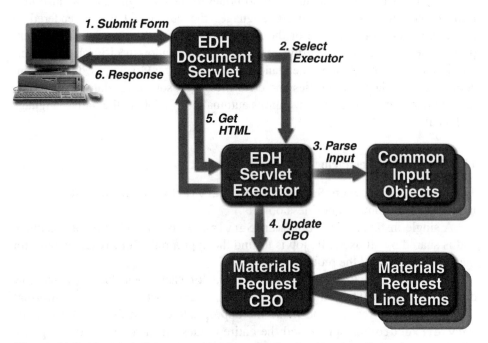

Figure 11.3 Electronic Document Handling Application Runtime Scenario

As shown in Figure 11.3, the steps in processing a form are

1. When the user submits the HTML form, the `DocumentServlet` uses the session cookie to identify the correct `ServletExecutor` instance. If there is no `ServletExecutor` for the document in the current session, the servlet creates a new instance.

2. The `DocumentServlet` then calls the `ServletExecutor` so that it can process the user's input.

3. The `ServletExecutor` first makes a call to each of the CIOs so that they have an opportunity to interpret the user's input.

4. If the CIO successfully interprets the form data, the `ServletExecutor` then calls the corresponding `setX` method on the CBO. The CBO either accepts the new value or throws a `ConstrainedPropertyException`, indicating that the value is not valid.

   If either the parsing of the user input or the `setX` method call of the CBO failed, then the CIO is set to error state, which appears to the user as an error message (see Figure 11.4).

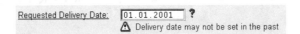

Figure 11.4　Date Input Object Showing Error Message

After all the CIOs have been processed, the `ServletExecutor` returns control to the document servlet.

5. The `DocumentServlet` then makes a call to the `getHTML()` method of the `ServletExecutor` that generates the HTML representation of the document by using an HTML template.

6. Finally, the `DocumentServlet` sends the resulting HTML back to the user.

11.3　Migration to EJB: First Steps

As a first step in the migration to the EJB component model, one of the simpler CBOs was re-implemented as an EJB component.

The Currency CBO was chosen because it is a self-contained bean with a simple interface, without dependencies on other parts of EDH, and is based on a single table.

The Currency CBO is defined according to Figure 11.5

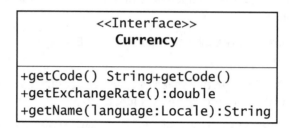

Figure 11.5 The Currency Business Object
Interface

All the CBOs are defined as interfaces with an underlying implementation class. It was designed this way so that the implementation could be replaced at a later date, without having to change any client code.

The Currency CBO uses only a single database table. Each instance of a Currency CBO maps to a single row in the EDHCUR currency table (see Figure 11.6).

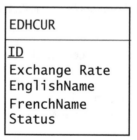

Figure 11.6 The Currency Table

The CurrencyHome provides the definition of the finder methods (see Figure 11.7). Because the Currency CBO is read-only, there is neither a create() method in the Home interface, nor setXXX() methods in the actual bean. Within a servlet, the program obtains a reference to a class that implements the Currency-Home interface by calling the findByName("X") method of the HomeHome interface.

The HomeHome interface performs the same role as the lookup() method in a JNDI context. The implementation does not make use of JNDI, but instead

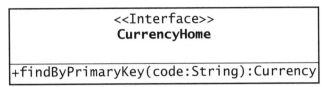

Figure 11.7 The CurrencyHome interface

employs `Class.forName()` to obtain a reference to an implementation of the `Home` interface.

The `CurrencyService` supplies the interface to the relational database (see Figure 11.8). As a measure to improve the maintainability of EDH, all the SQL for a particular CBO was located in a single class, rather than spread over the code. By grouping together all the SQL into one place, it is easier to identify which statements need to be changed if the underlying tables change their definition (as they have done in the past for tables provided by third-party products). JDBC is preferable for dynamic SQL, and SQLJ for static SQL. Developers often use SQLJ because it gives the ability to embed static SQL in Java code, thereby raising the level of abstraction, resulting in increased productivity. The Oracle JDBC drivers support the JDBC 2.0 standard. They also provide support for Oracle-defined extensions for Oracle datatypes, connection pooling, and distributed transactions.

Figure 11.8 The CurrencyService Class

11.3.1 The Currency Bean

In updating the application to an EJB implementation, the `Currency` and `CurrencyHome` interfaces were kept, but were implemented using EJBs. The remainder of the EDH application could then conveniently be used to test the new EJB implementation. Eventually, the interface could be extended to also allow updates of the exchange rate (restricted to the accounting department).

A wizard in Oracle JDeveloper allows for the creation of a Container-Managed Persistence (CMP) Entity Bean by pointing to the existing currency table, EDHCUR, and indicating the primary key and which columns need persisting. By default, the field names of the EJB correspond to the column names in the table, but you can override this. With this information, the wizard creates the remote interface (Currency.java), the home interface (CurrencyHome.java), its implementation (which was called CurrencyCMPBean.java), and the standard deployment descriptor (Currency.xml), as well as the vendor-specific descriptor (Currency_oracle.xml).

Oracle EJE provides a hook to plug in custom Object Relational (O/R) mapping through the Persistence Storage Interface (PSI). This is a Java API that allows container-managed persistence (CMP) providers, such as Oracle Business Components for Java, to manage O/R mappings from entity beans to database entities. You can use JDeveloper's wizards to design an O/R mapping that Oracle Business Components for Java manages with the PSI. An entity Bean class also needs a primary key, corresponding to one or more columns of the table, that allows instances to be retrieved using the findByPrimaryKey() method. CMP beans can also make use of other business component classes: domains that allow EJB fields to be based on Oracle object types, and secondary-view objects corresponding to EJB finder methods. Using the EJB/Oracle9i Deployment Object Wizard in Oracle JDeveloper, CMP persistence can be added to the entity bean.

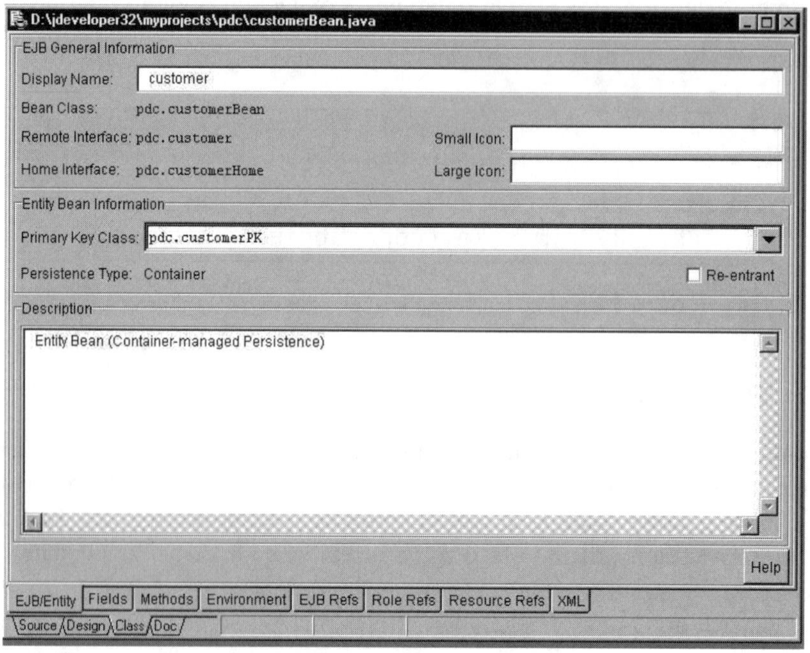

Figure 11.9   Oracle JDeveloper EJB Designer Screen

The following code excerpt shows the method declarations for the Currency.java interface.

```
public interface Currency  extends javax.ejb.EJBObject
{
    public String getName(Locale lang) throws java.rmi.RemoteException;
    public double getExchangeRate()    throws java.rmi.RemoteException;
    public void setExchangeRate(double newExchangeRate)
                                       throws java.rmi.RemoteException;
...
```

In the following excerpt from Currency-oracle.xml, the Oracle-specific deployment descriptor mainly defines the mapping of the Currency bean (in the package cern.base) to its JNDI name ais/base/Currency. In addition, it specifies the CMP provider (here the simple reference implementation PSI-RI was used) and the mapping of the columns in the database table to their field names.

```
<oracle-descriptor>
    <mappings>
      <ejb-mapping>
      <ejb-name>Currency</ejb-name>
      <jndi-name>ais/base/Currency</jndi-name>
</ejb-mapping>
</mappings>
<persistence-provider>
    <description> demo persistence manager </description>
    <persistence-name>psi-ri</persistence-name>
    <persistence-deployer>
       oracle.aurora.ejb.persistence.ocmp.OcmpEntityDeployer
    </persistence-deployer>
</persistence-provider>
<persistence-descriptor>
    <description> simple persistence-mapping  </description>
    <ejb-name>Currency</ejb-name>
    <persistence-name>psi-ri</persistence-name>
    <psi-ri>
       <schema>demo</schema>
       <table>edhcur</table>
       <attr-mapping>
          <field-name>CurrencySymbol</field-name>
          <column-name>CUR</column-name>
```

```
    </attr-mapping>
    <attr-mapping>
        <field-name>EnglishDesc</field-name>
        <column-name>ELG</column-name>
    </attr-mapping>
    <attr-mapping>
        <field-name>ExchangeRate</field-name>
        <column-name>EXG</column-name>
    </attr-mapping>
    ...
```

The EJB designer in JDeveloper can be used to further define the remote and home interfaces. After this, business logic is added to the bean implementation. For example, in the setExchangeRate() you could check whether the new value is within the same range of the existing value, to reduce data-entry errors. The getName() method was also added to support more languages in the future, without changing the interface. After this, the bean is ready to be deployed to the Oracle container.

Because Container-Managed Persistence was chosen, the container automatically invokes a persistence manager on behalf of the bean, without any extra programming to load or store the data in the database. In addition, you automatically get many CMP-only finder methods to perform a SQL query against the persistent data table (findAllCurrencys takes a string that denotes the "where" clause of a SQL query). Assuming the CurrencyHome, curHome, was obtained, all Currencies can be listed (Collections are not currently supported).

```
Currency cur;
Enumeration e = curHome.findAllCurrencys("");
while(e.hasMoreElements())
{
    cur = (Currency) e.nextElement();
    System.out.println (" name = " +  cur.getName(Locale.ENGLISH)+
                        " has rate = " + cur.getExchangeRate() );
}
```

11.3.2 The Converter Bean

With the Currency Bean defined, a facility was added to convert any amount from one currency to another through a converter Stateless Session Bean in the same *cern.base* package. After creating the bean through the appropriate wizard in JDeveloper, the interface files, the bean implementation, and the deployment descriptors are automatically generated. The remote interface in Converter.java is

```
public interface Converter extends javax.ejb.EJBObject
{
        double convert (Currency from, Currency to, double amount)
                        throws  java.rmi.RemoteException;
}
```

Its implementation in the bean is as follows:

```
public double convert (Currency from, Currency to, double amount)
            throws java.rmi.RemoteException
{
    return ( to.getExchangeRate() / from.getExchangeRate() ) *
    amount;
}
```

After deploying to the container, you can now write the following client code.

```
// Create the currencies we want to convert from their primary key
// (ISO Code)
Currency swissFrancs = curHome.findByPrimaryKey("CHF");
Currency euro = curHome.findByPrimaryKey("EUR");

// Obtain a new Exchange Calculator from the
// ConverterHome interface convHome
Converter myXChangeCalc = convHome.create();

System.out.println("150 " + swissFrancs.getEnglishDesc() +
                " corresponds to " +
                myXChangeCalc.convert(swissFrancs, euro, 150f)
                + " " + euro.getEnglishDesc());

// Clean up neatly
myXChangeCalc.remove();
```

Which produces the following:

```
 150 Swiss Franc corresponds to 97.4 Euro.
```

11.3.3 Taking Stock

The `Currency` Entity Bean can be accessed by anyone through its JNDI name. During deployment of the EJB, access rights are set up so that exchange rates can be updated only centrally from the accounting department, with the `setExchangeRate()` method. Because the beans and the database table reside in the same database, the loading and storing of data is efficient. Any changes to the underlying database table will affect only our bean.

Any application that wants to use the `Converter` retrieves these new rates immediately. The remote `convert` method call will access the exchange rates of the two `Currency` beans that reside in the same container, and there is no further overhead.

After the first simple EJB was completed, we were ready to tackle a more complex example.

11.4   The CERN Material Request

The CERN Material Request is a Web-based electronic document that allows any of the 10,000 people working on CERN activities to purchase any of 16,000 standardized items from the *CERN Stores Catalogue*.

The Material Request document resembles almost any on-line order form, as you can see in Figure 11.10. It consists of a simple *header* that holds information about the customer, and how the goods are to be paid for, followed by one or more line items that contain quantity, description, and price fields.

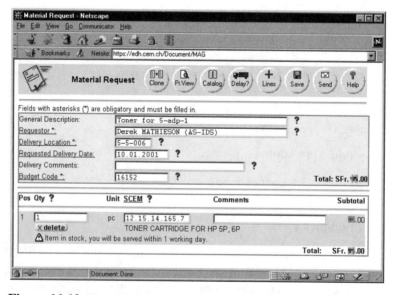

Figure 11.10 The EDH Material Request Document

One of the first steps in converting the document to EJB is to identify the existing objects:

- BudgetCode
- CatalogItem
- Currency
- Location
- MaterialRequest
- MaterialRequest Line Item
- Person

The list is divided into "simple" objects (`Person`, `Location`, `Budget Code`, and `CatalogItem`) that were converted to EJBs in the same way as were the `Currency` object, and the more complicated updatable objects.

11.4.1 The CERN Stores Catalog

Every item in the CERN catalog has a unique identification number (the SCEM[1] code) that allows for identification in the Materials Management System (MMS) database. CERN uses a commercial MMS from Baan running on an Oracle database. The CERN Stores Catalog itself is a separate custom application that provides two primary interfaces.

1. A set of tables in an Oracle database that contain all information available for every item in the catalog

2. A Web application (written in Oracle's PL/SQL programming language) that has the ability to "paste" a chosen product ID to another Web form, using Java-Script

These intefaces are designed to ensure that although CERN plans to reimplement the Web application with Java technologies, no changes will be required to this infrastructure.

The Material Request form accepts the product ID pasted into it, and then revalidates it on the server.

---

[1] Standard de Classification pour Equipement et Matériels

11.4.2 The Material Request Bean

The `MaterialRequest` bean is the primary business component in the application. It contains all the business logic for implementing our Material Request document (see Figure 11.11).

At this stage, bean-managed persistence was chosen, rather than defer it to the container because our `MaterialRequest` maps to more than one table and has relationships to other EJBs that must be persisted.

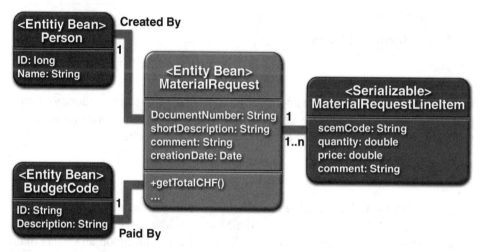

Figure 11.11 UML Diagram of `MaterialRequest` Bean and Object Associations

Persistence Methods

With bean-managed persistence, you must provide implementations for the `ejb-Create()`, `ejbLoad()`, `ejbStore()`, and all the finder methods.

The database schema for the Material Request consists of two tables, one that holds the main contents of the documents (EDHMAG), and the other that holds the individual line items (EDHMAGLI). The following is the start of the Material-Request bean implementation.

```
public class MaterialRequestBean implements EntityBean {
    transient  EntityContext ctx;

    String     shortDescription;
    String     comment;
    Date       creationDate;
```

```
ArrayList  line_items;
Person     creator;
BudgetCode budCode;

   ...
```

11.4.3   Object Relationships

The preceding Unified Modeling Language (UML) code shows that the `Material-Request` also references two other objects, a `BudgetCode` that indicates the account being charged for the purchase, and a `Person` object corresponding to the document creator. These objects will be stored as attributes of the EJB, and the relationship will be persisted by storing the primary key of the referenced objects in the `ejbStore()` method and then refinding the `Person` and `BudgetCode` objects again in the `ejbLoad()` method (see the following code) from the appropriate home interface through its `findByPrimaryKey()`. Alternatively, you can also do this in the getter method if the related object is not always needed (lazy initialization).

```
InitialContext ic  = new InitialContext();
BudgetCodeHome bch = (BudgetCodeHome)ic.lookup
                        ("java:comp/env/ejb/BudgetCode");

        budCode =  bch.findByPrimaryKey(budCodePK);
   ...
```

Notice that the Oracle EJB container does not require you to use `Portable-RemoteObject.narrow()` when obtaining object references through JNDI. Instead, a simple Java cast is all that is needed.

Business Methods

The business methods of the `MaterialRequest` are where the business-specific logic is implemented.

The business methods fall into two categories.

1. The business logic specific to the `MaterialRequest`—for example, the methods responsible for validating the consistency of the materials request, and for calculating its total value in a specific currency

2. The methods responsible for manipulating the line items

The Material Request Line Items

The `MaterialRequestLineItem` objects are simple Java language objects. They implement the `serializable` interface so that they can be transported over the network by value. The infrastructure support needed to enable this communication is performed using RMI-IIOP, which is supported in the Oracle EJE environment. The line items are not implemented as EJBs for two reasons. First, they exist only within the context of a `MaterialRequest` object, and would never be referenced outside that context. Second, EJBs are relatively heavyweight objects that consume resources on the server and, therefore, should be used only where their added capabilities (such as transactions) are required.

As the previous illustrates, `MaterialRequestLineItem` objects are contained within the `MaterialRequest`. This is achieved by extending the `ejbLoad()` and `ejbStore()` methods so that the line items are retrieved along with the header in the `ejbLoad()` method, and stored at the same time as the header in the `ejbStore()` method.

Although it doesn't currently, plans are for Oracle JDeveloper to provide support for the Unified Modeling Language. Initially, it will consist of two UML modelers: a class modeler and an activity modeler. Developers will be able to use the class modeler to generate Java classes or Oracle Business Components for Java applications. In addition, a reverse engineering facility will allow developers to build UML models from existing code. The code will be automatically synchronized with the UML model so that changes you make in the class modeler are immediately reflected in your code, and the converse.

11.5   Deployment Descriptors

Every Enterprise JavaBean component has a set of deployment descriptors contained in a deployment descriptor file in XML format. This allows a developer to specify the bean's transactional and security attributes declaratively. The container reads the deployment descriptors and enforces transaction and security constraints, state management, lifecycle, and persistence.

11.5.1   The Material Request Bean

One of the benefits of using a tool like JDeveloper is that it helps you to create the XML deployment descriptor through a series of wizards. In the case of the Material Request Bean, JDeveloper is used to create deployment descriptors for transaction control, EJB relationships, and the deployment environment.

Transaction Control

All the business methods in the `MaterialRequest` bean have the transaction attribute set to `Requires`. This means that a new transaction context will not be created if the method is called within an existing one. This will usually be the case, because the session bean controlling the Web interface will create a transaction context before calling the `MaterialRequest` bean methods. This is achieved by using the `RequiresNew` transaction attribute on the methods of the session bean.

Oracle9*i* database and the Oracle9*i*AS support declarative and programmatic transactions using JTA APIs. The Oracle J2EE container supports both JTA client and server-side demarcation and propagation of transaction contexts. Propagation of transaction context is necessary for including the invoked object into the global transaction. The JDBC drivers supplied by both Oracle9*i* database and the Oracle9*i*AS are also JTA-enabled, giving them the capability to incorporate client-side transaction demarcation.

EJB Relationships

In common with many EJB applications, the `MaterialRequest` bean must interact with other EJBs in the system. To do this in a portable way, you can define an EJB relationship within the deployment descriptor.

```
<ejb-ref>
  <description>BudgetCode Entity</description>
  <ejb-ref-name>ejb/BudgetCode</ejb-ref-name>
  <ejb-ref-type>Entity</ejb-ref-type>
  <home>cern.base.BudgetCodeHome</home>
  <remote>cern.base.BudgetCode</remote>
  <ejb-link>BudgetCodeBean</ejb-link>
</ejb-ref>
```

Doing this allows the `MaterialRequest` bean to always refer to the Budget-Code bean using the logical JNDI name "`java:comp/env/ejb/BudgetCode,`" giving a degree of independence. If the implementing class or the environment changes in some way, only the deployment descriptor would need updating, without having to modify any Java code.

The `<ejb-link>` tag in the deployment descriptor gives the name of the entity bean. (See the following code, which is part of an Oracle-specific deployment descriptor) Currently, Oracle implements this differently from the EJB1.1 standard. In this case, the name relates to a mapping entry in the vendor-specific deployment descriptor that maps the name of an EJB to a specific JNDI path.

```
<ejb-mapping>
  <ejb-name>BudgetCodeBean</ejb-name>
  <jndi-name>ais/base/BudgetCode</jndi-name>
</ejb-mapping>
```

Deployment Environment

Another important aspect of the deployment descriptor is the section that defines the EJB environment. You can use this feature to define resources that the EJB can retrieve in a platform-independent way at runtime. The following sample shows the part of the descriptor that is needed to connect to the database.

```
<resource-ref>
  <res-ref-name>jdbc/localDB</res-ref-name>
  <res-type>javax.sql.DataSource</res-type>
  <res-auth>Application</res-auth>
</resource-ref>
```

The database connection can then be obtained at runtime, using JNDI as follows.

```
if (ic == null)
  ic = new InitialContext ();

DataSource                    localDS =
     (DataSource)ic.lookup("java:comp/env/jdbc/localDB");

return localDS.getConnection();
```

How you bind the `DataSource` object to the JNDI namespace depends on the application server you are using. With Oracle9*i*, you bind a `DataSource` using the `binddS` command in the session shell, as in the following.

```
binddS  /edh/DataSource/localDB -rebind -url
     jdbc:oracle:thin:@edhdb:1521:ORCL
     -user scott -password tiger
```

Oracle provides support for transaction application failover (TAF). In case of connection failure, the application is automatically reconnected. Developers should also be aware that Oracle supports strong connection pooling to improve performance when interacting with the database.

11.5.2 The Material Request Executor (Session) Bean

The code for the Material Request Executor remains largely unchanged with the introduction of EJB. As stated previously, the Executor bean is responsible for maintaining the conversational state information. The Executor bean also plays the role of coordinator as it passes the HTTP request from the client to the user interface components and then obtains the resulting HTML stream for passing back to the browser.

This Executor bean is implemented as a stateful session bean; it has relatively few methods, and most of them simply delegate their implementation to other objects.

Transaction Control

As with many EJB applications, the session bean has responsibility for demarking transactions. This is done, in this case, mainly for efficiency. The entity beans have been defined such that all their business functions run in an existing transaction context if one exists (the Requires attribute in the application assembly section of the deployment descriptor). When users submit the HTML forms, it is possible they have updated many fields in the forms. This means that the Material Request Executor bean will make several calls to the MaterialRequest entity bean. By making all the calls part of the same transaction, the container will commit the changes to the database only after all the updates are complete.

The CatalogItem Bean

The CatalogItem bean is the representation of a product in the *Stores Catalog*. As with many the objects in the material request, it is effectively a read-only object (maintenance of the catalog is performed using a previously existing administration tool build, using Oracle Forms). One extra piece of functionality that has been added to the CatalogItem bean is an interface to the delivery lead-time information. This is provided through a stateless session bean.

Obtaining the Delivery Lead Time

For efficiency, a local copy (snapshot) of the catalog database table from the MMS database is taken nightly. This allows faster access to the catalog than through a database link, and the content of the catalog does not change often enough to require more-frequent updates. One piece of information that does change often, however, is inventory information. If an order can be fulfilled from stock, delivery happens within 24 hours. Otherwise, an order must be placed with an external supplier, which usually implies a longer delivery time. In order to give the EDH users some idea of the expected delivery time, live feedback from the MMS is required.

Minimizing the number of round trips between the business-logic tier and database tier can influence the response time. The relative percentage of read-only tables in the business-logic tier application can have an effect in the number of round trips your application has to perform. Database caches are effective in multitier environments in which databases are located on separate nodes. These caches reduce the load on the database tier by processing the most common read-only requests to data sets on the business logic tier. Oracle9iAS's database cache keeps track of queries and can intelligently route to the database cache or to the origin database, without any application code modification. Oracle9iAS database cache is not just an in-memory cache—it is also disk-backed cache. This combination does not limit the cache size of the memory footprints and also means that the cache is not "cold" immediately after a machine reboot.

This case provides a good example of where to use stateless session beans. This particular bean requires only a single method to call a stored procedure on the MMS database which returns a *value* object containing the delivery lead time and an associated comment. This feature creates a nice separation of the two systems; the ordering application (EDH) has no idea of how lead times are calculated—it knows only what service to ask (see Figures 11.12 and 11.13).

To simplify the use of this bean, a simple helper method, `getLeadTime()`, was added to the `CatalogItem` bean. This method obtains an instance of the Stores bean and calls its `getLeadTime()` method.

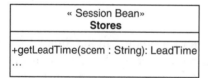

Figure 11.12 The Stores Stateless Session Bean

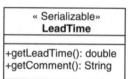

Figure 11.13 LeadTime *Value* Object

11.6 Putting It All Together

Oracle JDeveloper, a powerful interactive development environment for creating Java applications, was used to great benefit in creating this EJB application. It's wizards allowed rapid creation of the EJB components, and its integrated debugger supported debugging EJB implementations, even when running within the database. When the project-wide JNDI namespace was defined, the built-in JNDI browser allowed convenient access to entities within (see Figure 11.14).

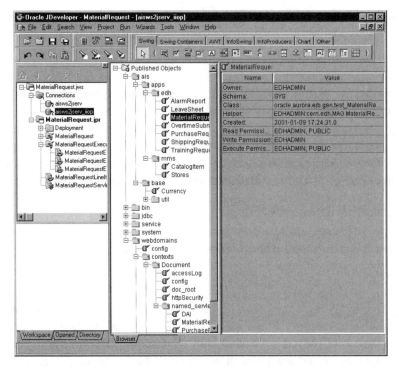

Figure 11.14 Using JDeveloper to Browse the JNDI Namespace

11.6.1 The Oracle Enterprise Java Engine (Oracle EJE)

The choice of Java virtual machine can have a large influence on the overall performance and stability of a Web application written in the Java programming language. Oracle has addressed this problem by developing its own Java virtual machine implementation that runs within each server product—Oracle9*i* database and Oracle9*i*AS. By running *within* the database, Java applications can leverage all the scalability and reliability of the database server. In the application server, Oracle EJE runs within the mid-tier SQL cache, allowing the data proximity benefits to exist in the application server as well. It is the only JVM implementation that uses the scalability of an RDBMS to be able to support thousands of concurrent users.

The developers of Oracle EJE have been able to make significant improvements compared with traditional Java virtual machines designs. For example:

- Accelerator[2]

  An innovative feature of Oracle EJE is its use of native compilation. In a server environment, the portability offered by interpreted Java bytecode is not necessary. Server applications are typically longer lived than those of a client, which means it is worthwhile investing more CPU cycles to produce highly optimized native code than could be done by a just-in-time compiler such as HotSpot. Native code compilation can significantly improve server performance.

- Generational Scavenging Garbage Collector

  Oracle EJE uses an advanced garbage collection strategy that greatly improves the memory utilization of Java applications.

  A generational garbage collector (GC) distinguishes objects by their ages in various memory spaces (new space, old space). Objects in older spaces are less frequently reclaimed than objects in newer spaces. OracleJVM allocates and manages memory at the individual session level, without any impact on other sessions, providing stable and predictable behavior (as opposed to thread-based virtual machines in which all threads stop during GC).

- Scalability

  Oracle has made significant advances in reducing the amount of memory required for a typical stateful Java session. On Oracle EJE, each session appears to be running on its own private JVM, yet the memory overhead is typically under 50K.

  Sessions are per-user memory structures used to keep the user's state across calls. Scalability in OracleEJE is enabled by the execution framework that allows a large number of sessions to be scheduled and executed by a small number of shared servers.

- Database Integration

  Because most e-business Web sites typically involve extensive use of relational databases, it is vital that Java applications efficiently access the database. By integrating the JVM within the database, the communications overhead imposed by running in an external JVM is eliminated. Oracle has

---

2   Accelerator has been used to natively compile all the standard Java classes provided with the JVM. It became available for application developers to compile their own classes in Oracle8*i* Release 3 (version 8.1.7).

also supplied a special "server" JDBC driver that can be used to directly access the database's SQL engine through the same high-performance APIs that were previously available only to PL/SQL-stored procedures.

Oracle EJE is a relatively new feature, yet the CERN team has used it successfully in production with EDH for the past two years and found it to be a very stable implementation.

11.6.2 Java Virtual Machine Overload

One area that was identified very quickly when developing EDH was the need to spread the load of the application on several Java virtual machines at the same time. This was because a single virtual machine rapidly became overloaded with only a relatively small number of users. The problem usually manifested itself with the virtual machine running out of available memory, even though it had been allocated 64 MB of RAM. This is because the virtual machine gets loaded and the garbage collector fails to keep up with the number of objects being freed. The result is that new memory allocation calls fail, even when there is plenty of free memory (albeit, all of it waiting to be marked free by the garbage collector).

In the past, this problem was solved by spreading the user population across several virtual machines (up to 20) running on the same host. This effectively created 20 garbage-collector threads, each managing a smaller pool of objects. This type of load balancing is necessary on any large-scale, Java technology-based Web application, and can significantly complicate its design.

With Oracle EJE memory architecture, this scheme is no longer necessary; in fact, each session (user) runs in its own *virtual* VM. Typical thread-based servlet engines use threads to isolate concurrent users. This becomes a bottleneck when there are a large number of users and a stateful application. True, a good design will limit session state to only the essentials; however, even this can cause resource (thread) contention within the container. Oracle's approach is to use a virtual machine architecture that isolates concurrent users. The result is less contention and a container that is more resilient to application failures within an individual session.

In addition, when many users share the same virtual machine, it is almost impossible to prevent the activity of one user from affecting the others. By using Oracle EJE, however, the resources consumed by a session can be strictly controlled using standard Oracle tools. Limits on memory, CPU, and other resources can all be set.

11.6.3 Load Balancing

Another area identified when developing EDH was the need to understand how load balancing is handled by the platform on which J2EE components are deployed. This led to an effort to understand how the server platform dealt with response times and how Oracle9*i* platform distributes connection loads across multiple servers to provide no single point of failure. Oracle's clustering technology is used to load-balance and provide fault tolerance.

Oracle supports several load balancing techniques.

- Round-Robin DNS for distributing HTTP requests across the cluster. This simple mechanism works well for Web traffic in which multiple IP addresses are assigned for the same name in the DNS name space. Requests are alternated among the hosts that are presented in rotational order.

- Use of hardware load-balancing devices and IP sprayers. In order to address the scalability problem, a router, or IP-sprayer is placed between the clients and a cluster of application servers to spread the load evenly over the nodes.

- Spawning a number of HTTP processes to handle load. Spawning multiple HTTP processes increases the ability of the server to handle thousands of client requests. Load balancing is used to distribute the load among the running instances.

- Using Oracle HTTP servers in reverse proxy mode. In this mechanism, Oracle HTTP Server can be used in front of origin servers simply configured as a reverse proxy—that is, proxy for content servers. This mechanism relieves the origin server load by taking advantage of the caching features of the proxy server.

In addition, Oracle9*i*AS offers techniques to improve the performance of servlets, EJBs, and J2EE components delivering dynamic content. J2EE components rely on HTTP for communication among Web clients and servers, and RMI-IIOP for communication among objects requesting service from each other in a distributed computing environment. In Oracle9*i*AS, different components work together to intelligently route HTTP and IIOP requests to nodes, thereby providing smooth response times and no single point of failover.

As a result, when an HTTP request arrives, the load-balancing device redistributes the load over Web caches that sit in front of the application server farm. Oracle9*i*AS Web Cache distributes the HTTP requests according to the relative capacity of each application server, which is configurable. If one of the application servers in the farm were to fail, Web Cache automatically redistributes the load among the remaining servers. Oracle9*i*AS Web Cache reduces application server load not only on Oracle9*i*AS, but on other application servers too.

Oracle HTTP Server load balances servlet processes that use the Apache JServ servlet engine. Several JServ processes can serve single or multiple instances of Oracle HTTP Server. This is done using a weighted load-balancing algorithm that can be configured, depending upon the load-handling capability of the target machines.

Oracle9*i*AS listener/dispatcher architecture provides a fault-tolerant and resilient environment, without a single point of failure. With this architecture, each physical machine has a listener on a designated port and a number of dispatchers to service J2EE container requests. The bridge in this paradigm is that each dispatcher registers itself with any number of nodes in the application server farm. Thus, if a particular node is no longer able to service requests, the listener will send incoming requests to another dispatcher on another node. It is important that an application server redirects both HTTP and IIOP requests intelligently for the purpose of load balancing. Redirection is essential to load balance at a *protocol level*. However, there is no concept of "redirection" in HTTP—but there is one for IIOP. Oracle leverages its listener/dispatcher architecture with Apache modules to provide HTTP redirection. For example, mod_ose load balances servlet requests across nodes by redirecting HTTP requests.

Oracle9*i*AS provides mechanisms to load-balance incoming requests IIOP or other network formats in multithreaded server mode. This has great benefits to enterprise components residing on multiple nodes. The listener process has the ability to load-balance across these nodes using IIOP redirection. This is possible because of the listener's ability to inspect IIOP headers for session IDs and redirect to the appropriate node. Incoming IIOP connections are redirected to dispatchers on the node with least load. The load is computed based on number of parameters, including CPU utilization, number of sessions in progress, and so on. With load balancing, you can split the load across multiple servers. The Listener process within Oracle9*i*AS performs load balancing by distributing EJB lookup across multiple application servers. Services that are located in a number of places can be grouped together by specifying a service name in the URL. Listener handles HTTP connections by transferring such requests to configured dispatchers on a node.

11.7 CERN's Experience

The EDH application has been running using an EJB-style component model since November 1998 (already old in terms of Java technology!). This design strategy has been extremely positive. The well-defined and relatively simple structure makes the architecture very effective for developing a variety of e-business applications.

CERN's experience with Oracle's EJB container has been reasonably successful. Although, the dream of complete application-server independence is tantalizingly close, most EJB containers still have some way to go before an application can be moved from one to another without modification.

Once the relatively minor incompatibilities have been resolved, application developers will be able to choose an application server based on factors such as performance, scalability, and maintenance tools.

11.7.1   Expensive Entities

In the EDH application, several entities (`Currency`, `CatalogItem`) could have been implemented as simple value objects, obtained from a session bean. It was possible to do this because they were simple.

It is important to remember that entity beans are relatively expensive in terms of resources, and they should be used only where the complicated machinery for authorization, transaction control, and persistence is necessary. Although the `CatalogItem` bean exists, it would *not* be a good choice for implementing the on-line catalog. When the user browses the catalog, the system should not have to create thousands of instances of the `CatalogItem` bean. Instead, a session bean should access the database directly. Only once the user had made a selection would a `CatalogItem` bean instance be created.

It would, of course, be preferable not to need this hybrid approach. In fact, the choice of when to use Entity Beans may eventually depend on the level of optimization of your EJB container. Hopefully, with time, the EJB specification will evolve to make this decision unnecessary (the EJB 2.0 specification does address this issue). In so doing, it will simplify application design and reduce the amount of code that needs to be aware of the actual database design.

11.7.2   Oracle EJE Accelerator

Currently, the Oracle EJE Accelerator has been available to application developers for only a short time. In recent tests, it was found that Oracle EJE Accelerator was two to three times faster at running the EDH application, compared with the previous fastest Java virtual machine (Symantec JIT).

The response time of any interactive application is a critical success factor, and using Oracle EJE Accelerator gives a significant advantage compared with EJB application servers relying on classical Java virtual machine technology.

11.7.3 Future Work

Although this is early in the life of EJB containers, EJBs appear to be an excellent way to develop highly scalable Java Web applications.

EDH is part of a larger set of AIS (Advanced Information System) applications that manage all corporate information at CERN, including financial, accounting, supplier, purchasing, materials management, HR, and payroll data. CERN aimed at acquiring 80 percent of the functionality through best-of-breed ERP suites in the various areas, all running Oracle on top of Sun servers. The remaining 20 percent was implemented at CERN for specific needs.

The integration and communication among the developed and acquired software modules is currently achieved with a foundation layer, which consists of a set of database tables with an extensive interface through stored procedures. The aim is to rearchitect this layer on top of the EJB component framework in which all business objects are truly unique and have a well-defined interface to the outside world. Areas such as portals, wireless, business intelligence, dynamic Web services, collaboration, and process integration are already part of the Oracle9*i*AS infrastructure. This would greatly simplify integration of enterprise components and prepare the EDH application for use on any wireless or mobile device.

For more information about Java technology and Oracle, visit http://otn.oracle.com/tech/java/. For more information about the Oracle application server, visit http://www.oracle.com/ip/deploy/ias/index.html. For more information about CERN, visit http://www.cern.ch.

SunPS/USMTMC

About the Contributors

Lieutenant Colonel Hank Abercrombie, FSD product manager, Military Traffic Management Command, Alexandria, Virginia, is responsible for providing Department of Defense transportation and freight traffic managers with information management systems for the procurement of commercial freight transportation services, with an emphasis on service, economy, and readiness.

Todd Lasseigne is a Java architect with Sun Microsystems Java Center, in Mclean, Virginia. Todd has in-depth knowledge and experience in object technologies, including the Java 2 Platform, Enterprise Edition (J2EE), Enterprise Java-Beans, Java Servlets, Java ServerPages (JSP), and XML. While at Sun, Todd has been architecting enterprise solutions for many Fortune 500 and government customers. Todd has an undergraduate business background, with a concentration in information systems, and an MS in information systems technology. He not only has the ability to provide highly technical solutions, but also the ability to deliver with a business expertise.

CHAPTER 12

USMTMC Overhauls Small Package Shipping with SunPS

$\mathbf{A}$s part of a continuing quest to align its operations with twenty-first century business practices, the Freight Systems Division (FSD) of the U.S. Army's Military Traffic Management Command (MTMC) is adopting the latest advances in Internet technology to improve user productivity and responsiveness, reduce operational costs, and streamline application development and maintenance. Working with the Java Center of Sun Professional Services, the FSD used Java 2 Platform, Enterprise Edition (J2EE), technology to develop a new application to manage the shipment of small packages using multiple domestic and international carriers. Development of the first phase of the application was completed in just 3 months, thanks to a highly granular component-based architecture and a well-structured development process. The FSD expects a full return on its investment within the next 18 months. Taking advantage of the standard system-level services built into the J2EE platform and implemented by J2EE-compliant application servers also helped reduce development time and will make maintenance much easier.

The use of thin-clients to access the application is saving the agency an estimated 60 percent annually on the cost of software upgrades and distribution. Since the application accommodates interfaces to multiple carriers, the FSD doesn't need to install dedicated terminals for each carrier—saving the FSD up to 70 percent in costs.

The FSD is also migrating its older Java applications to the J2EE platform to enhance their scalability, reliability, and ease of maintenance. In all of these efforts, the FSD expects to benefit from significant reductions in development cycle time—in some cases, by as much as 50 percent.

As the first agency in the Department of Defense (DoD) to implement the J2EE standard, the FSD will serve as a model for other agencies and help reduce the risk these agencies might perceive with regard to adopting the new technology.

12.1   Global Freight Management, Military Traffic Management Command, Mission

As a core agency in the MTMC, the FSD is responsible for supporting the procurement of commercial freight transportation services for the DoD—serving the Army, Navy, Air Force, Marine Corps, the Defense Logistics Agency (DLA), as well as the U.S. Coast Guard and the Federal Emergency Management Agency (FEMA). These transportation services provide a key capability within the logistical operations of the armed forces.

Taking its cue from the private sector, the DoD has been working for several years to implement time- and cost-saving concepts, such as just-in-time logistics, which help to reduce stockpiles of raw materials and finished components. This new approach requires forging relationships with material vendors, as well as with transportation companies that deliver products to destinations only when they are needed, instead of requiring the destinations to keep surplus inventory. Along these lines, it was the FSD's mission to provide DoD traffic managers with an automated e-commerce capability for the procurement of commercial freight transportation services and to provide real-time feed data to war fighters.

Playing a central role in the establishment and management of these relationships, the FSD is tasked with selecting freight carriers, costing, generating shipping documentation, and managing the freight movements by road, rail, air, and sea. More than 3,000 traffic managers in 800 FSD locations across the United States perform these tasks through an e-commerce and EDI system called Global Freight Management system (GFM). The GFM system incorporates multiple applications, including the Freight Acquisition Shipping Tool (FAST), the main shipment processing application; Spot Bid, a tool for posting open shipments for bid on the Web; Guaranteed Traffic (GT) Bid Submission, which allows electronic submission of tenders against GT traffic solicitations; and various reporting and traffic management mechanisms. All told, GFM manages 800,000 shipments per year, worth approximately US$600 million.

12.2   Technology Evolution

Deployed in 1998, GFM represented a huge improvement over the paper-based logistics and transportation processes that had previously prevailed within the

FSD and throughout the DoD. But migrating from paper-based to electronic processes was just the first step in bringing the DoD's transportation systems in line with Twenty-first century business practices. The next step was enabling these electronic systems to take advantage of browser-based user interfaces, cost-effective IP networks, and Web-based business process technologies that improve responsiveness, productivity, and cost-effectiveness.

The process of Web enabling existing business applications not only changed the way users interact with these applications, but also called into question the way the applications were developed and maintained. For example, until recently, the FSD's GFM system housed all its data and programs for tender management, carrier rating and ranking, as well as payment and shipment tracking, on a host computer residing in Falls Church, Virginia. As the number of applications within the GFM system grew, and as the functional requirements for each application evolved, the FSD experienced increasing complexity in managing new application development.

While the need to protect long-standing investments in legacy hardware, databases, and applications remained a key factor in its IT decisions, the FSD was quick to begin implementing the DoD's vision for the Twenty-first century. Guided by the foresight of FSD product manager, Lieutenant Colonel Hank Abercrombie, the FSD became the first DoD department to migrate its operations to the Web, complying with a 1997 directive from the Office of the Secretary of Defense, called MRM 15.

In accordance with DoD directives, the FSD adopted an IP-based network and instituted Web browsers as the standard client interface. And since 1998, all new FSD applications have been written in Java technology. The cross-platform portability of the Java language and its object-oriented structure have given the FSD greater flexibility in providing a wide range of application services to a large user base. FAST, Spot Bid, and the Small Package system are all server-side Java applications.

Working with Sun Microsystems, Inc., FSD developers have been incrementally improving the performance and availability of their Java applications by taking advantage of new technologies, such as Enterprise JavaBeans (EJB). And in 1999, the FSD made its latest stride in ensuring the openness and extensibility of its transportation systems by adopting the Java 2 Platform, Enterprise Edition (J2EE).

12.2.1 Why J2EE Technology?

The FSD's migration to the J2EE platform was the combined result of an overall drive to improve the efficiency of the FSD's business processes, enhance application scalability and performance, and reduce application development and maintenance costs. In late 1999, a Java Architecture Assessment performed by the Sun Professional Services Java Center revealed that the FSD had much to gain by

- Standardizing its development processes

- Building a well-defined component-based application architecture

- Relying on standards-based containers to provide system-level functionality

- Creating a services framework with generic components that could be reused in other FSD applications

All these findings naturally pointed to the adoption of the J2EE platform, with its inherent specifications for system-level logic and its clear separation of applications into multiple tiers. These features provide both a highly standardized application framework and the flexibility to leverage that framework to quickly create new applications that meet specific demands.

The Defense Information Systems Agency (DISA), which is responsible for setting standards for application deployment within government agencies, had reached similar conclusions. In 1996, prior to the release of the J2EE standard, the DISA released a standard called the Defense Information Infrastructure Common Operating Environment (DII COE). Among other things, the DII COE specified that all new applications developed for the DoD should be self-contained—that is, have limited code dependency on other applications. Where such dependencies exist, they must be clearly defined to reduce the complexity of new development efforts.

Around the time of the Sun assessment, the need arose within the FSD for a new application to handle overnight domestic and international shipment of small packages. Based on the recommendations of the above assessment and a successful J2EE technology proof-of-concept demonstrated by a consultant from the Sun Professional Services Java Center and FSD developers, the FSD decided to apply the J2EE framework in developing the new Small Package application. In doing so, it became the first DoD agency to apply J2EE technology to a production application.

With the assistance of the Sun Professional Services Java Center, two FSD developers completed the first phase of the application in just three months. A high level of componentization within the application makes it easy to enhance the application with additional functionality. And just as important, the development effort yielded a number of reusable services components, which will significantly speed up the development of new applications at the FSD, as well as the migration of existing applications, such as FAST, to a J2EE-based architecture.

Lori Barnhill, MIS specialist at the FSD, notes that the agency is a pioneer within the DoD in the implementation of the industry and DII COE standards. "We are the first agency in the Department of Defense to develop a Web-enabled J2EE technology-based application that complies with the DISA specifications," she says. "We are also the first agency to interface with a commercial system— such as our shipping vendors—using the J2EE technology-based framework."

12.3   The Small Package Application

The FSD was originally organized to handle large items, such as equipment and supplies, not small packages. The FSD agreed to help implement this contract because it realized that its customers send large packages, as well as thousands of small packages (less than 150 lbs.) each year to various domestic and international destinations. Until recently, these customers shipped all their small packages using dedicated terminals with software from FSD's domestic small-package carrier, FedEx.

However, the FSD was concerned about the high cost and lack of flexibility in this process. The FedEx software, which relied on a server at the carrier's facility to handle the entire shipping transaction process, did not give the FSD enough control to ensure that the process conformed to all its business rules, and it did not integrate with its billing system. Moreover, the FSD wanted to be able to select from multiple carriers to handle its international shipments, and installing and maintaining carrier software on multiple dedicated terminals for each of its 3,000 users was prohibitive from both cost and resource perspectives.

Another obstacle was that these small-package shipments, which need to be delivered overnight or within two business days, could not be handled through the FSD's existing Web-based transport application (FAST). The main reason: FAST was developed for the transport of larger items and equipment that used complex bills of lading, which required several days to complete.

While the Small Package application was built from scratch in the sense that it initiated the construction of a new application framework based on J2EE technology, it still leveraged the FSD's existing Sun servers and Oracle and Unidata databases. Furthermore, because the vendors of the existing Web and application servers offered J2EE-compliant versions of their products, the developers were able to make use of the new releases of the already familiar software.

12.3.1   Collaboration with Sun Professional Services

Sun Microsystems has been serving the MTMC since 1997 with hardware and software technology solutions. Soon after the MRM 15 directive was issued in

1997, the Sun Professional Services Java Center assisted the FSD in migrating its FAST system—then a DOS-based systems written in FoxPro—to a system based on Java technology that enabled the use of standard Web browsers. The use of thin clients eliminated the need to install and maintain client software on each desktop, which in turn enabled the FSD to cost-effectively accommodate a growing user base.

In late 1999, the Sun Professional Services Java Center conducted a Java Architecture Assessment of one of the FSD's primary Java applications. Among other findings, the assessment pinpointed that the FSD was spending a great deal of time developing much of its own system-level code—for services such as object caching, distributed garbage collection, for remote method invocation (RMI), lifecycle management, transactions, and so on. These elements were already standardized within the framework of the J2EE-based platform. Sun suggested that the FSD could rely on its J2EE-compliant container vendors to implement these services within their products, freeing the FSD developers to focus on the business logic and the presentation parts of the applications.

Other findings and recommendations of the assessment included the following.

- The core business logic, written in Unibasic, could be managed more easily if it were ported to an object-oriented design. This would allow the system to easily evolve as needs and requirements changed.

- Some objects within the system were much too coarsely defined and, consequently, were consuming exorbitant amounts of memory within the system, causing the system to require frequent restarts. This could have impaired future scalability as more users began to use the system.

- To keep the FSD project moving forward and to prevent project members from becoming completely engaged in maintaining the current system, a more componentized architecture was needed. Such an architecture would provide maximum scalability and flexibility if it were based on open standards and designed as a collection of services. Further benefits would result if the architecture focused on the reuse and abstraction of proprietary implementations.

- As technology evolves and requirements change, new interfaces with the host rating and ranking system should be developed. For example, extensible markup language (XML) can be used to design interfaces for the exchange of data between the rating and ranking system and other applications.

Todd Lasseigne, an enterprise Java architect with the Sun Professional Services Java Center, worked with the FSD on assessment and the development of the Small Package application. He sums up the recommendations: "With the goals expressed by the FSD management—scalability, reliability and maintainability, among other things—a J2EE technology-based architecture became the natural choice. J2EE technology would not only inherently provide all of these capabilities but also allow the FSD development staff to focus on the business logic and not the internal plumbing."

In addition to performing the architectural assessment and delivering the ensuing recommendations, Sun also played a critical role in mentoring the FSD developers on the implementation of the J2EE technology specifications. The FSD was familiar with J2EE technology but had no practical experience and thus needed some guidance in applying the new architecture to the application at hand. "We discussed the use of stateful and stateless session beans and how to integrate the Web tier with back-end services," recalls Lasseigne. "We also covered concepts in object modeling and object design, such as starting with use cases, creating a high-level object model, and sequence diagrams—essentially introducing a very structured process into their design." These concepts are the core of the services-driven architecture from Sun, which incorporates elements of the Rational Unified Process (RUP).

To demonstrate the benefits of J2EE technology, Lasseigne turned his attention to the FSD's Spot Bid application, a reverse-auction service that allows freight carriers to bid on ad hoc shipments for the agency. Although relatively simple, the Spot Bid application had been created by copying and customizing the FAST application, and as a result, was becoming difficult to maintain. Every change to the business logic in FAST required an update to Spot Bid.

Using the process inherent to the services-driven architecture, Lasseigne and two FSD consultants created a general-purpose reverse-auction service to serve as a proof-of-concept to the FSD management. "The key was to introduce the concept of services," Lasseigne explains. "When I design something using J2EE technology, I think of it as a generic service; it's no longer a requirement of a specific application."

One of the prerequisites to enabling the development of such generic services is a clear separation of services and the infrastructure from the specifics of each application.[1] By applying the J2EE patterns developed by the Sun Java Center, the development team could address the core issues of each problem. This ultimately offered solutions that represented an applicable distillation of theory and practice. These patterns were used to assist in addressing the complicated navigational issues in the presentation tier. The key pattern used was Sun Professional Services' Service-to-Worker pattern. The J2EE platform specifies a clear distinction between the roles of Java ServerPages (JSPs), Java Servlets and EJBs to ensure

---

[1]   Lasseigne, Todd, "Dynamic Servlet to JSP Page Navigation," *The Java Report*, November 2000.

maximum scalability and ease of maintenance. The Servlets are tasked with handling the initial requests from the Web server and delegating them to the application (business logic) tier; JSPs focus solely on presenting responses to the client tier; and EJBs, with their associated worker beans and business delegates, are responsible for executing the business logic.

However, a servlet is still faced with the administrative overhead of deciding which worker bean to use to process each request, and which JSP to invoke to present the response. A navigation service fills this role, thus abstracting the navigation from the servlet. As illustrated in Figure 12.1, the navigation service stores the information that matches incoming requests with the appropriate worker beans and JSPs in a database. It uses a caching mechanism to ensure efficient loading of the navigational information into memory.

With the navigation service in place, the servlet needs to contain only the code necessary to pass on the request to the navigation service. The navigation service returns the relevant information to the servlet, which then invokes the designated worker bean(s) and JSP(s).

The reverse-auction function is one example of a practical implementation of the navigation service concept. Another example is a user login service. And as Lasseigne explains, one generic service can be embedded within another. For instance, the login service can be used by the reverse-auction service.

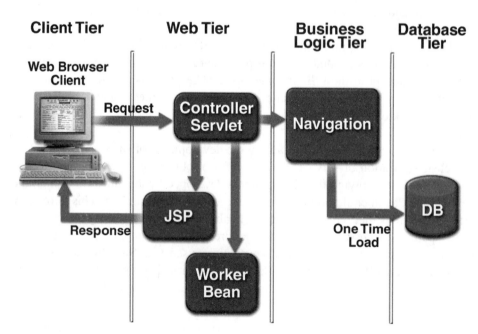

Figure 12.1 A Typical Navigation Service

Because they make use of stateful and stateless session beans, supported by the J2EE-based platform specifications, these generic services can reside anywhere on the enterprise network, where they can be accessed by any application that requires them. Consequently, they don't need to be maintained separately for each application.

As a result of the successful prototype, the FSD gave the go-ahead to build the Small Package application on the basis of a fully compliant J2EE-based architecture, enlisting Sun Professional Services to assist in design and implementation. "The dot-com consultants from Sun Professional Services did a fantastic job of helping us to architect and integrate an extensible infrastructure," says Lieutenant Colonel Abercrombie. "This architecture not only enables us to leverage our existing systems, but also positions us for future innovation."

12.3.2 Solution Analysis

The solution analysis for the Small Package application follows two scenarios, a use scenario and a transaction scenario.

Use Scenario

The following scenario illustrates a typical transaction that a user would perform on the Small Package application.

1. A user logs on to the system through a log-on screen on a secure FSD Web page.

2. Once the user's identity and authorization are verified, the system presents a form in which the user can enter the details of a new shipment, or reuse the information from a previous shipment sent to the same location.

3. The system stores the information in a database and concurrently transmits the information to the carrier, which returns a confirmation number and a shipping label.

4. At this point, the user can decide to either cancel the transaction or complete it. If the user cancels the transaction, the system notifies the carrier, the carrier confirms the cancellation, and the system sends a cancellation notification to the user and then presents the user with the option of creating a new shipment.

5. If the user decides to complete the initial transaction, the system stores the transaction details in a completed-items database. The carrier, which already has the shipping request, will proceed to schedule pick up and delivery of the package. Meanwhile, the user can print out the shipping label and attach it to the package.

6. Once a day, the system collects all the completed transaction data and applies a bundling discount to groups of packages addressed to the same location. This is in accordance with the FSD's contract with the carrier. After the discount is applied, the payment information is sent by file transfer protocol (FTP) to a Unidata database in the FSD's host system. The host system creates an EDI transaction which the FSD uses to pay the carrier.

This is a description of the major functionality provided by the first-phase implementation of the Small Package application. Currently, the application provides domestic shipping through FedEx only. Future phases of the application will enable selection of carriers for domestic and international shipments.

Architecture

The Small Package application consists of four logical tiers—client, Web, business logic and databases (see Table 12.1).

The client tier consists of numerous clients running Netscape version 4 or higher or Microsoft Internet Explorer.

The Web tier, which accepts requests from iPlanet Web Server 4.1, runs on the FSD's existing cluster of four Sun Enterprise 4500 servers. This tier consists of the following objects.

- Controller servlet (called the generic controller)—handles all the incoming requests from the Web server.

- Navigation service—generates a generic controller that determines for the servlet which worker beans and which JSPs to invoke based on the incoming request.

- JSPs—handle the dynamic presentation for the outgoing requests.

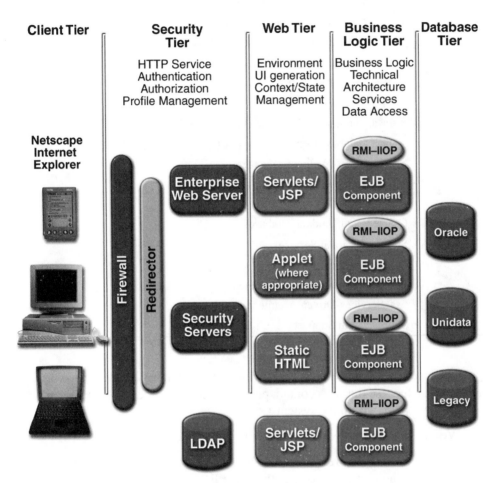

Figure 12.2 Three-tier Architecture for the Small Package Application

Table 12.1 Technology Environment

Hardware	• Sun Enterprise 4500 and 6000 servers
	• Sun StorEdge A5200 disk arrays
Software	• Solaris Operating Environment 2.5
	• Java 2 Platform, Enterprise Edition (J2EE)
	– Enterprise JavaBeans (EJBs)
	– Java ServerPages (JSPs)
	– Java Servlets
	– Java Naming and Directory Interface (JNDI)
	– Java Database Connectivity (JDBC)
	• Sun Enterprise Volume Manager
	• iPlanet Web Server 4.1
	• BEA WebLogic Server 5.1
	• Oracle8i and Unidata databases
Services	• Sun Professional Services
	– Sun Java Center
	• Java Architecture Assessment
	• Services-Driven Architecture
	• SunSpectrum Support

- Session objects—provide the JSPs with information they need from the worker beans. (Because the JSPs contain pure presentation logic, they cannot call any business logic within the system.)

- Worker beans—serve as an interface to the business-logic tier.

- Helper classes (also referred to as business delegates)—provide the worker beans with appropriate access paths to the EJBs.

The business-logic tier runs on the same server as the presentation tier and consists of the following objects contained in BEA WebLogic Server 5.1.

- EJBs (stateful and stateless session beans)—contain the application's primary transaction-related business logic.

- Domain objects—Java classes defining each of the entities participating in the shipping transaction process.

- Data-access objects (DAOs)—contain the SQL code that defines how the domain objects access the databases. In this way, the system hides the data-access methods from the domain objects. The data-access layer is highly granular, containing separate DAOs for each domain object, for each database. This allows the FSD developers to redefine domain objects or create new ones, without affecting the database access code for the other objects. It also allows the developers to reuse the Oracle and Unidata DAOs, which were created for the FAST system, in the Small Package application. Finally, the segmentation makes it relatively easy for the FSD to switch databases in the future, with minimal impact on the application.

- FedEx Ship—the shipment service package from FedEx, with a Java API wrapper that enables it to be called from within the Java application. Similar packages from other carriers will be added in the future.

The database tier consists of Oracle and Unidata databases running on a cluster of two Sun Enterprise 6000 servers supported by 10 Sun StorEdge arrays for backup and recovery.

Transaction Scenario

The following is a partial description of what happens within the system in a typical user interaction, as described in the use scenario above. A package shipping transaction begins when a user logs into the system from a standard Web browser, as shown in Figure 12.3. The initial HTML screen presents the user with a choice of tasks. We'll assume the user elects to create a new package by clicking on the appropriate menu item. The request is posted to the servlet, which takes the incoming request and forwards it to the navigation service.

The navigation service looks at two hidden fields within the incoming HTML request: the `ToScreen` and the `FromScreen` (See Table 12.2). The `FromScreen` field tells the navigation service where the user came from within the application, and the `ToScreen` field tells the navigation service where the user wants to go. Using these fields, the navigation service finds the appropriate worker beans for the specified screen. The navigation service then passes control back to the servlet, providing an object called a generic controller, on which the servlet invokes its call process request.

The generic controller knows that every incoming request involves two steps: (1) saving the information from the incoming screen, and (2) loading information for the out-going screen. For step one, it retrieves the same worker bean that the navigation service found and invokes the process incoming on the associated worker bean, passing on the `ToScreen` and `FromScreen` variables. Based on these variables, the worker bean determines which services to access on the business-logic tier.

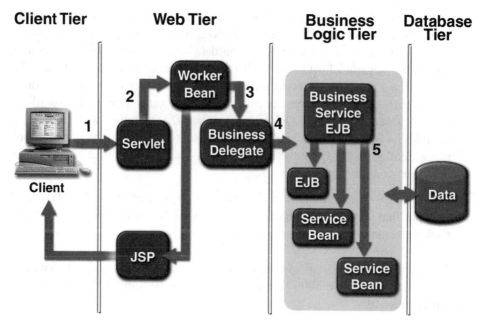

Figure 12.3 A New Package Request Transaction in the J2EE Technology-based Application

Table 12.2 Save and Load

SAVE

ToScreen	FromScreen	Role	Worker Bean	Error JSP	Order
ListScreen	LoginScreen	User	Com.sun.exampleWB	ListError	1
ListScreen	LoginScreen	User	Com.sun.example2WB	ListError	2
MainScreen	ListScreen	User	Com.sun.example3WB	MainScreenError	1
MainScreen	ListScreen	Admin	Com.sun.example4WB	MainScreenError	1

LOAD

ToScreen	FromScreen	Role	Worker Bean	Success JSP	Error JSP	Order
ListScreen	LoginScreen	User	Com.sun.loadListWB	List	ListFailure	1
MainScreen	ListScreen	User		MainMenu	MenuError	1
MainScreen	ListScreen	Admin	Com.sun.mainWB	MainMenu	MenuError	1

The worker bean prompts the business delegate it needs to access these EJBs and then invokes the appropriate EJB to call that service.

The EJB recognizes the request to create a new shipment and passes the new shipment arguments to the DAO for that user. The DAO accesses the Oracle database to get a new shipment ID and returns it in a domain object to the EJB (most likely a stateful session bean).

The EJB then returns control to the worker bean, across the tier, which may or may not serialize that domain object, depending on the method signature (that is, pass the shipment domain object back to the worker bean). The worker bean then stores that shipment ID (the shipment object) in the `HttpSession` object.

It's now time for step two—displaying the next screen the user needs (specified by the `ToScreen` field). In this case, that means getting the shipment details of the new package. The generic controller invokes the appropriate load information JSP, which accesses the session object, pulls out the shipment ID that was just created and creates an HTML screen that displays the shipment ID and requests the address information for the package.

The user fills out and submits the HTML form. When the servlet receives the HTML and forwards the request to the navigation service, the generic controller calls out a new worker bean, which initiates the same kind of process as before, putting the appropriate information back into the session object and then returning control to the servlet.

Figure 12.3 represents a componentized approach to a service-based architecture. A distinct separation of responsibilities allows for a clear understanding both of the system structure and the transactional flow, which proceeds as follows.

1. The servlet handles the incoming request.

2. It passes the data to the worker bean, which then does the low-level syntactical validation. The worker bean holds the data pertaining to the business services available to it, as well as the process workflow.

3. The worker bean requests the use of these services via the business delegate.

4. The business delegate is responsible for abstracting out the network communication necessary to use the EJB services.

5. The business services have the ability to process the request, by working in conjunction with service beans to handle the business logic.

12.3.3 Benefits

As the first organization in the DoD to comply with the DISA specification, the FSD is demonstrating several positive results of implementing a J2EE technology-based architecture.

Operational Benefits

- Improved productivity. Using the J2EE technology-based system-level services provided by the BEA WebLogic Application Server, the Small Package application exhibits high performance, enabling the users to complete a new shipment transaction in three minutes, with 700 concurrent users online. Overall, the FSD expects the Small Package system to handle 10,000 shipments per day.

- Freedom in carrier selection. The Small Package application accommodates interfaces to multiple carriers through a single Web-browser-based interface. This cuts costs by up to 70 percent by eliminating the need to install dedicated terminals for each carrier, or alternatively, by no longer being locked into a single carrier. This also strengthens the FSD's control over its shipping processes.

- Ability to expand user base cost effectively. Through the use of thin clients, the FSD estimates that it will save up to 60 percent annually on the cost of client software upgrades and distribution. In effect, client software maintenance will no longer be a cost consideration in the deployment of future applications.

- Rapid return on investment. Rolled out in Fall 2000, the Small Package application enables 700 concurrent users to schedule and manage 10,000 daily shipments. Through these productivity improvements, the reuse of the application's components in other applications, and the ensuing reduction in application development time, the FSD estimates it will achieve a 100 percent return on its investment in the Small Package application within 18 months. Additional returns will be achieved when the Small Package system is enabled for multiple domestic and international carriers.

Lieutenant Colonel Henry Abercrombie concludes, "As a result of Sun's technologies and services, the tremendous relationships we have built with our industry partners and the instructions we receive from the top, such as MRM15, we are achieving our goals and conducting business the way it will be done in the future."

Table 12.3 Overview of Achieved Business Results of the FSO Small Package Application

Business Process Area	Nature of Benefit	Actual Result
Return on investment	Improved user productivity, reduced development costs	Projected 100 percent ROI in 18 months
Customer service	Improved productivity	Approximately 3,000 transportation officers can send and manage small-package shipments in real-time from their desktops
Vendor (carrier) options	Reduced costs, more options	Will be able to use more than one carrier for shipments, resulting in up to 70 percent reduction in costs
Time to market	Quick deployment of new applications, functionality	Met aggressive three-month time to market using service-driven architecture, which would have taken as much as 66 percent longer using previous development approach

IT Benefits

Use of J2EE technology for application development provides a number of benefits to IT professionals.

- Better utilization of development resources and freedom in vendor selection. EJB developers don't need to worry about creating or maintaining system-level infrastructure services. These services are provided by any J2EE-compliant container vendor, allowing the FSD developers to concentrate on specific application functionality. Further, since the FSD can rely on the fact that all J2EE-compliant containers will provide at least a minimal set of infrastructure services, the organization is not locked into a single vendor. The need for this type of flexibility should provide an impetus for container vendors to update their products to the J2EE technology specifications and motivate developers to upgrade their existing container products to these J2EE-compliant versions.

- Improved application performance. The J2EE technology-based platform, because it reduces, rather than increases, the proliferation of coding, improves application response times and transaction reliability.

- Reduced time to market. Thorough documentation and adherence to the principles of the J2EE platform—especially the separation of tiers using the Sun-Connect Solutions Stack Architecture—provided two main benefits. First, it enhanced developer productivity by minimizing the complexity of the evolving code and making testing easier. The architects were able to reuse up to 50 percent of the business logic. Second, it mitigated the effects of staff turnover. The FSD's Small Package project experienced a complete turnover of its two-person team in mid-project, yet the new team was able to get up to speed and complete the entire project in an aggressive three-month time frame. Lasseigne estimates that the Small Package application would have taken five to eight months to complete, or as much as 66 percent longer, using the previous development approach under the same conditions. The reuse of generic services developed for the Small Package application is also expected to help reduce the development cycle time for subsequent FSD applications by as much as 50 percent, and these new applications will be completely independent of changes in the Small Package application.

Table 12.4 Technical Results of the FSO Small Package System

Technical Process Area	Nature of Benefit	Actual Result
Application development	Enhanced productivity	Up to 25 percent reduction in development time and reuse of 50 percent of business logic; up to 50 percent reduction in future development cycles
Site performance	High performance, scalability	Depending on transaction type, delivers three-second response time on average; support for up to 700 concurrent users scheduling and managing 10,000 packages daily
IT operations	Reduced costs, improved productivity	Able to avoid future client software upgrades through thin client, resulting in 60 percent reduction in IT costs
System integration	Reduced costs, cost avoidance	Able to integrate with disparate systems from multiple carriers to seamlessly connect front-end Web transactions with disparate back-end legacy systems

- Easier and less costly application maintenance. As previously noted, the J2EE-based architecture, and the navigation service created by Sun Professional Services, are making it easy to enhance, modify, and scale the initial Small Package application. For example, adding new carriers will require only the addition of the appropriate third-party APIs and minor screen changes to add the new carrier selection to the screens. It will not require any changes in the overall business logic. Alternatively, if the FSD wants to enhance the user interface, modifications to the JSPs need not affect any other part of the application. Database changes will also have minimal impact on the application, as the only development effort would be the creation of new DAOs. And because each of these updates can be made by developers who don't need to be familiar with the entire application model, the FSD can complete these upgrades quickly and, likely, at a lower cost.

On this note, Barnhill comments, "We have a clear migration path into the future and can grow our platforms to meet the coming data demands of our customers. And because our team was able to meet our deadline for the Small Package application, we have gained significant credibility with the Office of the Secretary of Defense and our customers."

Glossary

This glossary defines terms according to their usage in the context of the Java™ 2 Platform, Enterprise Edition (J2EE platform). Many of the terms have more general usage. For example: the term handle has general currency in modern programming languages, but here is defined in terms of its use in Enterprise JavaBeans™ (EJB™) technology.

access control The methods by which interactions with resources are limited to collections of users or programs for the purpose of enforcing integrity, confidentiality, or availability constraints.

ACID The acronym for the four properties guaranteed by transactions: atomicity, consistency, isolation, and durability.

activation The process of transferring an enterprise bean from secondary storage to memory. See passivation in this glossary.

applet A component that typically executes in a Web browser, but can execute in a variety of other applications or devices that support the applet programming model. See component in this glossary.

applet container A container that includes support for the applet programming model.

Application Component Provider A vendor that provides the Java classes that implement a component's methods, JSP page definitions, and any required deployment descriptors.

Application Assembler A person that combines containers and modules into deployable application units.

application client   A client-tier component that executes in its own Java virtual machine. Application clients have access to some (JNDI, JDBC, RMI-IIOP, JMS) J2EE platform APIs.

application client container   A container that supports application client components.

application client module   A software unit that consists of one or more classes and an application client deployment descriptor.

authentication   The process by which an entity proves to another entity that it is acting on behalf of a specific identity. The J2EE platform requires three types of authentication: See basic authentication, form-based authentication, and mutual authentication. It supports digest authentication.

authorization   The process by which access to a method or resource is determined. Authorization in the J2EE platform depends upon the determination of whether the principal associated with a request through authentication is in a given security role. A security role is a logical grouping of users defined by an Application Component Provider or Assembler. A Deployer maps security roles to security identities. Security identities may be principals or groups in the operational environment. See access control and role (security).

authorization constraint   An authorization rule that determines who is permitted to access a Web resource collection.

basic authentication   An authentication mechanism in which a Web server authenticates an entity with a user name and password obtained using the Web client's built-in authentication mechanism.

bean-managed persistence   Entity bean management of data transfers between an entity bean's variables and a resource manager.

bean-managed transaction   A transaction whose boundaries are defined by an enterprise bean.

business logic   The code that implements the functionality of an application. In the Enterprise JavaBeans model, this logic is implemented by the methods of an enterprise bean.

business logic tier   The tier of a multi-tier distributed application that contains the business logic. In a J2EE application, this tier is implemented by the EJB server

business method   A method of an enterprise bean that implements business logic or rules of an application.

callback methods   Component methods called by the container to notify the component of important events in its life cycle.

caller   Same as caller principal.

caller principal   The principal that identifies the invoker of an enterprise bean method, or a servlet method.

client certificate authentication   An authentication mechanism in which a client uses a X.509 certificate to establish its identity.

client tier   The tier of a multi-tier distributed application (see distributed application) that presents the application to the end user. The client tier of a J2EE application can be provided through a standalone Java application or a Web browser.

commit   The point in a transaction when all updates to any resources involved in the transaction are made permanent.

component   An application-level software unit supported by a container. Components are configurable at deployment time. The J2EE platform defines four types of components: enterprise beans, Web components, applets, and application clients. A component type embodies a programming model implementing the component's contract with it container. See component contract and container.

component contract   The contract between a component and its container. The contract includes: life cycle management of the component, a context interface that the instance uses to obtain various information and services from its container, and a list of services that the container must provide for its components.

connection   See resource manager connection.

connection factory   See resource manager connection factory.

connector   A standard extension mechanism for containers to provide connectivity to enterprise information systems. A connector is specific to an enterprise information system and consists of a resource adapter and application development tools for enterprise information system connectivity. The resource adapter is plugged in to a container through its support for system-level contracts defined in the connector architecture.

connector architecture   An architecture for integration of J2EE products with enterprise information systems. There are two parts to this architecture: a resource adapter provided by an enterprise information system vendor and the

J2EE product that allows this resource adapter to plug in. This architecture defines a set of contracts that a resource adapter has to support to plug in to a J2EE product, for example, transactions, security, and resource management.

container   An entity that provides life cycle management, security, deployment, and runtime services to components. Each type of container (EJB, Web, JSP, servlet, applet, and application client) also provides component-specific services.

container-managed persistence   Data transfer between an entity bean's variables and a resource manager managed by the entity bean's container.

container-managed transaction   A transaction whose boundaries are defined by an EJB container. An entity bean must use container-managed transactions.

context attribute   An object bound into the context associated with a servlet. See servlet context.

conversational state   The field values of a session bean plus the transitive closure of the objects reachable from the bean's fields. The transitive closure of a bean is defined in terms of the serialization protocol for the Java programming language, that is, the fields that would be stored by serializing the bean instance.

CORBA   Common Object Request Broker Architecture. A language independent, distributed object model specified by the Object Management Group (OMG). See also IDL and IIOP.

create method   A method defined in the home interface and invoked by a client to create an enterprise bean.

credentials   The information describing the security attributes of a principal. See principal.

CSS   Cascading Style Sheet. A stylesheet used with HTML and XML documents to add a style to all elements marked with a particular tag, for the direction of browsers or other presentation mechanisms.

CTS   Compatibility Test Suite. A suite of compatibility tests for verifying that a J2EE product complies with the J2EE platform specification.

database tier   The tier of a multi-tier distributed application that contains the data store or other enterprise information system. In a J2EE application, this tier is linked to the other tiers of the application through JDBC API or other API conforming to the J2EE Connector Architecture.

delegation An act whereby one principal authorizes another principal to use its identity or privileges with some restrictions.

Deployer A person who installs modules and J2EE applications into an operational environment.

deployment The process whereby software is installed into an operational environment.

deployment descriptor An XML file provided with each module and application that describes how they should be deployed. The deployment descriptor directs a deployment tool to deploy a module or application with specific container options and describes specific configuration requirements that a Deployer must resolve.

destination A JMS administered object that encapsulates the identity of a JMS queue or topic. See point-to-point message system, publish/subscribe message system.

digest authentication An authentication mechanism in which a Web client authenticates to a Web server by sending the server a message digest along with its HTTP request message. The digest is computed by employing a one-way hash algorithm to a concatenation of the HTTP request message and the client's password. The digest is typically much smaller than the HTTP request, and doesn't contain the password.

distributed application An application made up of distinct components running in separate runtime environments, usually on different platforms connected via a network. Typical distributed applications are configured in multiple tiers, for example, a two tier application may consiste of just client and server tiers, while a thrie tier application of consiste of client, middleware, and server tiers.

DOM Document Object Model. A tree of objects with interfaces for traversing the tree and writing an XML version of it, as defined by the W3C specification.

DTD Document Type Definition. A description of the structure and properties of a class of XML files. See XML.

durable subscription In a JMS publish/subscribe messaging system, a subscription that continues to exist whether or not there is a current active subscriber object. If there is no active subscriber, JMS retains the subscription's messages until they are received by the subscriber or until they expire.

EAR file   A JAR archive that contains a J2EE application.

EJB™   See Enterprise JavaBeans™ (EJB™).

EJB container   A container that implements the EJB component contract of the J2EE architecture. This contract specifies a runtime environment for enterprise beans that includes security, concurrency, life cycle management, transaction, deployment, naming, and other services. An EJB container is provided by an EJB or J2EE server.

EJB Container Provider   A vendor that supplies an EJB container.

EJB context   An object that allows an enterprise bean to invoke services provided by the container and to obtain the information about the caller of a client-invoked method.

EJB home object   An object that provides the life cycle operations (create, remove, find) for an enterprise bean. The class for the EJB home object is generated by the container's deployment tools. The EJB home object implements the enterprise bean's home interface. The client references an EJB home object to perform life cycle operations on an EJB object. The client uses JNDI to locate an EJB home object.

EJB JAR file   A JAR archive that contains an EJB module.

EJB module   A software unit that consists of one or more enterprise beans and an EJB deployment descriptor.

EJB object   An object whose class implements the enterprise bean's remote interface. A client never references an enterprise bean instance directly; a client always references an EJB object. The class of an EJB object is generated by a container's deployment tools.

EJB server   Software provides services to an EJB container. For example, an EJB container typically relies on a transaction manager that is part of the EJB server to perform the two-phase commit across all the participating resource managers. The J2EE architecture assumes that an EJB container is hosted by an EJB server from the same vendor, so does not specify the contract between these two entities. An EJB server may host one or more EJB containers.

EJB Server Provider   A vendor that supplies an EJB server.

enterprise bean   A component that implements a business task or business entity and resides in an EJB container; an entity bean, a session bean, or a message-drivenbean.

enterprise information system   The applications that comprise an enterprise's existing system for handling company-wide information. These applications provide an information infrastructure for an enterprise. An enterprise information system offers a well defined set of services to its clients. These services are exposed to clients as local and/or remote interfaces. Examples of enterprise information systems include: enterprise resource planning systems, mainframe transaction processing systems, and legacy database systems.

enterprise information system resource   An entity that provides some functionality of an enterprise information system to its clients. Examples are: a set of records in a database system, a business object in an enterprise resource planning system, and a transaction program in a transaction processing system.

Enterprise Bean Provider   An application programmer who produces enterprise bean classes, remote and home interfaces, and deployment descriptor files, and packages them in an EJB JAR file.

Enterprise JavaBeans™ (EJB™)   A component architecture for the development and deployment of object-oriented, distributed, enterprise-level applications. Applications written using the Enterprise JavaBeans architecture are scalable, transactional, and secure.

entity bean   An enterprise bean that represents persistent data maintained in a database. An entity bean can manage its own persistence or it can delegate this function to its container. An entity bean is identified by a primary key. If the container in which an entity bean is hosted crashes, the entity bean, its primary key, and any remote references survive the crash.

finder method   A method defined in the home interface and invoked by a client to locate an entity bean.

filter   A reusable piece of code that can transform the content of HTTP requests, responses, and header information. Filters do not create a response or respond to a request as Web components do, rather they modify or adapt the requests for a resource, and modify or adapt responses from a resource. A filter should not have dependencies on the Web resource for which it is acting as a filter. It should be composable with more than one type of resource.

form-based authentication   An authentication mechanism in which a Web container provides an application-specific form for logging in.

group   A collection of principals within a given security policy domain.

handle   An object that identifies an enterprise bean. A client may serialize the handle, and then later deserialize it to obtain a reference to the enterprise bean.

home interface   One of two interfaces for an enterprise bean. The home interface defines zero or more methods for managing an enterprise bean. The home interface of a session bean defines create and remove methods, while the home interface of an entity bean defines create, finder, and remove methods.

home handle   An object that can be used to obtain a reference of the home interface. A home handle can be serialized and written to stable storage and deserialized to obtain the reference.

HTML   Hypertext Markup Language. A markup language for hypertext documents on the Internet. HTML enables the embedding of images, sounds, video streams, form fields, references to other objects with URLs and basic text formatting.

HTTP   Hypertext Transfer Protocol. The Internet protocol used to fetch hypertext objects from remote hosts. HTTP messages consist of requests from client to server and responses from server to client.

HTTPS   HTTP layered over the SSL protocol. SSL protocol is used to obtain additional security in client accesses.

impersonation   An act whereby one entity assumes the identity and privileges of another entity without restrictions and without any indication visible to the recipients of the impersonator's calls that delegation has taken place. Impersonation is a case of simple delegation.

IDL   Interface Definition Language. A language used to define interfaces to remote CORBA objects. The interface definitions are independent of operating systems and programming languages. An IDL2Java compiler is used to obtain a Java representation of IDL interfaces. Similar compilers exist for other computer languages and programming systems. Also see CORBA.

IIOP   Internet Inter-ORB Protocol. A protocol used for communication between CORBA object request brokers (ORBs). Also see ORB.

initialization parameter   A parameter that initializes the context associated with a servlet. See context attribute and servlet.

ISV   Independent Software Vendor.

J2EE™   See Java™ 2 Platform, Enterprise Edition (J2EE).

J2ME™   See Java™ 2 Platform, Micro Edition (J2ME).

J2SE™   See Java™ 2 Platform, Standard Edition (J2SE).

J2EE application   Any deployable unit of J2EE functionality. This can be a single module or a group of modules packaged into an.ear file with a J2EE application deployment descriptor. J2EE applications are typically engineered to be distributed across multiple computing tiers.

J2EE product   An implementation that conforms to the J2EE platform specification.

J2EE Product Provider   A vendor that supplies a J2EE product.

J2EE server   The runtime portion of a J2EE product. A J2EE server provides EJB and/or Web containers.

JAR Java ARchive   A platform-independent file format that permits many files to be aggregated into one file.

Java™ **2 Platform, Enterprise Edition (J2EE)**   An environment for developing and deploying enterprise applications. The J2EE platform consists of a set of services, application programming interfaces (APIs), and protocols that provide the functionality for developing multi-tiered, Web-based applications.

Java™ **2 Platform, Micro Edition (J2ME)**   A highly optimized Java runtime environment targeting a wide range of consumer products, including pagers, cellular phones, screen phones, digital set-top boxes and car navigation systems.

Java™ **2 Platform, Standard Edition (J2SE)**   The core Java technology platform.

Java™ **2 SDK, Enterprise Edition (J2EE SDK)**   Sun's implementation of the J2EE platform. This implementation provides an operational definition of the J2EE platform.

Java™ **Message Service (JMS)**   An API for using enterprise messaging systems such as IBM MQ Series, TIBCO Rendezvous, and so on.

Java Naming and Directory Interface™ **(JNDI)**   An API that provides naming and directory functionality.

Java™ **Transaction API (JTA)**   An API that allows applications and J2EE servers to access transactions.

Java™ Transaction Service (JTS)   Specifies the implementation of a transaction manager which supports JTA and implements the Java mapping of the OMG Object Transaction Service (OTS) 1.1 specification at the level below the API.

JavaBeans™ component   A Java class that can be manipulated in a visual builder tool and composed into applications. A JavaBeans component must adhere to certain property and event interface conventions.

Java IDL   A technology that provides CORBA interoperability and connectivity capabilities for the J2EE platform. These capabilities enable J2EE applications to invoke operations on remote network services using the OMG IDL and IIOP. See CORBA, IDL, and IIOP.

JavaMail™   An API for sending and receiving email.

JavaServer Pages™ (JSP™)   An extensible Web technology that uses template data, custom elements, scripting languages, and server-side Java objects to return dynamic content to a client. Typically the template data is HTML or XML elements, and in many cases the client is a Web browser.

JDBC™   An API for database-independent connectivity between the J2EE platform and a wide range of data sources.

JMS   See Java™ Message Service (JMS).

JMS administered object   A preconfigured JMS object (a resource manager connection factory or a destination) created by an administrator for the use of JMS clients and placed in a JNDI namespace.

JMS application   One or more JMS clients that exchange messages.

JMS client   A Java language program that sends and/or receives messages.

JMS provider   A messaging system that implements the Java Message Service as well as other administrative and control functionality needed in a full-featured messaging product.

JMS session   A single-threaded context for sending and receiving JMS messages. A JMS session can be non-transacted, locally transacted, or participating in a distributed transaction.

JNDI   See Java Naming and Directory Interface™ (JNDI).

JSP   See JavaServer Pages™ (JSP™).

JSP action A JSP element that can act on implicit objects and other server-side objects or can define new scripting variables. Actions follow the XML syntax for elements with a start tag, a body and an end tag; if the body is empty it can also use the empty tag syntax. The tag must use a prefix.

JSP action, custom An action described in a portable manner by a tag library descriptor and a collection of Java classes and imported into a JSP page by a taglib directive. A custom action is invoked when a JSP page uses a custom tag.

JSP action, standard An action that is defined in the JSP specification and is always available to a JSP file without being imported.

JSP application A stand-alone Web application, written using the JavaServer Pages technology, that can contain JSP pages, servlets, HTML files, images, applets, and JavaBeans components.

JSP container A container that provides the same services as a servlet container and an engine that interprets and processes JSP pages into servlets.

JSP container, distributed A JSP container that can run a Web application that is tagged as distributable and is spread across multiple Java virtual machines that might be running on different hosts.

JSP declaration A JSP scripting element that declares methods and variables in a JSP file.

JSP directive A JSP element that gives an instruction to the JSP container and is interpreted at translation time.

JSP element A portion of a JSP page that is recognized by a JSP translator. An element can be a directive, an action, or a scripting element.

JSP expression A scripting element that contains a valid scripting language expression that is evaluated, converted to a String, and placed into the implicit out object.

JSP file A file that contains a JSP page. In the Servlet 2.2 specification, a JSP file must have a .jsp extension.

JSP page A text-based document using fixed template data and JSP elements that describes how to process a request to create a response.

JSP scripting element A JSP declaration, scriptlet, or expression, whose tag syntax is defined by the JSP specification, and whose content is written according to the scripting language used in the JSP page. The JSP specification describes the syntax and semantics for the case where the language page attribute is "java."

JSP scriptlet   A JSP scripting element containing any code fragment that is valid in the scripting language used in the JSP page. The JSP specification describes what is a valid scriptlet for the case where the language page attribute is "java."

JSP tag   A piece of text between a left angle bracket and a right angle bracket that is used in a JSP file as part of a JSP element. The tag is distinguishable as markup, as opposed to data, because it is surrounded by angle brackets.

JSP tag library   A collection of custom tags identifying custom actions described via a tag library descriptor and Java classes.

JTA   See Java™ Transaction API (JTA).

JTS   See Java™ Transaction Service (JTS).

life cycle   The framework events of a component's existence. Each type of component has defining events which mark its transition into states where it has varying availability for use. For example, a servlet is created and has its init method called by its container prior to invocation of its service method by clients or other servlets who require its functionality. After the call of its init method it has the data and readiness for its intended use. The servlet's destroy method is called by its container prior to the ending of its existence so that processing associated with winding up may be done, and resources may be released. Similar considerations apply to all J2EE component types: enterprise beans (EJBs), Web components (servlets or JSP pages), applets, and application clients.

message   In the Java Message Service, an asynchronous request, report, or event is created, sent, and consumed by an enterprise application, not by a human. It contains vital information needed to coordinate enterprise applications, in the form of precisely formatted data that describes specific business actions.

Message Consumer   An object created by a JMS session that is used for receiving messages sent to a destination.

Message Producer   An object created by a JMS session that is used for sending messages to a destination.

message-driven bean   An enterprise bean that is an asynchronous message consumer. It is created by the container to handle the processing of the messages for which it is a consumer. It has no state for a specific client, but instance variables may contain state across the handling of client messages, including an open database connection and an object reference to an EJB object. A client accesses a message-driven bean by sending messages to the destination for which the message-driven bean is a message listener.

method permission   An authorization rule that determines who is permitted to execute one or more enterprise bean methods.

module   A software unit that consists of one or more J2EE components of the same container type and one deployment descriptor of that type. There are three types of modules: EJB, Web, and application client modules. Modules can be deployed as stand-alone units or assembled into an application.

multi-tier application   A business system structured with two or more tiers or layers. See distributed application. A typical two tier configuration involves a Web-server application for processing HTTP protocol requests and producing HTML pages from corporate resources to be displayed on a Web browser. Tiered structuring allows wrapping of functionality in familiar application programming interfaces (APIs), and independent development and mainte- nance of the separate tiers.

mutual authentication   An authentication mechanism employed by two parties for the purpose of proving each's identity to the other.

naming context   A set of associations between distinct, atomic people-friendly identifiers and objects.

naming environment   A mechanism that allows a component to be customized without the need to access or change the component's source code. A con- tainer implements the component's naming environment, and provides it to the component as a JNDI naming context. Each component names and accesses its environment entries using the java:comp/env JNDI context. The environment entries are declaratively specified in the component's deploy- ment descriptor.

non-JMS client   A messaging client program that uses a message system's native client API instead of the Java Message Service.

ORB   Object Request Broker. A library than enables CORBA objects to locate and communicate with one another.

OS principal   A principal native to the operating system on which the J2EE platform is executing.

OTS   Object Transaction Service. A definition of the interfaces that permit CORBA objects to participate in transactions.

passivation   The process of transferring an enterprise bean from memory to sec- ondary storage. (See activation.)

persistence   The protocol for transferring the state of an entity bean between its instance variables and an underlying database.

POA   Portable Object Adapter. A CORBA standard for building server-side applications that are portable across heterogeneous ORBs.

point-to-point message system   A messaging system built around the concept of message queues. Each message is addressed to a specific queue; clients extract messages from the queue(s) established to hold their messages.

principal   The identity assigned to an user as a result of authentication.

privilege   A security attribute that does not have the property of uniqueness and that may be shared by many principals.

primary key   An object that uniquely identifies an entity bean within a home.

publish/subscribe message system   A messaging system in which clients address messages to a specific node in a content hierarchy. Publishers and subscribers are generally anonymous and may dynamically publish or subscribe to the content hierarchy. The system takes care of distributing the messages arriving from a node's multiple publishers to its multiple subscribers.

queue   See point-to-point message system.

realm   See security policy domain. Also, a string, passed as part of an HTTP request during basic authentication, that defines a protection space. The protected resources on a server can be partitioned into a set of protection spaces, each with its own authentication scheme and/or authorization database.

re-entrant entity bean   An entity bean that can handle multiple simultaneous, interleaved, or nested invocations which will not interfere with each other.

Reference Implementation (RI)   See Java™ 2 SDK, Enterprise Edition (J2EE SDK).

remote interface   One of two interfaces for an enterprise bean. The remote interface defines the business methods callable by a client.

remove method   Method defined in the home interface and invoked by a client to destroy an enterprise bean.

resource adapter   A system-level software driver used by an EJB container or an application client to connect to an enterprise information system. A resource adapter is typically specific to an enterprise information system. It is available as a library and is used within the address space of the server or client using it. A resource adapter plugs in to a container. The application components deployed on the container then use the client API (exposed by the resource adapter) or tool generated high-level abstractions to access the underlying enterprise information system. The resource adapter and EJB container collaborate to provide the underlying mechanisms-transactions, security, and connection pooling-for connectivity to the enterprise information system.

resource manager   A resource manager provides access to a set of shared resources in transactions that are externally controlled and coordinated by a transaction manager. A resource manager is typically in a different address space or on a different machine from the clients that access it. Note: An enterprise information system is referred to as a resource manager in the context of resource and transaction management.

resource manager connection   An object that represents a session with a resource manager.

resource manager connection factory   An object used for creating resource manager connections.

RMI   Remote Method Invocation. A technology that allows an object running in one Java virtual machine to invoke methods on an object running in a different Java virtual machine.

RMI-IIOP   A version of RMI implemented to use the CORBA IIOP protocol. RMI over IIOP provides interoperability with CORBA objects implemented in any language if the remote interfaces are originally defined as RMI interfaces.

role (development)   Distinguished functions performed by a party in the development and deployment phases of an application developed using J2EE technology. The roles are: Application Component Provider, Application Assembler, Deployer, J2EE Product Provider, EJB Container Provider, EJB Server Provider, Web Container Provider, Web Server Provider, Tool Provider, and System Administrator.

role (security)   An abstract logical grouping of users that is defined by the Application Assembler. When an application is deployed, the roles are mapped to security identities, such as principals or groups, in the operational environment.

role mapping   The process of associating the groups and/or principals recognized by the container to security roles specified in the deployment descriptor. Security roles are mapped by the Deployer before a particular component is installed in the server.

rollback   The point in a transaction when all updates to any resources involved in the transaction are reversed.

SAX   Simple API for XML. An event-driven, serial-access mechanism for accessing XML documents.

security attributes   A set of properties associated with a principal. Security attributes can be associated with a principal by an authentication protocol and/ or by a J2EE Product Provider.

security constraint   A declarative way to annotate the intended protection of Web content. A security constraint consists of a Web resource collection, an authorization constraint, and a user data constraint.

security context   An object that encapsulates the shared state information regarding security between two entities.

security permission   A mechanism, defined by J2SE, used by the J2EE platform to express the programming restrictions imposed on Application Component Providers.

security permission set   The minimum set of security permissions that a J2EE Product Provider must provide for the execution of each component type.

security policy domain   A scope over which security policies are defined and enforced by a security administrator. A security policy domain has a collection of users (or principals), uses a well defined authentication protocol(s) for authenticating users (or principals), and may define groups to simplify setting of security policies.

security role   See role (security).

security technology domain   A scope over which the same security mechanism is used to enforce a security policy. Multiple security policy domains can exist within a single technology domain.

security view   The set of security roles defined by the Application Assembler.

server principal   The OS principal of the executing server.

servlet   A Java program that extends the functionality of a Web server, generating dynamic content and interacting with Web clients using a request-response paradigm.

servlet container   A container that provides the network services over which requests and responses are sent, decodes requests, and formats responses. All servlet containers must support HTTP as a protocol for requests and responses, but may also support additional request-response protocols such as HTTPS.

servlet container, distributed   A servlet container that can run a Web application that is tagged as distributable and that executes across multiple Java virtual machines running on the same host or on different hosts.

servlet context   An object that contains a servlet's view of the Web application within which the servlet is running. Using the context, a servlet can log events, obtain URL references to resources, and set and store attributes that other servlets in the context can use.

servlet mapping   Defines an association between a URL pattern and a servlet. The mapping is used to map requests to servlets.

session   An object used by a servlet to track a user's interaction with a Web application across multiple HTTP requests.

session bean   An enterprise bean that is created by a client and that usually exists only for the duration of a single client-server session. A session bean performs operations, such as calculations or accessing a database, for the client. While a session bean may be transactional, it is not recoverable should a system crash occur. Session bean objects can be either stateless or they can maintain conversational state across methods and transactions. If a session bean maintains state, then the EJB container manages this state if the object must be removed from memory. However, the session bean object itself must manage its own persistent data.

SSL   Secure Socket Layer. A security protocol that provides privacy over the Internet. The protocol allows client-server applications to communicate in a way that cannot be eavesdropped or tampered with. Servers are always authenticated and clients are optionally authenticated.

SQL   Structured Query Language. The standardized relational database language for defining database objects and manipulating data.

SQL/J   A set of standards that includes specifications for embedding SQL statements in methods in the Java programming language and specifications for calling Java static methods as SQL stored procedures and user-defined functions. An SQL checker can be used to detect errors in static SQL statements at program development time, rather than, for example, with a JDBC driver at execution time.

stateful session bean   A session bean with a conversational state.

stateless session bean   A session bean with no conversational state. All instances of a stateless session bean are identical.

system administrator   The person responsible for configuring and administering the enterprise's computers, networks, and software systems.

three tier application   A business system structured as GUI presentation logic on the client machine, business logic on a server in the middle tier, and back-end access to corporate resources in a third tier. Placing business logic on the server allows better control and use of corporate resources. For example, database connections may be leveraged across multiple clients saving overhead and allowing use of legacy information systems. The architecture allows central control of security and implementation of business policy without distribution headaches. Three tier application structures have allowed the development of high-volume transaction processing.

tiered application architectures   See two tier application, three tier application, multi-tier application, and Web application in this glossary.

topic   See publish/subscribe message system.

transaction   An atomic unit of work that modifies data. A transaction encloses one or more program statements, all of which either complete or roll back. Transactions enable multiple users to access the same data concurrently.

transaction attribute   A value specified in an enterprise bean's deployment descriptor that is used by the EJB container to control the transaction scope when the enterprise bean's methods are invoked. A transaction attribute can have the following values: Required, RequiresNew, Supports, NotSupported, Mandatory, Never.

transaction isolation level   The degree to which the intermediate state of the data being modified by a transaction is visible to other concurrent transactions, and data being modified by other transactions is visible to it.

transaction manager   Provides the services and management functions required to support transaction demarcation, transactional resource management, synchronization, and transaction context propagation.

tool provider   An organization or software vendor that provides tools used for the development, packaging, and deployment of J2EE applications.

two tier application   A business system structured as a collection of operating system level application processes executing on a client machine. These applications typically implement business processes plus GUI presentation logic. The applications on the client machines communicate over a network with a second tier on a server comprised of enterprise resources. Enterprise resources include a database server controlling access to corporate information. The client application may access data in the second tier using Structured Query Language (SQL) on a relational database.

URI   Uniform Resource Identifier. A compact string of characters for identifying an abstract or physical resource. A URI is either a URL or a URN. URLs and URNs are concrete entities that actually exist; A URI is an abstract superclass.

URL   Uniform Resource Locator. A standard for writing a textual reference to an arbitrary piece of data in the World Wide Web. A URL looks like `protocol://host/localinfo` where protocol specifies a protocol for fetching the object (such as HTTP or FTP), host specifies the Internet name of the targeted host, and localinfo is a string (often a file name) passed to the protocol handler on the remote host.

URL path   The URL passed by a HTTP request to invoke a servlet. The URL consists of the Context Path + Servlet Path + Path Info, where Context Path is the path prefix associated with a servlet context that this servlet is a part of. If this context is the default context rooted at the base of the Web server's URL-namespace, the path prefix will be an empty string. Otherwise, the path prefix starts with a / character but does not end with a / character. Servlet Path is the path section that directly corresponds to the mapping that activated the request. The Servlet Path starts with a / character. Path Info is the part of the request path that is not part of the Context Path or the Servlet Path.

URN   Uniform Resource Name. A unique identifier that identifies an entity without specifying where it is located. A system can use a URN to look up an entity locally before trying to find it on the Web. Use of URNs allows the Web location to change while still allowing the entity to be found.

user data constraint   Indicates how data between a client and a Web container should be protected. The protection can be the prevention of data tampering or of eavesdropping on the data.

WAR file   A JAR archive that contains a Web module.

Web application   Any application written for the Internet. This includes applications built with Java technologies such as JavaServer Pages and servlets, as well as those built with non-Java technologies such as CGI and Perl.

Web application, distributable   A Web application that uses J2EE technology written so that it can be deployed in a Web container distributed across multiple Java virtual machines running on the same host or different hosts. The deployment descriptor for such an application uses the distributable element.

Web component   A component that provides services in response to requests; a servlet or a JSP page.

Web container   A container that implements the Web component contract of the J2EE architecture. This contract specifies a runtime environment for Web components that includes security, concurrency, life cycle management, transaction, deployment, and other services. A Web container provides the same services as a JSP container and a federated view of the J2EE platform APIs. A Web container is provided by a Web or J2EE server.

Web container, distributed   A Web container that can run a Web application that is tagged as distributable and that executes across multiple Java virtual machines running on the same host or on different hosts.

Web container provider   A vendor that supplies a Web container.

Web module   A unit that consists of one or more Web components and a Web deployment descriptor.

Web resource collection   A list of URL patterns and HTTP methods that describe a set of resources to be protected.

Web server   Software that provides services to access the Internet, an intranet, or an extranet. A Web server hosts Web sites, provides support for HTTP and other protocols, and executes server-side programs (such as CGI scripts or servlets) that perform certain functions. In the J2EE architecture, a Web server provides services to a Web container. For example, a Web container typically relies on a Web server to provide HTTP message handling. The J2EE architecture assumes that a Web container is hosted by a Web server from the same vendor, so does not specify the contract between these two entities. A Web server may host one or more Web containers.

Web server provider   A vendor that supplies a Web server.

Web tier   The tier of a multi-tier distributed application that provides services to access the Internet, an intranet, or an extranet. The Web tier of a J2EE application is implemented by a Web server that implements the Java Servlets and JavaServer Pages specifications.

XML   Extensible Markup Language. A markup language that allows you to define the tags (markup) needed to identify the content, data and text, in XML documents. It differs from HTML the markup language most often used to present information on the internet. HTML has fixed tags that deal mainly with style or presentation. An XML document must undergo a transformation into a language with style tags under the control of a stylesheet before it can be presented by a browser or other presentation mechanism. Two types of style sheets used with XML are CSS and XSL. See CSS, XSL and XSLT in this glossary. Typically, XML is transformed into HTML for presentation. Although tags may be defined as needed in the generation of an XML document, a Document Type Definition (DTD) may be used to define the elements allowed in a particular type of document. See DTD in this glossary. A document may be compared with the rules in the DTD to determine its validity and to locate particular elements in the document. J2EE deployment descriptors are expressed in XML with DTDs defining allowed elements. Programs for processing XML documents typically use SAX or DOM APIs. See SAX and DOM in this glossary.

XSL   Extensible Stylesheet Language. An XML transformation language used for transforming XML documents into documents with flow object tags for presentation purposes. The transformation aspect of XSL has been abstracted into XSLT with the XSL name now used to designate the presentation flow language. XSL is a direct descendent of the DSSSL style language for SGML (Standard Generalized Markup Language), the language from which XML was subsetted. It was designed to have all the capabilities of CSS, the stylesheet often used with HTML. XSL flow objects can be presented by specialized browsers, and themselves transformed into PDF documents for presentation by the product Acrobat. See HTML, XML, CSS, and XSLT in this glossary.

XSLT   XSL Transformation. An XML file that controls the transformation of an XML document into another XML document or HTML. The target document often will have presentation related tags dictating how it will be rendered by a browser or other presentation mechanism. XSLT was formerly part of XSL, which also included a tag language of style flow objects.

Index

The Java™ Series

 ISBN 0-201-70433-1

ISBN 0-201-31005-8

 ISBN 0-201-70323-8

 ISBN 0-201-70393-9

 ISBN 0-201-74622-0

 ISBN 0-201-48558-3

 ISBN 0-201-43299-4

 ISBN 0-201-75282-4

ISBN 0-201-75484-3

ISBN 0-201-71623-2

ISBN 0-201-31002-3

ISBN 0-201-31003-1

 ISBN 0-201-48552-4

 ISBN 0-201-71102-8

 ISBN 0-201-70329-7

 ISBN 0-201-30955-6

 ISBN 0-201-31000-7

 ISBN 0-201-31008-2

 ISBN 0-201-63456-2

 ISBN 0-201-70277-0

 ISBN 0-201-31009-0

 ISBN 0-201-70502-8

 ISBN 0-201-32577-2

 ISBN 0-201-43294-3

 ISBN 0-201-70267-3

 ISBN 0-201-74627-1

 ISBN 0-201-70456-0

 ISBN 0-201-71041-2

 ISBN 0-201-43321-4

 ISBN 0-201-43328-1

 ISBN 0-201-70969-4

 ISBN 0-201-72617-3

Please see our web site (http://www.awl.com/cseng/javaseries)
for more information on these titles.

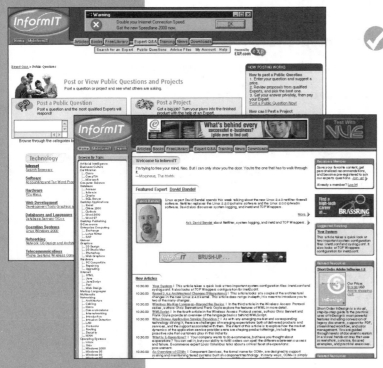

Register
Your Book

at www.aw.com/cseng/register

You may be eligible to receive:

- Advance notice of forthcoming editions of the book
- Related book recommendations
- Chapter excerpts and supplements of forthcoming titles
- Information about special contests and promotions throughout the year
- Notices and reminders about author appearances, tradeshows, and online chats with special guests

Contact us

If you are interested in writing a book or reviewing manuscripts prior to publication, please write to us at:

Editorial Department
Addison-Wesley Professional
75 Arlington Street, Suite 300
Boston, MA 02116 USA
Email: AWPro@aw.com

Addison-Wesley

Visit us on the Web: http://www.aw.com/cseng